Library of
Davidson College

# REFORM IN THE ROYAL NAVY

*Traditions of the Royal Navy?
I'll give you traditions of the Navy
—rum, buggery and the lash.*

> Sir Winston Churchill to the
> Board of the Admiralty, 1939

# Reform in the Royal Navy

*A Social History of the Lower Deck
1850 to 1880*

*by*

*Eugene L. Rasor*

*Archon Books*

*1976*

© *Eugene L. Rasor 1976*
*First published 1976 as an Archon Book,*
*an imprint of The Shoe String Press Inc.,*
*Hamden, Connecticut 06514*

*All rights reserved*

*Library of Congress Cataloging in Publication Data*

Rasor, Eugene L   1936-
    Reform in the Royal Navy.

    Bibliograph: p.
    Includes index.
    1. Great Britain. Navy—History. 2. Seamen—Great Britain. I. Title.
VA454.R32—1976        359.1'332'0941        76-20689
ISBN 0-208-01595-7

*Printed in the United States of America*

To Claire

# Contents

| | | |
|---|---|---|
| | Preface | 7 |
| I | Introduction: The Royal Navy of the Nineteenth Century | 9 |
| II | Recruitment, Impressment, and the Problem of Manning | 21 |
| III | Discipline Regulations and Punishment | 38 |
| IV | Mutiny, Desertion, Problems of Leadership, and Alcoholism | 62 |
| V | Other Problems and Issues | 87 |
| VI | Reform and Transition: The Naval Discipline Acts | 112 |
| | Appendix | 125 |
| | Notes | 131 |
| | Selected Bibliography | 171 |
| | Index | 207 |

# Preface

The Royal Navy of the nineteenth century is the object of numerous but limited studies. Accounts proliferate about design of ships, new technology in engineering and weaponry, and doctrinal rectification in strategy and tactics. Change is the theme: from sail to steam power, from propulsion using wind to paddle-wheels and screw-propellors, from guns using smooth-bore and muzzle-loading to rifled and breech-loading barrels, and from divergent basic doctrines to an analysis of sea power which all could espouse.

Change is the theme of this study but the emphasis is on social history, a neglected approach. Little has been written about the reform of conditions and welfare of the *bluejacket*, a term which originates about 1850, and his abode, the lower deck, a term which technically becomes obsolete about 1880. The life and times of the enlisted man are thoroughly reviewed and glorified during previous eras of victories and heroes, but little interest is demonstrated about the more mundane times after the Wars of the French Revolution and Napoleon.[1]

A contemporary, John Bechervaise, naval gunner of the 1840s, anonymously lamented that the seaman was ignored and

> undervalued.... The Bar, the Church, the Army, and the higher branches of the Naval Department, have spread volumes of their secret history before the public gaze; while the seafaring man of the lower class has, with scarcely one exception, been a sealed book; or if ever entered upon, it has been by shore-going writers, who know nothing of the true principles of the seaman.[2]

More recently Professor Charles Christopher Lloyd, a foremost authority on the history of the Royal Navy, hoped perhaps some day someone will give us a detailed study of the lower deck at the end of the nineteenth century: at present we know less about the sailor of that time than in earlier days.[3]

This monograph is intended to fulfill, at least partially, these aspirations and to provide some basis for a more balanced and comprehensive view of the Royal Navy during the third quarter of the nineteenth century.[4]

The five Naval Discipline Acts of the 1860s best exemplify the social reform in the Royal Navy. This study will describe the making of those acts.[5]

Expressions of indebtedness to those persons who have provided invaluable assistance on a project of this sort are undoubtedly insufficient reciprocity, but I feel obliged to somehow communicate sincere and grateful appreciation to Lea Booth, Thomas Chilcote, Robert Denham, Nicolas Edsall, John Grant, Oron Hale, Martin Havran, Landon Lane, Ronald Linker, Christopher Lloyd, Maurice Luker, Bryan Ranft, George Stevenson, and James Thorpe III. In addition, officials and staff persons of the following institutions have rendered assistance in research: Frederick Thrasher Kelly Library of Emory & Henry College; the university libraries at the University of Virginia, Duke University, the University of Chicago, Indiana University at Bloomington, Virginia Polytechnic Institute and State University; the Alfred Thayer Mahan Library at the Naval War College, Newport, Rhode Island; in England, the Public Record Office, the Institute of Historical Research, and the university library, University of London; the Reading Rooms of the British Museum and the National Maritime Museum, Greenwich, and the Naval Library at Earl's Court.

E. L. R.

Emory & Henry College
*Emory, Virginia*
December 1975

# I

# Introduction: The Royal Navy of the Nineteenth Century

During the year 1859 the Lords of the Admiralty, the executive authority of the Royal Navy located in Whitehall, instituted a number of reforms affecting the conditions and welfare of the seaman on the lower deck. Implementation was accomplished in comparative haste and in an ameliorating and moderating manner. This was unprecedented. Traditionally action, if any, would have been repressive and grudging, for the bluejacket was neither respected nor considered respectable. Moreover, the events triggering the unique response included a number of mutinies, the ultimate crime in the armed forces. Other indicators of trouble were deemed equally abominable: the recruiting situation was so desperate that the hated bounty had been offered with the usual complications; the rate of desertion exceeded the worst predictions; and the incidences of alcoholism and of venereal disease were particularly alarming.

Yet the Admiralty responded with uncharacteristic kindness and generosity to an exceedingly disruptive situation. Possibly for the first time it conceded that its enlisted constituency possessed human feelings, dignity, ambition, initiative, aspirations, and, yes, even respectability, that uniquely Victorian virtue. Admiralty consciousness of the need for fundamental change was obvious and sustained at a high level over a period of several years. The impetus was external, primarily from parliamentary and journalistic pressures. The transformation of conditions on the lower deck was concentrated during the administration of Edward Adolphus Seymour, Twelfth Duke of Somerset, First Lord of the Admiralty in the governments of Lords Palmerston and Russell, 1859-66. The reforms dealt with a variety of problems which had collectively contributed to low morale and to the disruptive situation of 1859. Previously fundamental practices such as impressment and corporal punishment were repudiated and replaced by more humane measures. Leave and liberty, once denied, were offered freely and cheerfully, virtually as a right. A number of measures contributed to a significant improvement of living conditions on the lower deck. All of this was legislatively consolidated into the Naval Discipline Acts, the first being passed by Parliament in 1860 and the last in 1866. Most of the reforms had been implemented fully by 1880. By 1900 indicators of success and improvement were recorded in virtually every category. Moderation of punishment practices and the granting of leave resulted in a reduction in desertions and in the incidences of drunkenness and venereal disease.

The Royal Navy of the nineteenth century enjoyed extraordinary preeminence, unchallenged between the battle of Trafalgar of 1805 and the end of the century. This superiority was based upon past exploits during warfare which ended in 1815. After that British imperial policy stressed consolidation. The requirements of the world's most powerful empire meant employment in an amazing variety of tasks. Patrolling to stop the slave trade in that region of the South Atlantic known as the "White Man's Grave" was obviously unhealthy and dangerous. Navigational surveys and related chart-making provided enormous contributions, unselfishly, to the advancement of all mankind but were tedious and boring for the participants. Ubiquitously "policing the seas" added to the Empire and contributed to the new imperialism but made life miserable for the common sailor. Transporting gold, encour-

# REFORM IN THE ROYAL NAVY

aging and protecting commerce, and chasing pirates and filibusters were financially rewarding to many, but little benefit accrued to the bluejacket. There were minor wars, for example in China and Burma as well as a colonial mutiny in India, and naval brigades campaigned ashore, collecting about twenty Victoria Crosses in the process—but for most there was little, if any, glory.[1]

The drudgery, boredom, danger, and misery were overlooked in the popular assessments which stressed the versatility and long, brilliant tradition of victories and successes. Myths and glorified slogans developed: the British were "the Sailor Race," "the Island People," "by the navy we must stand or fall," the navy was "the first line of defense," "whatever may be wrong ashore, nothing is wrong at sea," "the Royal Navy was British and Best," it was "the Senior Service," and "the Royal Navy always traveled first class."

However, there were chinks in the armor, and such appraisals of aloofness and superiority resulted from selective and limited knowledge. The navy had blundered through and emerged from the Russian War of 1854-56 relatively untarnished, but its performance can only be evaluated as unsatisfactory.[2] The plight of the bluejacket on the lower deck gained little attention or sympathy. The biographer of Admiral Sir Percy Scott, the gunnery expert, described a midshipman in the 1860s entering "this apparently splendid, but nevertheless deteriorating service."[3]

Other than myths, platitudes, and appellations there was little contemporary scholarly recognition of the navy. No significant historians came forward, and popular interest at a sustained level had to await the contributions of an important group of writers who began publishing after 1880. There then followed an outburst of analysis and revision of traditional views by an extraordinary school of intellectuals and professionals who ultimately transformed the strategy and tactics of naval warfare.[4] Admittedly during our period, 1850 to 1880, protests of passionate outrage and public demonstrations involving naval matters can be cited, but, compared to events of 1889 or 1909, they fell largely upon deaf ears. Concern about this deficiency and lack of interest was expressed at the time.[5]

A potentially explosive situation developed in 1859 with possible repercusions affecting the security of Great Britain and her empire. The royal Navy as "the first line of defense" was not a mythological illusion or innocuous appellation. The preamble to the Naval Discipline Act, around which the thesis of this study revolves, provided the rationale: " . . . the Navy, whereupon the good Providence of God, the Wealth, Safety and Strength of the Kingdom chiefly depend. . . . "[6] Therefore, crises affecting the navy were of concern to the empire.

The citing of the year 1859 as a critical and cardinal landmark is not unique. For a variety of reasons this year, deemed *annus mirabilis,* has been singled out: perhaps it was "at once the climax of the Enlightenment and source of disillusionment for the Generation of Materialism," or a watershed in the careers of Charles Darwin, Karl Marx, and Richard Wagner, all of whom contributed significantly to the heritage of modern western civilization, or perhaps the year was decisive for the breakup of the Peelites, or for John Stuart Mill, who, incidently, was one of the radical critics demanding reform in the navy.[7]

Certain other episodes impinged more directly, to one degree or another, upon the responsibilities of the navy and the events of 1859. For reasons of foreign policy, national security, budgetary retrenchment, and reform, the manning level in the Royal Navy fluctuated drastically during the 1850s, this being a major factor in arousing disgruntlement and a rebellious spirit among the bluejackets. A number of incidents contributed to this instability at the international level. The detente with France, England's ally in the Russian War, was seriously strained because of suspicion, competition, resentment, and fear of invasion: specifically, the French initiative in building the Suez Canal, rumors of a Franco-Russian alliance, the Orsini conspiracy, a general distrust of

Emperor Napoleon III, French interference in the Italian War, unpredictable advances in warship construction techniques, and lamentations and warnings of unpreparedness by Admiral Sir Charles Napier, Alfred Lord Tennyson, and the *Times*. At the height of an invasion scare, when there was panic along the Dover coast in May 1859, the *Times* published a poem by "T" (the poet laureate, Tennyson) entitled "Riflemen, Form!" or *The War*, which stirred the country. The government responded by sponsoring the Volunteer Rifle Corps as a militia which attracted 60,000 men in two months.[8] Elsewhere before 1859 the Indian Mutiny and a China War had exacerbated the situation. Relative calm was restored in the autumn of 1859, and the signing of the Cobden-Chevalier trade agreement early in 1860 signified a resumption of the entente with France.

Domestically the period was identified with reform and political complexity. The dominating influences were humanitarianism and administrative innovation. A new liberal and rational consciousness pervaded the country and influenced such reforms as moderation of punishment and penal practices and improvement of sanitary and health arrangements. Professor David Roberts, among others, has described this as an administrative "revolution in government."[9]

Politically the situation was confused and complex; no exclusive party programs or identifiable political dichotomy can be delineated. The Peelites remained "in the Wilderness"; William Gladstone had not emerged as the obvious leader of the Liberal Party, and the Tories were regrouping. Lord Palmerston was liberal only on matters of foreign policy or, at least, he was "most English" in that sector. His last government, 1859-65, during which the important legislative reform of the navy was passed, has been called "an interlude before the resumption of clear cut party division." That government was possible only because Lords Palmerston and Russell agreed to disagree. Henry Adams, for other reasons, described this regime as one of "arrested development." In the same vein, Professor Kitson Clark referred to the period as "a lull, a centre of indifference." A more recent student, Professor Colin Baxter, has called it a "period of repose."[10]

Specifically the two Lord Derby governments in the 1850s initiated studies leading to reforms concerning manning, and Lord Palmerston's and Russell's governments enacted the series of five Naval Discipline Acts or amendments during the 1860s. The reforms cannot be credited to one political group nor can one person claim exclusive accomplishment. Paradoxically, Lords Palmerston and Russell had often spoken in favor of corporal punishment, yet the major steps leading to its suspension took place under their regimes.[11]

Economically and financially for the navy during the nineteenth century the story was repetitious: annual budgets to get through Parliament every spring, incessant demands for retrenchment, especially from radicals such as Joseph Hume, ever increasing costs for more sophisticated materiel, and higher expenses for personnel and their welfare. Chronologically, the period from 1815 to 1880 can be identified by trends. Budget totals decreased after 1815 and were characterized by parsimony, "with warship construction continuing at a leisurely pace" through the mid-1830s. Spending slowly increased, spurred on by occasional invasion scares, the Russian War, and increased costs. There then followed two decades of hesitancy and a pause in fiscal matters because of uncertainty about design and construction and a moderating international situation associated with free trade and arbitration. After 1880 came a resumption of the upward trend and the beginning of the classic arms race.[12]

Socially a transformation took place in the navy between 1850 and 1880. The life, conditions, and environment of the typical bluejacket underwent drastic alteration. The Admiralty "began consciously to care for the sailor in all his needs, physical, mental, moral. . . ."[13] Elaboration of this particular process will be the theme of subsequent chapters.

Personnel of the navy in nineteenth-century Britain were

divided into two classes or ranks, the dichotomy being quite formal with little or no mobility between the status of officer and enlisted. Sources of supply and availability presented interesting comparisons. For the lower class, the enlisted man whose place was the lower deck, there existed a dangerous shortage; for the upper class, the officer symbolically placed on the quarterdeck, there was superfluity. Those enlisted men just entering the service who were not yet eighteen years old were called "boys."

Enlisted men were sometimes subdivided into formal "classes," there being several criteria: conduct, training status, and eligibility for leave. For example, men in the first class for conduct were immune from flogging; boys in the first class had completed a year aboard a training ship; and men in the third class for leave were least eligible for time ashore.

About one-quarter of the crew of Her Majesty's warships comprised the Royal Marines whose functions included sharpshooting, boarding, repelling boarders, landing parties, and, quite important for discipline, guarding for internal security, ". . . constant reinforcement to the powers of law and order." When they were attached to ships, the marines were subject to the same statutes and regulations as the seamen. Between 1756 and 1871 the Marine Mutiny Act, passed annually as for the army, regulated discipline ashore for the Royal Marines.[14]

Living conditions on the lower deck, what today is called habitability, can only be described as deplorable. Excessive crowding and an unhealthy atmosphere prevailed, there being only fourteen inches allotted for each hammock, the typical bedding facility. The atmosphere was

> . . . quite nauseating. The place was perennially damp; in cold weather incredibly cold, and in hot weather intolerably stuffy.[15]

Among the hundreds of extant memoirs and recollections of

the period there is general agreement even among those who became high ranking officers that conditions were harsh and debilitating. For months, sometimes years, at sea a man endured confinement, monotony, and isolation in an existence where he was subject to the dangers of exposure, disease, and rotten food. There was no privacy or female companionship. Overwork literally wore him out at an early age.[16]

The Admiralty exhibited little appreciation for such dedication and sacrifice and was reluctantly and belatedly influenced by the more humanitarian spirit coming to the fore in British life. Philosophically the naval establishment conformed to the classic conservative view about the worth of the individual: man was basically evil. The seaman could not be trusted; he was degenerate, despicable, immoral, and barely distinguishable from the common criminal. The worst was always expected, and there was little, if any, mutual trust. Statistics appeared to reinforce this stance, and, even more persuasive, predominant opinion in national politics supported it, at least until the radicals became more vocal. Seamen were recruited from the most illiterate, ignorant, and primitive sources. Discipline policies were predicated upon what was claimed to be a delicate balance between the low caliber of personnel and stringent measures of punishment. No mitigation was possible. Any variation, however slight, would result in anarchy, according to the consistent prediction from the authorities.

This prevalent attitude of reaction was strengthened by a peculiar combination of circumstances related to naval officers: promotion by seniority, no mandatory retirement, and the absence of wars with resultant casualties. The consequence was an excessive number of superannuated officers largely lamenting the past. Senility, mediocrity, and inertia prevailed. Much has been written about the effect of this dead hand upon engineering, weapons, and tactical innovations, and there was similar obscurantism against social changes. "It was personnel problems at all levels that showed the least sign of amendment."[17]

Exceptions to these trends can be cited. Sensitive and perceptive officers consciously created an atmosphere of mutual respect, trust, and confidence without resort to harsh and brutal measures. Experiments in granting generous leave resulted in dramatic decreases in the rate of desertion. Moderation aboard individual ships led to improved performance and fewer discipline problems. In the 1840s Captain Sir Bartholomew James Sulivan, commanding officer of H.M.S. *Philomel*, conducted a four-year commission in an extraordinary manner. He granted generous leave in port and permitted much freedom ashore. Over a two-year period there were no entries on the Quarterly Punishment Returns; over the four years there was only one case of drunkenness and not a single case of desertion. The commanding officer of H.M.S. *Merlin* achieved exemplary discipline also.[18]

However, these internal attempts to improve conditions did not exert much influence on the Admiralty. For the most part external pressures forced the Admiralty to conform to contemporary humanitarian and administrative trends and to alter attitudes toward treatment of the bluejacket. Reform was not an internally initiated, magnanimous, voluntary contribution to a cause or campaign. The Admiralty was the passive object of a movement, not the active instigator.

These outside forces influencing change comprised a variety of vehicles of public expression articulating concerns for reform and rationalization. The media of public opinion broadened and intensified its capabilities to influence at the same time that the public able to comprehend and to respond continued to increase. The importance of the pressures of public opinion evoked contemporary comment, for example, from Louis Blanc, the French statesman in exile in England, and from another who credited it as being "the great force of the present day." The measurable extent of that "great force" and whether it was leading or being led was difficult to determine.[19]

There were several reasons for these altered circumstances.

The traditional newspaper was relieved of debilitating encumbrances and as a result was able to expand greatly. The *Times,* enjoying the commanding heights for so long, was now successfully challenged by what would evolve into mass-circulation, "yellow-journalist" competitors. Abolition of an excise duty on paper in 1861 stimulated newspapers, periodicals, journals, pamphlets, essays, and novels toward increased output. The monthly shilling magazine was established.[20] Richard D. Altick has characterized the period as the age of "the universality of print, the omnipotence of ink."[21]

Two of these printed approaches exerted particular influence upon the navy: the service journal and the didactic novel. Of the former, two were established around 1860: the *Journal of the Royal United Service Institution* (1857) and the *Army and Navy Gazette* (1860). Though both generally came down on the side of reaction, they did provide a platform for healthy debate.[22] The most significant of the didactic novels in Great Britain was a series by Captain Frederick Marryat of the Royal Navy. An American admiral claimed *White-Jacket,* written by Herman Melville in the 1840s and reputedly sent to every member of Congress, was instrumental in the decision to abolish corporal punishment in the American navy.[23]

The proliferation of written materials coincided with increased utilization of oral techniques: the Dispatch Box and back bench in Parliament, the public platform and association hall outside, and campaigns, demonstrations, and crusades involving petitions and letters of complaint. One sensational and ultimately successful example was the campaign to repeal the Contagious Diseases Acts. Though less organized and ostentatious, equally successful results were achieved in the movement to abolish the practice of corporal punishment.

The Admiralty was not pleased about being the object of so much Parliamentary, journalistic, and public debate. In 1861, Sir John Pakington, a once and future First Lord, exclaimed that there seemed "to be a feeling that any man who wants to write a pamphlet or make a speech cannot do better than attack the Admiralty." Regulations were explicit prohibiting any communication by service personnel with the newspapers, and the Admiralty was consistently aroused when such communication was suspected, taking immediate punitive action if confirmed.[24]

The Admiralty reluctantly submitted to these influences and pressures, both by instituting reforms and by adopting measures to improve the image of the Royal Navy. More importantly, the navy had to be made to appear more desirable (or less repulsive) to attract the higher caliber enlisted man capable of functioning effectively under the changing demands of technical and mechanical revolution. Rationalization was mandatory in a competitive situation demanding continued dominance of sea power, and one of the prerequisites was higher quality personnel. Thus, convincing the recruit with better potential and ability that the navy should be his choice for a career was high on the list of priorities. A particular effort was made to revive the close association with the merchant service, previously held as the "nursery" of naval seamen, an association that had deteriorated primarily at the expense of naval recruiting. The contemporary merchant seaman saw the Royal Navy as the last resort for employment, and since compulsion had been abandoned as an option, a serious dilemma confronted the recruiter. Young, inexperienced, and career-oriented boys could fill the annual quotas during peacetime, but only the merchant service could provide a reliable source of rapid expansion in the more critical time of war.[25]

There was also need to restore credibility and to convince powerful critics of personnel and social practices in the navy that reform and change for the better were a reality. The complaining and questioning back bencher, the crusading journalist, the Radical politician, and the outraged relative had to be shown in a number of different ways that the Admiralty cared for and provided for its own. Socially, philosophically, and psychologically the navy must molt; it must abandon its old shell and skin which had sufficed for one stage of its development and replace that with new growth capable of sustaining life under different and more modern circumstances. Mere appeasement was insufficient; there must be fundamental change which would be readily apparent and obviously dramatic. The methodology of reform must include a broad-based advance against a wide spectrum of problems, complaints, and inadequacies in order to reverse the trends toward decline and disgruntlement.

The rhythm of the evolution and execution of the various reforms can be ascertained by the analyst who has perused the *Admiralty Digests,* that "monstrous but invaluable" accumulation of summaries of day-to-day administration peculiar to naval records.[26] Initial and hesitant efforts can be seen in the early 1850s. The process broadened and accelerated during the critical year of 1859; the zenith occurred in 1864-66, and the movement back to a relative equilibrium began in 1867-68. By 1880 there were numerous indications of success.[27]

The policies adopted in order to transform the conditions and welfare of the constituency of this deteriorating service affected in one way or another every aspect of the life of the bluejacket. Perhaps a phase-by-phase review of a typical career from recruitment to pensioning would provide a basis for a better understanding of his environment, say in 1850, and for an appreciation of the effect of the reforms which had been fully implemented by 1880. This method of presentation should illustrate by contrast the significant and dramatic improvement which occurred.

Secondarily, this approach will provide an opportunity to fill a lacuna in the social history of the Royal Navy. There have been a number of thorough accounts of the period up to about 1850, and Professor Arthur J. Marder covers some of the field after 1880, but there has yet been no publication to fill the void, as a number of scholars and observers have indicated.[28]

# II

# Recruitment, Impressment, and the Problem of Manning

An important goal of the reforms instituted by the Royal Navy at mid-century was attracting sufficient numbers of higher caliber and better quality seamen. To achieve this, the Admiralty must find a solution to a complex and enduring problem which had plagued it, and the army also for that matter, for some time: a reliable and politically acceptable method of recruitment which would guarantee adequate sources of enlisted personnel in peacetime and fulfill greatly expanded needs in wartime, this latter being the crux of the problem. The security of Great Britain and her empire depended upon the capability to rapidly expand the fleet in an emergency. An insufficient number of seamen in the service that was the first line of defense could mean disaster.

The typical bluejacket of the nineteenth century would first encounter the Royal Navy through some phase of recruiting. Entry into Her Majesty's naval service could be accomplished by a number of methods. A combination of several possibilities might be in operation at any given time. The volunteer system was always the most desirable both from the perspective of the man and the naval authorities, but the need for manpower fluctuated radically, and attractions and inducements for volunteers in the navy and the army in the first half of the nineteenth century were minimal. Those who joined of their own volition generally proved to be objectionable; indeed, precisely the type of man most attractive to the armed forces was repulsed by the bad reputation and inferior image which the services projected. At a time of technical and mechanical transformation, the navy must abandon its traditional philosophy of accepting criminals and the "dregs of society" and redirect its efforts toward the type of person capable of learning sophisticated skills. As will be seen, this involved some trial-and-error.

The seaman might enlist because of the offer of a bounty, a one-time monetary award paid upon induction. This alternative was frequently used by the army but was resorted to by the navy only in extraordinary circumstances when other approaches had proved insufficient, as in 1858 and 1859. On that occasion this inducement only exacerbated an already deteriorating situation.

A quota system had provided needed personnel in the past, though this technique too had caused disruption and created notoriety. Backed by Quota Acts passed by Parliament, the Admiralty would allot a number of men to a local political unit, usually inland, which could fill the quota by any method suitable to it. The products, called "Quota-men," were too often the worst types of criminals and ne'er-do-wells, "the scourings of gaols." Some were given an option from criminal court, imprisonment or service in the navy. Quota-men were blamed for causing the mutinies of 1797. As was the case with impressment, the quota system was not used after 1815.

Another possibility was a ballot or lottery system, a form of compulsory service involving arbitrary selection. This process was considered occasionally but never implemented in England, though it was used on the continent, most notably by the French.

Despite the fact that England and France had fought as allies in the Russian War, their relations remained strained both before and after that episode. France was frequently depicted as England's ultimate enemy, and critics of recruiting practices often warned that the effectiveness of any system might well mean the difference between victory and defeat. They often presented the French system of naval recruiting, the *Inscription*

# REFORM IN THE ROYAL NAVY 23

*Maritime*, in the best light as especially productive, efficient, and fair. It incorporated a combination of registry, ballot, and quota systems, no substitutes being permitted. It was claimed that 50,000 trained seamen could be provided in an emergency whereas the Royal Navy could, at best, produce only 9,000. The Admiralty listened politely but kept its options open, relying most heavily during the first half of the century upon hire-and-discharge, and, if necessary, impressment.[1]

In an evolutionary review of the most important recruitment practices in the nineteenth century, four processes require elaboration: impressment, hire-and-discharge, continuous or long-term service, and the reserve. Impressment, the practice of augmenting the number of seamen in the navy in times of need such as preparation for and during war, had been the primary method of acquisition of large numbers of personnel before 1815, but no occasion arose subsequently to necessitate reactivation of the process. Theoretically this compulsory service applied to all able-bodied males whose potential occupation was associated with or whose residence was in close proximity to the sea. Certain critical occupations and the wealthy gained exemptions. Determination of eligibility was the responsibility of a "press gang," headed by a naval officer attached to the Impress Service. In practice a roving band of toughs commandeered ostensibly eligible males from wherever they could be found, that being most often aboard inbound merchant ships. As it actually functioned the policy was grossly unfair, and the press gang created panic and terror in its wake. There must have been hundreds of thousands of individual tragedies linked to the process; in most cases young males unsuccessful in attempts at avoidance literally disappeared permanently from homes and families. Furthermore, stringent and abnormal precautions became necessary to retain the impressed seaman aboard. Naval ships became floating prisons; the granting of liberty and leave during a commission, a period of three to five years, became impossible because large numbers would abscond. This meant volunteers could not go ashore either; they were innocently punished to maintain a manning system which was counterproductive and excessively costly. During the last years that impressment had been used, 1811 to 1813, the press gangs commandeered 29,405 men; during the same period 27,300 deserted.[2]

In fact, the subject of impressment should have no relevance to this study because the practice had not been implemented for decades. The immediate need to continue an active policy ended in 1815 and never recurred, and thus, from the perspective of hindsight, the policy could safely be abandoned. Nevertheless, the Admiralty, always supported by governments of all political persuasions, insisted upon leaving the option open. Permanently setting aside compulsory service was never seriously considered. The giving up of the practice, or the right, as they would define it—in fact, it was deemed one of the ancient prerogatives of the Crown—must endanger national security. All of this was sanctioned, indeed, almost sanctified, by Parliament.

The Admiralty did not reactivate the practice of impressment after 1815, but debate over the subject developed into a serious controversy. All of the pressures of public opinion were brought to bear against the policy and, oddly enough, few arose in defense; apologists were indeed rare.[3] The authorities perceived the popular prejudice against conscription and universal obligation and generally acted quietly to insure the option remained a viable one. For example, in 1835, after he had left office as First Lord of the Admiralty, Sir James Graham piloted through Parliament an act which secured "statutory recognition of the Crown's ancient right in common law to the compulsory service of its subjects."

Scarcely anyone supported the practice of impressment—it was a "bad thing," but it was necessary. The attitude was similar to that of *Junius* who had said a century before, "I see that right founded originally upon a necessity which supersedes all argument."[4] Over and over again in the various debates in and out of Parliament and in the written media, opponents lambasted the policy, and the authorities responded by admitting the evil and pleading extenuating circumstances. J. R. Hutchinson in the authoritative account of impressment concluded:

> ... it perhaps constitutes the greatest anomaly, as it undoubtedly constitutes the grossest imposition any free people ever submitted to.... it yearly enslaved, under the most noxious conditions, thousands against their will.... it ground under its heel the very people it protected and made them slaves in order to keep them free.... [5]

The heated polemics generated over the issue continued for half a century. Captain Frederick Marryat, an outspoken critic of this and other abuses (corporal punishment, incompetent officers, and brash midshipmen), pamphleteered against it as early as 1822.[6] A reviewer in the *Edinburgh Review* of 1824 editorialized: "... this miserable system, on the whole and in the long-run, deprives the fleet of more men than are obtained by other means." He linked this with other problems—low wages, cruel punishment, and excessive desertion—and called for complete reform of personnel policies.[7] In the same year Joseph Hume, in the House of Commons, called English sailors "White negroes." Another naval officer, Captain A. J. Griffiths, wrote a book in 1826 denouncing impressment, though he defended current discipline practices and discounted the "hue and cry" against them.[8] Retired Captain G. H. Gardner presented a devastating critique in 1871.

> The horrors of the press-gang and the barbarous discipline on board our men-of-war in former times, combined with the absence of good faith on the part of the Government towards the seamen while serving in the Fleet, were the chief causes of that aversion to impressment. ... how mischievously it works by destroying every patriotic feeling in our sea-faring population. ...
> The quality of the article obtained by means of it is

generally of the worst possible kind. . . . It involved the necessity of our men-of-war in former times being turned into prison ships . . . the remainder of the crews of necessity being made to suffer detention with it.[9]

One admiral in particular became noted as a critic of impressment after experiencing the consequences of a shortage of men on more than one occasion.[10] During the Russian War, Admiral Sir Charles Napier was Commander-in-Chief of the Baltic Expedition and was ordered to depart from England with inadequate numbers, the Admiralty advising him to "pick up some Norwegian sailors on the way." Later he was summarily relieved because he complained directly to the prime minister about his difficulties there, not all of which concerned this issue.[11] Later still after he had entered the House of Commons, Admiral Napier recalled a forty-year fight, beginning in 1816, to abolish impressment. His agitation apparently influenced the decision in 1858 to appoint the Royal Commission on Manning the Navy.

In fact the prerogative of impressment has never been formally abrogated by the Admiralty or the government, and it remained a precedent for twentieth-century universal military service.[12]

The second process, hire-and-discharge, became the standard practice of recruitment until 1853. Warships were fitted out and manned for a "commission" lasting from three to five years. The seaman signed voluntarily and was discharged upon completion (if he had not died or deserted), the only exception being the warrant officers who acted as caretakers of the ship between commissions, and a permanent core of gunners specially qualified aboard the training ship, H.M.S. *Excellent*. Each crew during a commission was trained from scratch and generally had reached optimum proficiency at about the time of termination, called "paying-off." Assembling or recruiting a new crew every commission for this short-term service was always a difficult process; often there were months of delay while sufficient numbers were found, the most consistent shortage being in the rate A.B. (able-bodied seaman). In practice this method proved to be unsatisfactory, offering no security or permanence to the man or the navy and no guarantee of re-employment. The seaman suddenly found himself a free agent, vulnerable to attractions outside the navy. One who had just been paid-off was often enticed into the merchant service, the American navy, or the English army. Conditions, wages, or punishment practices in those organizations may or may not have been better, but the bluejacket obviously thought that they were. Claims that the American navy was a major attraction for Englishmen have recently been verified. Professor Peter Karsten has concluded that in 1878 sixty percent of the enlisted men in the American Navy were foreign-born, and, of those, about half were from Great Britain and Ireland.[13] The only inducement to sign for another commission in the Royal Navy, and this presumably was of minor importance since so few participated, was the possibility of a pension; this after 1831.

Professor Christopher Lloyd has called hire-and-discharge "the fundamental weakness in manning the navy in the age of sail."[14] In the prize essay of the *Journal of the Royal United Service Institution* of 1882, Captain Lindesay Brine classified all of these methods of recruiting before 1853 as "most insecure and inexpedient." Hire-and-discharge, impressment, bounties, and quotas all contributed to a situation that proved to be excessively costly, inefficient, dangerously disruptive, needlessly complicated, and generally exasperating. The victim was the seaman.[15]

The third process was the Continuous Service system, the solution to the problem of peacetime recruitment in the nineteenth century, although success was not immediately apparent due to circumstantial complications. In the 1850s two formal investigations, a departmental committee and a Royal Commission, both appointed during separate governments of the Tory Lord Derby, searched for methods to alleviate the difficulties experienced in recruiting. The Committee on Manning the Navy of 1852, composed of professional naval officers, was chaired by Admiral Sir William Parker. Rear Admiral Sir Maurice Berkeley, Second Sea Lord, and Sir Charles Henry Pennell, Chief Clerk of the Admiralty, primarily influenced its recommendations, notably Continuous Service, which was implemented by Order-in-Council, 1 April 1853.

Continuous Service introduced long-term enlistments and provided for a relatively large annual input of "boys" to be trained and prepared for a career in the navy.[16] A boy would, with parental permission, voluntarily enter the navy, typically at age sixteen, serve aboard a training ship for a year and then aboard a warship until age eighteen, when he would sign a ten year engagement. After two consecutive agreements he would be eligible for pension. The seaman did lose his right of choice and much freedom of timing which he had enjoyed under hire-and-discharge, but proffered inducements and incentives compensated: additional pay (for the A.B., up twenty percent), more and faster opportunities for promotion, paid leave, and an improved pension arrangement. At last the Admiralty had faced an issue with some imagination and vision, but, alas, the immediate results were disappointing.

The circumstantial complications which hindered the proper functioning of Continuous Service involved radical fluctuations in the manning level of the navy in the 1850s, something which can be seen in table 1.

Chart 1 in the appendix graphically illustrates the drastic changes which occurred during this period. The situation was relatively stable during the 1840s.[18] Mobilization for the Russian War, just at the formative period for implementation of Continuous Service, meant a dramatic increase; indeed, there resulted a serious shortage which jeopardized the operations in the important though little publicized Baltic Sea expedition. Demobilization was carried out so rapidly and haphazardly that even Continuous Service men were dismissed, while men

Table 1. The Manning Level of the Royal Navy 1841-1866[17]

| Year | Seamen Voted | Boys Voted | Total number serving in the Royal Navy (includes Royal Marines) |
|---|---|---|---|
| 1841-42 | 30,500 | 2,000 | 41,389 |
| 1844-45 | 27,500 | 2,000 | 38,343 |
| 1847-48 | 27,500 | 2,000 | 44,969 |
| 1850-51 | 26,000 | 2,000 | 39,093 |
| 1851-52 | 26,000 | 2,000 | 38,957 |
| 1852-53 | 26,000 | 2,000 | 40,451 |
| 1853-54 | 31,000 | 2,000 | 45,885 |
| 1854-55 | 46,000 | 2,000 | 61,457 |
| 1855-56 | 50,000 | 10,000 | 67,791 |
| 1856-57 | 33,333 | 6,667 | 60,659 |
| 1857-58 | 27,530 | 5,470 | 50,419 |
| 1858-59 | 30,900 | 6,100 | 52,450 |
| 1859-60 | 40,100 | 7,900 | 66,509 |
| 1860-61 | 49,000 | 9,000 | 72,276 |
| 1861-62 | 42,900 | 8,100 | 71,297 |
| 1862-63 | 40,000 | 9,000 | 66,952 |
| 1863-64 | 39,900 | 9,000 | 63,225 |
| 1864-65 | 38,500 | 7,000 | 62,403 |
| 1865-66 | 38,000 | 7,000 | 60,846 |

with less potential were retained. Two or three years later a series of international incidents, including another French invasion scare, created increased demand and another shortage. The Admiralty found itself in an embarrassing dilemma. Admiral Sir Charles Napier, now retired and a member of Parliament nursing a vendetta against his former superiors, called for another investigation on manning.

This time a Royal Commission on Manning the Navy, the Earl of Hardwicke, chairman, was appointed, that particular investigative body being considered more important in the hierarchy than a mere departmental committee. As a last resort the Admiralty offered a bounty, ten pounds for an A.B., six pounds for an Ordinary Seaman, with the anticipation of 10,000 men. Not only did it fail to attract the necessary recruits (only 3,000 joined),[19] but it also antagonized those seamen already in the service. Many deserted and re-entered to collect the bounty, some more than one time. Those remaining felt so bitter that the Admiralty, to restore credibility, offered a half-bounty to any who would re-enlist for five years. Opposition to the bounty was vocal in Parliament, especially from Sir James Graham and Lord Clarence Paget. The overall effect of this was increased problems of discipline, retention, and desertion within the navy which significantly contributed to the disruptive situation that developed in 1859.[20]

The bounty offer had failed and the crises and rumors of war persisted, and still the Admiralty was unable to man the needed ships. Those placed in commission in 1857 and 1858 waited an average of four months longer than usual before departure. The worst example, in November 1857, was H.M.S. *Renown* which sailed 172 days late, and then short 62 men.[21] There existed no reserve of seamen the navy could fall back upon in an emergency. The merchant service, the traditional "nursery of seamen," had been alienated over the past decades. Numerous contemporary observers lamented the loss.

The members[22] of the Royal Commission on Manning of 1858 were selected on the basis of some attachment or expertise related to the merchant service. An underlying aim of the study was to restore the close and mutually beneficial relationship that had once existed between the armed and unarmed seagoing services. In its report, dated 19 February 1859, the commission endorsed Continuous Service and recommended that it be maintained as the primary source in peacetime. It then turned to the more fundamental problem of the antagonism.

It was the merchant seaman who had developed an aversion to the navy, a "suspicion, . . . a long-existing and deeply-rooted prejudice." The image of the Royal Navy from the perspective of the merchant seaman was "a black nightmare in which he would be scrubbed till clean and then flogged to death." This deterioration of relations was due to a number of factors: harsh conditions and brutal punishments, lower wages, less freedom, a loss of credibility, repeal of the navigation acts in 1849, and increasing demands for technical competence by the navy. An extreme instance was exemplified in a policy of the Seamen's Benefit Clubs in the North which "made taking service in the Royal Navy . . . a reason for expulsion and forfeiture of all claims on the funds."

Various schemes to institutionalize the attachment were attempted in an effort to restore relationships. In 1831 the Coast Guard service was founded as an adjunct to the navy, although it was originally under the Board of Customs (later the Board of Trade) and not transferred to the Admiralty until 1856. As a reserve it failed during the mobilization for the Russian War, primarily because many members were too old to serve. Later it did become a more reliable source. In 1834 Sir James Graham, while reaffirming the government's right of impressment, instigated a registration system within the merchant service to provide a pool of experienced seamen if needed. This approach was periodically altered and refined, for example by Sir Sidney Herbert, another Admiralty official, in 1845, but was never effective because there was no obligation which could be enforced. In 1846 a plan to organize dock workers as an alternative source of manpower was attempted, again without success largely because it was too costly. In response to still another French invasion scare in 1853, the Royal Naval Coastal Volunteers, operating under the control of the Coast Guard, was formed. Coastal fishermen, a previously untapped source, were organized as a "naval militia" for home defense, a restriction being imposed against their use long distances (over fifty leagues—150 miles) from Great Britain. This hindrance, the fact that their background rendered them useless aboard modern ships of war, and the perennial problem of insufficient numbers all contributed to the abolition of this expedient twenty years later.[23]

In the early 1860s, the recruiting situation stabilized. The Admiralty was able to make certain adjustments and to study Continuous Service operating under optimum conditions. In 1862, it was designated as the only method of voluntary entry into the navy, and in 1866, generous terms were offered to the "time-expired" man who agreed to re-engage while his ship was on foreign station. Expiration of enlistment at a time other than the end of a commission was an innovation not experienced under previous methods and had to be dealt with. It would be more feasible for the man simply to re-enlist where he was and save the considerable expense of bringing him home and sending out a replacement. In the 1870s additional pay and accumulated pensions were offered. By that time only a few hundred non-Continuous Service men remained active.

The long-range answer to the question of a reliable method of recruitment in peacetime proved to be Continuous Service; the corresponding answer for an emergency or mobilization was the Royal Naval Reserve, established in 1859. Sir Bartholomew James Sulivan, now an admiral serving at the Board of Trade, formulated the concept and Sir Charles Wood and Sir John Pakington at the Admiralty added their support, emphasizing the theme of reconciliation. Volunteers were recruited directly from the experienced merchant seamen, with the first class man receiving an annual retainer of six pounds and second class, two pounds, ten shillings. A drill period of twenty-eight days per year aboard a warship was required, for which the man was paid regular wages and subsistence. The Seamen's Union endorsed the new scheme and three years later merchant marine officers became eligible for commissions, an appeasing concession to W. S. Lindsay, a dissenting member of the Royal Commission.

The Royal Naval Reserve, which still exists, was to provide the much discussed, ready source of trained seamen, although achievement of projected manning levels was again delayed.

Only about 2,000 of the desired 6,000 men had been recruited by 1862, but the new concept soon achieved success and reached a figure of 18,000 by 1878.

In the 1870s and 1880s, Lord Thomas Brassey, M.P., advocated a shift of emphasis between the navy and the reserve. He was an articulate speaker and prolific writer in pamphlets, in his own *Naval Annual*, and in books, calling for a "beefing-up" of the Royal Naval Reserve and for maintaining a smaller professional navy, something that would save money and aggrandize the role of the merchant service. The Admiralty listened to all suggestions and did strengthen the reserve as the Royal Naval Coastal Volunteers was phased out, but did not incorporate Lord Brassey's plan.

By the end of our period the Royal Naval Reserve had become recognized as the major source of experienced manpower in an emergency. Table 2 indicating the total strength from all sources of the Royal Navy and Royal Marines in the years 1871-72 and in 1885 demonstrates the relative importance and disposition of these schemes:[24]

Our typical bluejacket experienced another disruptive transition after mid-century. Technical and professional advances

Table 2. Navy and Marine Strength

| Classification | Number | | |
|---|---|---|---|
| | 1871-72 | | 1885 |
| Officers and seamen | 30,235 | (seamen only) | 34,737 |
| Boys (in training) | 7,505 | | 5,900 |
| Coast Guard | 3,985 | | 4,693 |
| Royal Marines | 14,000 | | 12,400 |
| Ashore services (dockyards) | | | 995 |
| Royal Naval Reserve | 14,438 | | 19,000 |
| Pensioner Reserves | c. 6,000 | | 1,950 |
| Royal Naval Artillery Volunteers | | | 1,600 |
| Royal Naval Coast Volunteers | 2,200 | | |
| Totals | 78,364 | | 81,275 |

contributed a new dimension and weakened and complicated the long-standing, simplistic, and hierarchical organization of the lower deck in existence during the age of sail. In that era "each task has its man, and each man has his place," and each man knew his place. In two watches, fore-, main-, and mizen-top-men on the upper level and forecastle men and the after-guard on the lower level above deck handled all evolutions, combining the two watches on special occasions such as during storms and maneuvering in confined waters. The superior positions within this structure favored the upper levels and toward the bow, e.g., fore-top-men were most superior and the after-guard most inferior above deck. Waisters, mostly landsmen, and scavengers were in the lowest positions of the adults, and then came the "boys," teenagers, "whom everybody kicked and cuffed when they came within reach."

The advent of the skilled professional associated with progress—the stoker, the engineer, the gunner, and the diver—caused complications in the hierarchical structure and created strained relations. The trend toward specialization and the emphasis upon professional competence, often acquired at instructional institutions, was resented by the traditional seaman. The newcomer was an encroacher who threatened his vested interests. This conflict over status led to alienation and even violent eruption among the identifiable groups in the dichotomy of old versus new. A parallel competitive situation existed at the officer level. Inevitably under the circumstances, the outcome favored the specialist who acquired privileges in such matters as wages and inducements, while the others felt neglected and abandoned. In the final analysis neither was satisfied, and the divisiveness has never been fully resolved.[25]

Not only was the old-time seaman forced to change his attitude, but also the Admiralty found that it must alter its philosophy toward the bluejacket. To keep up with progress the navy was obliged to abandon sail, wooden hulls, and simple guns, all of which had been standard for centuries, and cultivate and prepare a new type of seaman, a more sophisticated professional capable of manipulating the new equipment and weapons. The higher caliber man who possessed potential to learn the new skills was more discriminating, less docile, and more difficult to please than his predecessor. He unhesitatingly questioned such established practices as flogging and lack of leave. Intensive, complicated, and delicate relations with the bluejacket on the lower deck involving sympathetic consideration of his concerns and interests was something new and foreign to the naval authorities at Whitehall. As will be seen below, the Admiralty did submit to the changing situation and proceeded to radically alter its own attitudes, forcing subordinates to do likewise. The navy was "forced to nurture its own seamen," something which had only been necessary for officers in the past.

A large number of boys must be convinced annually to consider the navy as a career, and the concerns of parents must also be satisfied since their permission in writing must be obtained. Under the impressment system the navy enjoyed a captive audience; under Continuous Service, a volunteer arrangement, the program virtually had to sell itself. The Admiralty organized an elaborate propaganda campaign, eventually including distribution of pamphlets, handbills, and newspaper announcements, all "advertising the advantages." Roving recruiting teams projecting very different images from the press gangs traveled throughout the country, and after 1870 even actively recruited in Ireland. Admiralty sensitivity on the matter of attractiveness to the boy and his family was discernible in the 1870s, for example, when it immediately suspended corporal punishment of boys following complaints in Parliament and the press against birching of boys aboard training ships.

Another innovation was the establishment of an elaborate and extensive basic training program for several thousand boys per year. Previously when the merchant service had been the primary source, such preparative responsibilities had been left to that unarmed service. In conjunction with Continuous Service, Sir James Graham, First Lord of the Admiralty, established formal training facilities for the new boys, subsequently called "Jimmy Graham's novices." H.M.S. *Illustrious* with Captain Robert Harris as commander was designated a training ship and an ambitious program was implemented with significant expansion occurring later. Captain Harris remained a key figure in naval educational reform during this period.[26]

One extraneous factor which contributed to the success of the recruiting campaigns was a deteriorating economic situation, especially the so-called "Great Depression" which began in the early 1870s. The matter of conditions, whether external and economic, as in this case, or internal and environmental, aided or hindered recruiting efforts.

Despite these new conflicts the most pressing problems of manning had been solved by Continuous Service and the Royal Naval Reserve. Professor Michael Lewis called those two measures "essential to the whole structure of the modern Navy.... They revolutionized ship-life, and especially life as lived on the Lower Deck." Since no major crisis occurred during the rest of the century to require mobilization, the value of the Royal Naval Reserve could not be demonstrated; that had to wait until the twentieth century. Continuous Service was more immediately appreciated. Numerous testimonials can be cited praising the innovation, noting its success, crediting it with attracting the higher quality and better behaved seaman, and designating it, along with the reserve, as the alternative to impressment. By the end of our period the navy had become a popular institution. It was Continuous Service that created "a permanent regular Navy" and "the long-service, career-oriented, professional naval rating."[27]

The numerous problems and issues facing the Royal Navy at mid-century cannot be investigated in isolation. One affected another; one was linked with others, and changes relating to one caused altered circumstances elsewhere. Critics of the navy often enumerated major problems and with few exceptions explained that the inability to attract sufficient numbers of recruits was primarily because of harsh discipline and brutal punishment practices.

# III

# Discipline Regulations and Punishment

By 1859 some relief was experienced from the pressures of recruitment, and the Admiralty was able to turn its attention toward the Continuous Service man and toward enticing him into renewing his engagement. The environment on the lower deck must be made more attractive. As was the case with impressment, a vigorous debate was conducted outside the navy during the first half of the nineteenth century over discipline regulations and punishment practices, most notably concerning the use of corporal punishment in the army and the navy. Again the Admiralty resisted change, admitting the brutality of flogging but insisting upon the compelling danger of anarchy and pleading for the necessity of controlling an inferior class of men. At a time when the quality of seamen was improving, such arguments lacked credibility. Reform and improvement in one area invariably caused alterations in others.

Identifiable discipline regulations for the armed forces of Great Britain can be traced back to King Richard I in the twelfth century. A code of discipline, Draconian in character, was drawn up for the forces employed on the Third Crusade in 1190. Two hundred years later *The Black Book of the Admiralty*,[1] a compilation especially for the navy named for the color of the binding, delineated punishments for theft, brawling, and disobedience as well as specifying food and wine rations.

During and after the English Civil War, naval discipline regulations divided along two tracks: the Articles of War, formalized in 1661 and amended in 1749, and *The King's or Queen's Regulations and Admiralty Instructions*. The former, codified by the Earl of Sandwich from regulations used under the Commonwealth, contained thirty-four, then thirty-six, basic rules of conduct along with specified punishments, which in every case were ruthless and in most cases, capital, the recurring phrase being "... shall suffer death or such other punishment as a Court-Martial may direct." Admiral Lord George Anson was identified with the amended articles of 1749, about twenty of the thirty-six remaining unchanged, and that version became notorious for its harshness.[2] The Articles of War as a distinct entity applicable to the navy were superseded by the Naval Discipline Act of 1860, though the descriptive term continued to be used. The latter track consisted of more detailed and timely guides for discipline and was frequently revised, there being thirteen editions in the eighteenth and six in the nineteenth century before 1850. Examples of content included procedures for conducting a court-martial, responsibilities of commanding officers, and authority to punish summarily, i.e., without trial by court-martial.[3]

Discipline regulations for the navy provided for two judicial processes, summary punishment and the court-martial. Theodore Thring, author of a basic supplementary aid for naval judicial matters widely used at this time, said that the origin of the right to punish summarily was from the seventeenth century when minor offenses were punished "according to the order and custom of the sea."[4] The authority has traditionally been more powerful in the navy than in the other services, largely because naval units of necessity operated more independently and more remotely from normal channels in the chain of command. Since there has always been emphasis upon rapid and effective punishment, higher authorities have allowed wide latitude, meaning, for instance, power to execute sentences immediately without awaiting permission or confirmation. During the 1860s the Admiralty actively limited and confined the powers of discipline of naval commanders but the basic right of summary punishment was unaltered.

The more formal judicial proceeding which dealt with serious offenses was the court-martial, the first one dating from the sixteenth century. Within a hundred years precedent had established the practice that the court-martial must be held aboard a King's (or Queen's) ship, that all admirals and captains in the vicinity must sit as members or judges, and that it must sit continuously, except Sunday, until sentence. The proceedings were quite elaborate and awesome, and some of the guarantees and procedures available in civil cases were incorporated.

Composition of the court, in addition to the members, consisted of a prosecutor who was generally a designated officer of the accused's ship, and, after 1860, a representative of the naval judge advocate to act as legal overseer. The accused had the right to a civilian defense counsel, but this was of doubtful value. Outside legal experts at these "public" trials could speak only with the indulgence of the court; the accused could and did speak for himself, and a barrister could quietly give advice. A thorough review of a large number of courts-martial records, called Minutes and Proceedings, and other pertinent sources supports the conclusion that civilian attorneys were prejudicial to the accused's interests, presumably because the court members resented "outside interference."[5] Counsel was deemed "a heavy and grievous expense," and few received legal aid. Most often each defended himself. There were a few instances of the Admiralty providing a defense counsel to a constituent in a civil case.

Judicial review occurred automatically at two levels, sometimes more. The elaborate Minutes and Proceedings were first scrutinized by the convening authority, the pertinent commander-in-chief, who could make remarks and recommendations but could not change any feature. The Board of the Admiralty then reviewed every trial and followed one of several options. It could approve, remit part or all of the sentence, remonstrate any participant—member, prosecutor, witness, judge advocate, or accused—question procedures used, order the case reviewed again at some specified future time for possible remission, and cancel, annul, order a new trial, or reassemble the original court. It could not increase the punishment. The Crown must rule on all capital sentences. Legal questions which the Admiralty or any other governmental department might have were directed to the Law Office for an official legal opinion by experts. The *Admiralty Digests* contained numerous entries describing inquiries to the Law Office on a multiplicity of issues not the least of which concerned personnel and discipline. The Crown was available for final appeal and pardon, though there was little evidence of use of this alternative by naval personnel during our period.[6]

Ancillary forces attached to the Royal Navy were subject to the same discipline regulations. The Royal Marines, when aboard ship, were governed by the Naval Discipline Acts, but they organized separately as a unit and were not integrated with the seamen. As will be seen, their presence at times of disturbance and mutiny could be decisive, and if they refused to respond to authority, all was lost. The coast guard generally utilized naval regulations. In the nineteenth century most of its members had previously served in the navy, and customs and traditions were quite similar.[7]

Discipline had originally been the responsibility of the boatswain, at one time second-in-command. In the eighteenth century he lost considerable status, relinquishing police powers to the master-at-arms and his subordinate, the ship's corporal. The boatswain and his "mates" retained one function, wielding of the cat-of-nine-tails for corporal punishment. "Boatswain, do your duty!" was the order by the commanding officer to commence flogging.[8]

Punishment practices in the fleet were supervised and analyzed from Whitehall. In 1810 the Admiralty instituted warrants containing details of the offense, past record of the accused, and type and amount of punishment. These had to be signed by the commanding officer twelve hours before execution, a delay to encourage mitigation. The next year detailed reports of all punishments administered, the Quarterly Punishment Returns, were required. These and the Minutes and Proceedings of courts-martial provided the Admiralty with information about every event of legal punishment awarded; on the other hand, every other incident of punishment was illegal.

Extensive bureaucratic machinery was mobilized to maintain strict scrutiny and control over all punishments inflicted in the navy and marines. Guides, tables, reports, logs, books, inspection provisions, and other methods of supervision were developed, mostly in the early 1860s, to insure compliance and uniformity.[9] Subsequently these records and returns, which became increasingly elaborate and detailed, would be inspected and appraisals would be made. The ultimate step in the trend toward standardization was taken in 1862. William Hickman, the clerical expert on punishment, recommended use of a Table of Summary Punishments created by Captain A. P. Ryder of H.M.S. *Hero*, and the Admiralty ordered them distributed to the fleet, two thousand copies being printed. The guide consisted of six large-size, cardboard pages containing lists of minor punishments specified in the new instructions and designating exactly who might be punished by what punishment in table form from highest to lowest. Every summary punishment must be entered in the Defaulter's Book and reported on the Quarterly Returns. None but the twenty-nine authorized punishments listed could be awarded. Discharge with disgrace was first; corporal punishment was third. Numbers twenty-seven and twenty-eight applied only to boys: birching on the bare breech for second class boys and caning on breech—clothes on, for first class boys. The only punishment which might be interpreted as demeaning was number twenty-two, "carry hammock and clothes." Gags, irons, and handcuffs were specifically excluded.[10]

Critics outside the navy characterized punishment practices

as excessively brutal and capricious. They had successfully achieved moderation in the civil sector. In the 1840s they concentrated their efforts upon the services. In 1846, after several previous failures, Joseph Hume, radical M.P., moved that the punishment returns for the Royal Navy for 1845-46 be laid before the House. Passage meant a major breakthrough, the effect being to make each ship's punishment records public knowledge. The practice of publishing annual statistical returns continued until 1864; the returns for 1862-63 even being commercially printed in pamphlet form by the Council of Military Education, a quasi-official body which sponsored lectures and classes for men in the armed services.[11]

The accumulation of data about punishment provided the material for maintaining intensive bureaucratic supervision over subordinates. To the researcher of the *Admiralty Digests* it is clear that the authorities significantly increased their scrutiny of these two sets of records beginning about 1860, and that commanders were intimidated, upbraided, and in other ways forced to rigidly adhere to the regulations. The following were excerpts:

> ... unsatisfactory return. ... punishments irregular. ... disproportion appears. ... Captain ___ to explain excess number of punishments. ... My Lords much dissatisfied at receiving a Return showing such a want of discipline and good conduct. ... too lenient. ... Captain ___ censured, to adhere to form. ... Commander ___ reprimanded for careless way in which charges were drawn up. ... grave displeasure to Commanding Officer for lack of discipline. ... to Commander ___; only his disabled state saves him from being superseded. Lieutenant ___ has no such excuse. Dismiss ship [transfer him, possibly to half-pay]. ... state of discipline most lax and discreditable. ... serious displeasure ... too many lashes,

especially 50 to men in the navy. . . . explain Marine Officer awarding punishment.[12]

Such disparaging appraisals and high-handed methods abounded. No equivalent acceleration and sustained intensity of these provocative measures can be found before about 1860 or after about 1867.
The patterns and methodology of reform centered on discipline regulations and punishment practices. The Admiralty became increasingly authoritarian. Capriciousness and excessive use of corporal punishment were primary complaints of critics. In effect guilt was admitted when the Admiralty rigorously demanded uniformity, standardization, and conformity, on occasion resorting to punitive measures. The Admiralty pointed out illegal punishments and irregular procedures directly to commanding officers or, more effectively, indirectly through the commander-in-chief of the squadron or station who was ordered to convey the displeasure of the authorities.[13]

Commanding officers and commanders-in-chief were not the only targets. Circular Order No. 17 of 4 July 1862, reviewed the duties of the judge advocates at courts-martial and admonished them, the advisors, to be more careful. A list of "cases where irregularities have invalidated the sentences of Courts-Martial" was enclosed.[14]

The Admiralty was determined to make examples of recalcitrant officers who failed to adhere to the new regulations and submit to uniformization. Captain C. F. Hillyar of H.M.S. *Queen* was censured in 1861 for flogging a man belonging to the first class, a new classification of conduct providing immunity from corporal punishment. The court-martial of Commander B. G. W. Nicolas, H.M.S. *Trident*, provided a particularly good example of the cruel and unusual punishments that so outraged the public and raised the ire of the Admiralty. It is therefore worth recounting in some detail. On 9 November 1861, two boys returned aboard *Trident* forty-three hours late. At the court-martial of Commander Nicolas a month later, the first lieutenant described them as "generally good characters." Neither had appeared in the Defaulter's Book previously, which technically meant that the offense was their first. Commander Nicolas asked them no questions but ordered them flogged immediately. Every witness estimated differently the number of lashes on this and four subsequent occasions. The Lieutenant said "60 to 70 strokes each time." Each boy claimed he made an accurate count on at least one occasion, one said 115 and the other, 116. Both recalled that they had become insensible during at least one of the floggings. Immediately afterward Commander Nicolas ordered them to holystone the quarterdeck where they remained without food from noon to midnight. Both were flogged again on 11 November and one a third time on 12 November. The ship's corporal testified that this punishment was no more severe than usual. Commander Nicolas was tried by court-martial for irregular and cruel punishment and for failure to properly investigate the charges. He apologized at the end of the trial: "I committed a grave and serious error of judgment." The court found him guilty and sentenced him to discharge with disgrace, the most severe punishment for an officer short of death. The Admiralty circulated a memo relating all details throughout the fleet.[15]

In the case of Captain R. Moorman of H.M.S. *Cossack*, exoneration by court-martial did not prevent censure. He was "acquitted, charge not proved" in a trial for illegal punishment and cruelty, yet the Admiralty still denounced the punishments as "not in conformity with regulation." He responded with an appeal, but to no avail. In another case, Captain John H. Alexander of H.M.S. *Forte* was dismissed from his ship for failure to delay punishment the required time after the warrant was signed.[16]

Another approach resulting from this intensive scrutiny at Whitehall involved remission of sentences coupled with condemnation of those administering them. The phrase "too severe," followed by cancellation of part or all of the sentence, recurred. There were increased instances of the Admiralty impatiently observing that a court-martial was unnecessary in this or that case. For example, a court-martial of an engineer on H.M.S. *Wolverine* for "persisting in playing cards in his hammock while on the sick list," awarded a severe reprimand and loss of three month's seniority. The Admiralty threw out the entire proceeding, there being "nothing unreasonable" in playing cards "so long as gambling is avoided." Late in 1866 a confidential letter was promulgated warning all commanders that the Admiralty had determined that many courts-martial sentences were "unnecessarily severe" and some had been reduced, that periods of imprisonment were too long, that the punishment "discharge with disgrace" was being "abused," and that other discharges were being awarded "for trivial acts." When interrogated in the House of Commons about excessive punishment in 1866, Sir John Pakington, the new First Lord, answered that he too had been concerned and sent out the memo "calling attention to the severity of sentences, and expressing an opinion that their severity ought to be relaxed." In the House of Lords in 1863 the Earl of Hardwicke questioned the procedure of the Admiralty reviewing and changing courts-martial judgments, those being independent judicial decisions. A long debate also ensued in the House of Commons.[17]

Two persons had been assigned to administer the policy of extended supervision by the use of quarterly returns and courts-martial records: William Hickman, a clerk and legal expert, was responsible for the former, and William G. Romaine, Second Secretary of the Admiralty, perused and analyzed the Minutes and Proceedings of courts-martial. It was they who ruthlessly pointed out discrepancies, inconsistencies, and irregular procedures and even, on occasion, resorted to punitive measures[18] against recalcitrants, all, of course, in the name of the Admiralty and through the proper channels.

About 1867 the Admiralty discontinued accumulating extensive statistics on punishment, the returns for the previous year having been withheld from publication. William Hickman was released from his responsibilities after 31 March 1867, with thanks for a job well done; subsequently the legal branch was to "superintend" this area. On the last day of 1868, the Admiralty Board altered the policies relating to the review of courts-martial and in 1870, a formal procedure was promulgated. These were indications that the intensive scrutiny over the past decade had paid off and was no longer necessary. A variety of sources confirmed that punishment practices had been moderated and that discipline had improved.[19] Our typical bluejacket now faced discipline regulations and punishment practices considerably moderated, and he could reasonably expect that his interests were being protected in the highest echelons of the service.

The recipients of these aggressive and intimidating methods to moderate punishments did not all submit quietly and docilely. Another reason for curtailing wide distribution of statistics and relaxation of scrutiny stemmed undoubtedly from numerous complaints from commanders in the fleet. In their appraisals of reform requested by the Admiralty in 1865, there were many denunciations: ". . . of doubtful value. . . . misleads the public. . . . delusive and unsatisfactory bases. . . . an unmitigated evil. . . . least beneficial of all reforms." Captain F. B. Seymour of H.M.S. *Royal Adelaide* was most outspoken:

> I must most respectfully express dissent. . . . Nothing can be more fatal to the discipline of the service, than that an idea should become prevalent that the professional prospects of an officer depend upon the absence of crime on board the ship he commands. . . . [20]

In an article on manning reforms Roy Taylor summed up:

> Some captains . . . were said to be reluctant to punish as

they should for fear of Admiralty censure, and the Admiralty itself was accused of pandering to public opinion, which was becoming more sensitive on matters of discipline.[21]

Commanders objecting to the high-handed methods and permissiveness were appeased by being allowed to expel personnel who had continuously caused discipline problems. A less severe process of punitive dismissal, "discharge as objectionable," was permitted, indeed, encouraged. There had been complaints of a number of incorrigibles who could not be adequately controlled, especially after the moderating measures, but whose conduct did not justify "discharge with disgrace," a serious punitive device. The fact that the Admiralty would permit the free release of personnel was a sign that the critical manpower shortage on the lower deck had passed. The effect was that of a relief valve. As higher caliber Continuous Service men came into the navy, undesirable and troublesome ones could be released. Commanders had much praise for the success of this practice.[22]

The transformation which resulted from the abandonment of impressment and the institution of Continuous Service for recruiting exemplified one of the primary reforms in the Royal Navy between 1850 and 1880; another was the elimination of corporal punishment and its replacement by some form of confinement. Here the change was dramatic, and the evolution of reform can be readily followed step-by-step, once the pressures of public opinion had reached that optimum point at which the Admiralty was forced to react, however reluctantly. In 1850, corporal punishment, awarded summarily and by courts-martial, was the principal method of punishment; in 1880, it had been declared officially illegal. The trend can be followed graphically by referring to charts 2 and 3 in the appendix.

Mention of corporal punishment generally brings to mind flogging with the infamous "cat-of-nine-tails" against a half-naked common seaman or soldier strung up before formal ranks of his peers either aboard ship or on some regimental parade ground. No doubt that depiction was the most common form, but there were other methods and devices for punishment which were "corporal," i.e., administered upon the body. The use of handcuffs, gags, rattans, ropes' ends or "stomicky," hammock clews, canes, birches, "cobbs" or "firks," "nettles," putting men in irons or strait jackets, the practice of blistering, branding or "marking," and even keelhauling were all forms of corporal punishment used from the seventeenth century to 1880, most of them unsanctioned and illegal. By the latter date all use of any of these devices had been suspended in the Royal Navy with the exception of the cane and birch, and those only for juveniles.

As for flogging in the classic depiction, it was introduced in the seventeenth century and soon became the most common form of punishment in the navy. Previously the term "whipping" described a thrashing by using stout switches or rods, the maximum strokes being thirty-nine for the number noted in a Biblical reference.[23] In the interim, fines had been assessed as punishment, the money going to the Chatham Chest, a kind of charity.

The instrument to administer flogging was the cat-of-nine-tails, constructed of that number of hand-twisted cords of cotton or flax about eighteen inches long fastened to a wooden handle. At the end of each cord was a hard knot or pellet of lead. During execution of a punishment the boatswains alternated every dozen lashes. Dudley Pope, a writer of naval history, actually conducted an experiment with a duplicate of one of the last cats made in 1867. A person weighing 152 pounds struck a piece of wood (pitch-pine) and broke it. "A man not lashed to a grating would be knocked down by the first blow," Pope concluded.[24]

Typically, flogging was administered before all hands at formal quarters with the Royal Marines on the Quarterdeck above and the surgeon behind the grating upon which the accused was "seized-up." The time was usually 7:30 a.m. The large number of personally maintained logs and journals, usually in the form of diaries kept by midshipmen, now collected in the National Maritime Museum, Greenwich, shows this early morning time for corporal punishment to have been common practice. The phrase "as per warrant" when noting corporal punishment execution persisted, indicating a special consciousness of that provision for a formal document.[25]

Severity of corporal punishment increased in the eighteenth century, especially during the regime of Admiral Lord George Anson at the Admiralty. He emphasized "manual correction" as a way to improve discipline and provided for extreme versions of corporal punishment: "flogging round the fleet," consisting of a dozen lashes before the gangway of every ship present, and "running the gauntlet," in which the whole crew participated in whipping the accused. Scott Claver, author of the only authoritative survey of the practice of corporal punishment, concluded that the incidence of flogging reached a maximum during the first decade of 1800 and decreased subsequently.[26]

The history of flogging in the army was much the same, but most of the instances of rumors and actual observations of large numbers of lashes—500, 1000, 1500, even 2000—pertain to army punishment, and most occurred in the eighteenth and early nineteenth centuries. Nevertheless, there was general agreement that flogging in the navy was more severe. "Punishment in the Navy was four times as heavy as in the Army." "Forty-eight lashes in the navy equalled 100 lashes ashore." Testifying before the Royal Commission on Military Punishment, a surgeon who had treated recipients of floggings from both services concluded that navy punishment was "much more severe. The cat is heavier, the blow is heavier, but the stripes are fewer." *Queen's Regulations and Admiralty Instructions* limited the number of lashes by the commanding officer in summary punishment to twelve; a court-martial could award up to forty-eight. The former restriction was ignored.[27]

Numerous detailed and even autobiographical accounts of actual floggings can be found, and many were available for contemporaries to read and to use in the campaign against corporal punishment, including exposition during debates in Parliament.[28]

The use of corporal punishment in the navy, and also in the army, became the object of increasing controversy in the nineteenth century. Beginning in the 1810s and reaching intensity in the late 1840s, a campaign was waged in Parliament and among the public to abolish what was depicted as a dastardly punishment. The Parliamentary campaign against flogging was led by radicals, notably William Cobbett,[29] Sir Francis Burdett,[30] and Joseph Hume.[31] A Royal Commission on Military Punishment studied the question as it related to the army in 1835-36 and endorsed the practice if the number of lashes would not exceed 200.[32] After a perusal of the perennial debates in Parliament, it becomes apparent that the arguments were redundant and stereotyped. Statistics and analyses of the punishment returns were used by both sides. Opponents of the practice aired claims of instances of hundreds of lashes, delineated accounts of fatalities which resulted, and put forward the examples of other nations, especially Prussia, France, and the United States, which did not resort to or had recently abolished flogging without mishap. This group consistently presented corporal punishment as degrading. Proponents pleaded that abolition would be desirable from a humanitarian point of view but impossible if order and disipline were to be maintained and anarchy avoided, and that the effects had been moderated and future abuses precluded by checks and controls.

The authorities continued to insist that the practice of corporal punishment was vital to maintain discipline in the armed forces which were necessary to protect the empire and domestic security. As late as 1861 Theodore Thring in *A*

*Treatise on Criminal Law in the Navy* concluded, "corporal punishment is, in the opinion of the best authorities, necessary for the maintenance of discipline." Admiral Sir Astley Cooper Key acknowledged "the inevitability of flogging." It was associated "in the people's minds with any of the ordinary and routine—or inevitable—operations to be carried out on board ships, such as scrubbing decks or loosing sails to dry," he continued. The first flogging punishment awarded by a new commanding officer was "generally taken as a criterion of his future conduct towards the ship's company, in the way of supporting his officers." An undated (probably about 1880) pamphlet by the noted reformer of discipline practices, Admiral Sir William Fanshawe Martin, called for retention of corporal punishment because it was vital to England's existence; "the use of the 'cat' rests upon absolute necessity." To recruit from a better source of men, discharge those who were troublesome, or substitute the punishment of imprisonment were all merely palliatives, he believed.[33]

Outside Parliament, campaigns for and against corporal punishment were conducted utilizing various media: newspapers, pamphlets, didactic novels, journals, petitions, public meetings and demonstrations, what Professor W. L. Burn has called "the discipline of publicity."[34] Throughout the period the *Times* kept the public informed on incidents of flogging in the armed forces including feature articles, coverage of sensational (especially fatal) cases, reprints of statistics on crime and punishment, accounts of public demonstrations against flogging, public praise and congratulations, letters to the editor, and reports of decrease in the incidence of flogging in their coverage.[35] Other newspapers and journals provided significant coverage, notably *The People's Journal, The Annual Register, Tait's Edinburgh Magazine, Nautical Magazine, Fraser's Magazine, Blackwood's Magazine, The Nineteenth Century*,[36] and the two new service journals, *The Journal of the Royal United Service Institution* and *The Army and Navy Gazette*.[37]

Selective examples of the written debate illustrate the tenor of the arguments. A passionate indictment of flogging in the navy "by an old officer" appeared in *Tait's Edinburgh Magazine* in 1834. Flogging was an "inhuman custom" carried out by "that modern substitute for thumbscrews and racks, the cat-o'-nine tails." He related in lurid detail the effects of a punishment of over 100 lashes. He concluded that those commanders who resorted least to corporal punishment experienced the least problems.[38] William Howitt wrote in *The People's Journal*:

. . . dogs in England are protected by a whole act of Parliament. . . . The soldier of this country has not even the consideration of a dog. . . . This revolting barbarity cannot and will not longer be tolerated![39]

On the other side, an article in *The Nineteenth Century* in 1879, at a time when the practice of corporal punishment had practically ceased, called for its retention. By the use of exaggerated stereotypes, the author compared English servicemen with German, French, and Russian; the former inherently "needs more coercive treatment" and was more prone "to get into trouble." "Universal compulsory service" was the only alternative in England to the continued use of corporal punishment, it was claimed.[40] *The Annual Register* printed summaries of several cases including a court-martial of a commanding officer found guilty of cruelty and discharged.[41]

Several naval officers and others wrote didactic novels presenting opposite views on the practice of corporal punishment. The most famous critic was Captain Frederick Marryat, who in *The King's Own* presented a description of a flogging round the fleet. Captain Frederick Chamier was an apologist for corporal punishment in a series of novels in the 1830s. In the United States Herman Melville, who had served in the navy, wrote *White-Jacket*, an autobiographical novel containing several chapters critical of the practice.[42]

Corporal punishment, especially fatalities, led to public

demonstrations, petitions, and irate letters. One observer described the public as "hypersensitive" over the issue. William Heritage of Bethnal Green claimed his fifteen-year-old son jumped overboard from the *North Star* to avoid flogging. Residents of Bethnal Green met in a demonstration of protest and petitioned Parliament "to put an end to the barbarous and unchristian practice of tearing the living flesh from the backs of our fellow creatures. ('Hear, hear!')." A professional surgeon, Anthony Carlisle of Langham Place, in a letter to the *Times* after a fatal flogging in the army, claimed excessive flogging could disrupt physiological functions to an extreme degree. Corporal punishment was not justifiable if death could result, he concluded. In 1841, the "Easter Sunday flogging episode" at Hounslow barracks involving the Earl of Cardigan created sensation and notoriety.[43]

The Admiralty occasionally responded to these outside pressures against corporal punishment. A circular order of 1830 urged "safe forbearance." The 1844 edition of *Queen's Regulations and Admiralty Instructions* cautioned "great discretion and all due forbearance." The 1862 edition admonished commanding officers "to exercise the power vested in them with the greatest discretion and forbearance." This latter edition contained other restrictions not previously enunciated: authority to administer corporal punishment could not be delegated, and execution of corporal punishment was suspended on Sundays.[44]

Meanwhile more decisive action was being taken at Whitehall. In 1853, an important circular order set forth strict guidelines for summary punishment; in 1859, another circular order created classes based upon appraisals of conduct and exempted all men in the first class, the majority, from corporal punishment. All of this was followed by the previously described measures of administrative supervision. In 1866, a circular order summed up current policy. In 1871, A. J. Otway, M.P. for Chatham, questioned G. J. Goschen, First Lord of the Admiralty, about the continued use of corporal punishment. The latter responded that the Royal Navy now proposed to suspend the use in peacetime.[45] The exceptions were mutiny under circumstances precluding early imprisonment and the special situation of juveniles in training. The First Lord concluded that

> the higher education of our seamen, and the general condition of the Navy, will enable us to make these changes without detriment to the efficiency of our Fleets, and with much advantage to the popularity of the service.[46]

This was confirmed by Circular Order No. 66 of 18 December 1871, subjecting corporal punishment to "further restrictions." Until 1879 theoretically the limitations applied only to peacetime, but in that year the First Lord extended the suspension to all contingencies. However, suspended did not mean abolished. In the Royal Navy, corporal punishment could still be awarded for mutiny and gross personal violence to an officer until after the end of World War II, the Cadogan Committee of 1938 recommending its continuation.[47]

Corporal punishment of boys and officer cadets remained an exception to the rule of suspension, something insisted upon by training administrators. They claimed that their circumstances were different from those aboard a warship and that large numbers of juveniles in an environment of instruction could only be effectively disciplined by use of "the birch (supplied from the dockyards) and not the cat." Students must be motivated and protected, and other forms of punishment were potentially corrupting. Boys under eighteen could be awarded not over twenty-four "cuts... on the bare breech... in the presence of the officer next under the Commanding Officer, the Medical Officer, two or more petty officers, and all other Boys." They were not subject to courts-martial. This punishment required a warrant and an entry in the Quarterly

Returns. Boys over eighteen were to be treated as other seamen.

Sensitivity to public opinion was exemplified in the late 1860s over the matter of birching officer cadets aboard the training ship *Britannia*. Questions were raised in Parliament, and the First Lord, H. T. L. Corry, explained the Admiralty's philosophy about the uniqueness of this situation. Cadets were potential officers, and these practices were the same as those administered at the best public schools and were not used elsewhere in the navy. This was in March 1867. The same complainant revived his charge of excessive cruelty in July, and this time birching was discontinued, though not permanently. In 1873, birching cadets in the second and third class for conduct was revived.

Minor controversy continued to arise over the question of corporal punishment. The *Digests* contained a few entries of its execution after 1871: instances of up to 48 lashes, mostly for insubordination and striking a superior officer. A confidential letter of 1879 to commanders-in-chief ordered that the maximum limit be reduced to twenty-five lashes for a court-martial sentence. Simultaneously a pattern of the standard navy cat-of-nine-tails was issued to all ships. There continued to be complaints that discipline was deteriorating, for example from Admirals Sir Alexander Milne and Sir William Fanshawe Martin, and even some lamentations from seamen that flogging should be revived. Presumably the Admiralty was never truly convinced that suspension of corporal punishment was in the best interests of the Royal Navy. Outside pressure and sensitivity to the navy's public image were the decisive factors.[48]

As has been noted, flogging was only one form of corporal punishment. An explanation of the disposition of some other types will present a more comprehensive perspective of life on the lower deck experienced by our typical bluejacket. The punishment of "starting," i.e., the beating of a seaman with sticks, broomsticks, rattans, ropes' ends, etc., was officially prohibited by the Admiralty in 1809 after a celebrated court-martial and reprimand of Captain Robert Corbet of H.M.S. *Nereide*. Regulations were ignored and illegalities continued. Seamen diarists during our period, Lionel Yexley and Sam Noble, recalled that "starting" was commonly practiced by petty officers.[49]

Placing a seaman "in irons" was restricted in 1853, the first step toward abolishing the practice.[50] An incident, projected into a public scandal in late 1867, caused the Admiralty to outlaw another restraining device, the use of gags. Ordinary Seaman George Addison, H.M.S. *Favorite*, was gagged using "three turns of a small piece of rope," and handcuffed upon returning to the ship drunk and violent. Two hours later he was found dead, and a lieutenant and the master-at-arms were court-martialed for "unlawful assault, improper and excessive punishment, and manslaughter." Both were acquitted. The incident evoked a question in Parliament, and the Admiralty was most displeased. In the circular sent to the fleet abolishing the use of gags, the Admiralty suggested that men who were noisy or otherwise violent should be confined in a cell.

Branding or "marking"[51] was practiced in the Royal Marines as late as 1870, though the process had been declared illegal five years earlier. This punishment was never used against personnel in the navy.[52]

In these evolutionary steps leading to the cessation of the use of corporal punishment, the navy lagged behind the army and the civil sector. After a second study by a Royal Commission in 1868, the army complied with the recommendation that the practice be suspended. Sir Samuel Romilly was instrumental in the civil reform measures, the only exceptions being punishment for crimes of violence against the Royal Family and "garrotting," similar to "mugging." The alternative was imprisonment.[53]

In all the debate over the practice of corporal punishment, the defenders insisted that there was no feasible alternative which fulfilled the requirements under the special circumstances aboard a warship operating long distances from friendly bases, but, as in the case of impressment, those who could only argue necessity were overruled. The punishment selected as the replacement of flogging was confinement. The Report on Crime and Punishment in the Navy of 1862 contained the explanation:

> Imprisonment has of late years been substituted in a great measure for flogging, much to the discontent of the seamen themselves, though in deference to a popular outcry amongst civilians.[54]

The Earl of Hardwicke in the House of Lords called it "a step ... in accordance with public feeling."

There developed a kind of hierarchy of confinement punishments, from minor to serious: "confinement in cells" was a locally-executed, summary punishment; "solitary confinement" could be administered for very short periods locally, i.e., aboard ship, or it could be designated as part of a more serious "imprisonment" sentence; "imprisonment" meant in a jail ashore; "imprisonment at hard labor" was a more severe sentence; and "penal servitude" was most serious of all of the incarceration measures. The Admiralty ordered confinement cells built aboard large ships for summary punishment involving less than ten days and provided elaborate instructions on dimensions, ventilation, and location. Apparently commanding officers of steam warships attempted to improvise in the matter because one commander-in-chief made a point of prohibiting the use of coal bunkers in lieu of cells. "Confinement in cells on bread and water" was limited to three days. "Hard labor" did not mean industrial employment but irksome, fatiguing, and degrading tasks such as picking three to six pounds of oakum six to ten hours a day or manipulating the treadmill or a crank. Civil penal philosophy at this time sanctioned all of these practices. The emphasis was on deterrence, and attempts at moral regeneration were relegated to second place. The sentence of "transportation," common in the civil sector in the late eighteenth and early nineteenth centuries, was permanently discontinued in the 1850s.[55]

During the evolution of shifting emphases of punishment, the Admiralty went to great lengths to provide exclusive arrangements for the bluejacket sentenced to prison, the rationale being "to save our seamen from the contamination of prisoners in civil jails." Special facilities ashore were provided for naval prisoners on various foreign stations. In 1862 the Admiralty established its own prison at home, originally the county jail of Sussex at Lewes, containing 120 solitary confinement cells. "The only naval prison in the world" was supervised by a Board of Visitors consisting of the Speaker of the House of Commons, several senior naval officers, and the magistrates of Lewes. Administration incorporated a Governor, always a naval or marine officer, and eighteen "warders." Inevitably the prisoners were divided into classes for conduct, in this case three, and each prisoner wore distinctive clothing indicating his class. As a prisoner moved up from third to first class there were more privileges, increasing relaxation of restrictions, and less labor.[56] Corporal punishment was utilized but had to be reported to the Admiralty, this being another exception to the suspension in the navy. An observer given a tour was most impressed with the "good order and dead silence" at Lewes Naval Prison. Between 1862 and 1874 over six thousand prisoners passed through this penal institution with only three deaths occurring.[57]

The Admiralty itself exemplified the "positive approach" to discipline by offering rewards, medals, and badges demonstrating appreciation for long service and mitigating punishments because of prior good conduct or heroism. Each year during this period the *Digests* contained twenty to thirty pages detailing "Rewards and Gratuities." In 1862, for example, there were 288 separate entries of praise, rewards, promotions, pensions, foreign orders of merit, commendations, special favors, and privileges.[58]

Past conduct and performance influenced considerations for mitigation and remission of punishments; in addition to age, physical or medical disabilities, the *Digests* contained numerous references to

> prior good conduct, ... long service, ... heroic deeds, ... long service and wounds, ... youth and inexperience, ... performance of outstanding service while a prisoner, ... great provocation and high testimonials, ... heart condition, ... and skin disease.[59]

Unusual sensitivity, receptivity, and generosity in the matter of requests for remission of past punishments was demonstrated, statistically as in table 3.

Table 3. Remission Requests[60]

| Year | Number of Petitions Received | Number Acted Upon, Remitting All or Part | Refusals |
|---|---|---|---|
| 1861 | 17 | 11 | 6 |
| 1862 | — | — | — |
| 1863 | 26 | 22 | 4 |
| 1864 | 30 | 26 | 4 |
| 1865 | 34 | 27 | 7 |
| 1866 | 33 | 26 | 7 |
| 1867 | 31 | 26 | 5 |
| 1868 | 31 | 25 | 6 |
| 1869 | 15 | 14 | 1 |
| 1870 | 36 | 25 | 11 |
| 1871 | — | — | — |
| 1872 | 45 | 24 | 21 |
| 1873 | 59 | 45 | 11 |
| 1874 | 58 | 33 | 25 |
| 1875 | 48 | 28 | 20 |
| 1876 | 37 | 22 | 15 |
| 1877 | 28 | 20 | 8 |
| 1878 | — | — | — |
| 1879 | 25 | 16 | 9 |

In this study reference has been made to certain extreme contingencies about which the authorities speculated: if the prerogative of impressment were abandoned, England would be overwhelmed in an emergency and all would be lost; and if the practice of corporal punishment were abolished, anarchy would surely follow, England would be overwhelmed and all would be lost. In fact, both of those processes were voluntarily suspended by the Admiralty, and Armageddon did not follow. But what about the occurrence of mutiny, especially one as serious as that of 1797? If that happened, then England surely would be overwhelmed and all would be lost!

# IV

# Mutiny, Desertion, Problems of Leadership, and Alcoholism

## A. Mutiny: the Ultimate Defiance

Beginning in July 1859, and extending over a year's time, a series of riots and demonstrations aboard individual ships within the Royal Navy created considerable alarm at Whitehall. In contemporary Admiralty records the incidents are continually referred to as "mutinies." The Admiralty was most concerned about avoiding repetition of the events of 1797, "the Great Mutiny."

By legal definition, mutiny could incorporate a wide spectrum of acts: from those sensational insurrections at Spithead and the Nore in 1797, to the incident that same year when seamen murdered their officers and then turned over a frigate to England's enemy, to "the concerted refusal on the part of several seamen to obey the command of their superior officer—but without violence shown or threatened."[1] Whatever its degree, mutiny ranked as the most serious crime in the armed services; "the ultimate defiance," it undermined the very basis of authority and threatened the existence of the nation and empire. The discipline regulations treated the crime as extraordinary, much as treason in the civil sector. Maximum punishment was specified, and mutiny was the single exception to a number of general provisions and legal requirements.[2] Justification for such unique status was based upon the extreme seriousness of the offense, the potential danger involved, the compelling need to deter repetition, and the setting of an example for others to heed.

The panic of the authorities when confronted by potential mutiny was based upon precedents, notably the insurrections of 1797 which immobilized whole fleets, and, very recently, the Sepoy Mutiny in India in 1857 which did not directly involve the navy.

The definitive historians of "the Great Mutiny" have described the events of 1797 as "the most astonishing recorded in our, or perhaps any history."[3] What made these episodes so appalling was the fact that Great Britain was in the midst of a serious war with France and her allies, Spain and Holland, and that those powers were completing plans for a combined fleet-invasion campaign against the British. Thus one major difference in the situation in 1859 was the absence of such an awesome background.

There were two major and several minor outbreaks during 1797. At Spithead, the fleet anchorage between Portsmouth and the Isle of Wight, the crews of sixteen ships-of-the-line, during the period 16 April to 15 May, executed a well-organized take-over with "extra-ordinary restraint amounting almost to decorum, if mutinies can be decorus."[4] The authorities resumed control in an orderly manner after the government submitted to the principal demand for higher pay, and the mutineers received a royal pardon. All accounts conclude that the initiative of the enlisted men in this case was "justifiable."

By contrast, events at the Nore, the fleet anchorage in the Thames estuary, which began three days before the end of the mutiny at Spithead and continued for five weeks, exemplified irrationality, disruption, and violence[5] on both sides. The mutineers humiliated their officers, blockaded London, and threatened to sail away and join the enemy. The government lost patience and ruthlessly suppressed the rising, the Admiralty insisting upon maximum recrimination: over 400 courts-martial handed down 59 death sentences, 9 floggings, and 180 imprisonments. Twenty-nine[6] were actually executed, including Richard Parker, a Quota-man and leader of the mutiny. Risings did not end at Spithead and the Nore, for there were further mutinies at Plymouth, at Yarmouth, and in the Mediterranean Squadron where Lord St. Vincent resorted to execution of a dozen rebels. In September an especially bloody mutiny occurred aboard the frigate H.M.S. *Hermione*, 32 guns, off Puerto Rico. Ten officers were murdered, and the ship was turned over to the Spaniards. Eventually twenty-four mutineers were hanged.[7]

The mutineers of 1797 insistently and consistently demanded more pay, which was granted. Explanations about other causes and factors included everything from foreign intrigue, traitorous activities, and domestic revolutionary attempts linked to the Corresponding Societies and Irish insurrectionists, to revulsion against tyrannical officers and the press gang. Participants at Spithead, Plymouth, and in the Mediterranean did not specifically complain against flogging, though those at the Nore did. The definitive study stressed poor pay and the tyranny of officers.[8] As to outside influences, Geoffrey Marcus, a naval historian, discounted them, and E. P. Thompson, a social historian, speculated that there was some connection.[9]

Two mutinies involving single ships occurred before the end of the Napoleonic wars, one apparently partly caused by "starting."[10] No other important instances were recorded before 1859, though some comment and interest in England centered on the *Somers* mutiny in the United States Navy in 1842.[11]

The first signs of crisis were reported in July 1859, aboard H.M.S. *Liffey*, *Caesar*, and *Hero*; in a short time, incidents occurred on *Neptune* and *Orion*, but most serious were the eruptions aboard H.M.S. *Marlborough*, 121 guns and flagship of the Mediterranean Squadron, and *Princess Royal*, a 91-gun ship-of-the-line. The situation moderated during the winter of 1859-60, but disturbances resumed in March and April, again reaching serious proportions. H.M.S. *Terrible, Forte, Synx, James Watt, Calypso, Hero, Mars, Donegal,* and *Edgar* experienced disorders, in the last case exaggerated because the marines participated.

The causes of the instability were various. In all cases the primary complaint of the men was lack of leave. Reference has already been made to the extenuating circumstances of shortage of personnel, fluctuations in the manning level, and the damaging impact of the offer of a bounty, which nevertheless had failed to attract the necessary numbers. Simultaneously there existed an acute shortage of petty and warrant officers and a consequent excess of new and inexperienced men, a situation fraught with danger, especially if competent and conscientious officers were also lacking.[12] Other signs of crisis included unusually high desertion rates and large numbers of absentees without leave, so serious that several ships reported being unable to get underway.[13]

Signs of instability and disgruntlement abounded. Aboard the ships the men defied orders, audibly complained, mostly about lack of leave, and resorted to sabotage. Commodore G. P. Hornby recalled later that "no ship of any size... has gone through a Commission without the occurrence of an *emerite* (as they are called) [he obviously meant *emeute* for disturbance] involving the cutting of breechings, throwing overboard sights, linch pins, etc." The *Admiralty Digests* record receipt of an inordinate number of anonymous complaints, mostly demanding leave. The public became restive. There were questions in Parliament about "mutinous proceedings," reports in the newspapers, and letters to the *Times.*[14]

Three instances warrant detailed review. Aboard H.M.S. *Marlborough* in August 1859, "a few turbulent men... unaccustomed to discipline and excited by Reports in the Newspapers of occurrences at home, urged on their messmates. . . . They refused to change clothes and threw shot down hatchways." After order was restored four men were court-martialed, three receiving sentences of fifty lashes and two years' imprisonment each and the fourth, one year imprisonment. In this instance the Admiralty, after review, objected that the punishment was "much too lenient . . . , should have been death commuted to penal servitude for life," because the "mutineers" had "not a shadow of excuse."[15]

A more serious outbreak, described as "a disgraceful riot," took place in November aboard H.M.S. *Princess Royal*, this one involving a casualty among the ten men directly participating. Courts-martial sentenced all to imprisonment at hard labor: two to two years, five to eighteen months, and two to six months, the wounded seaman having been removed from immediate prosecution. Additionally, 109 men were charged with "being present at mutiny and not suppressing it" and sentenced to three months at hard labor. This incident generated major repercussions. Earlier that year in July, William Williams, M.P., had raised questions in the House of Commons about recent punishment returns of *Princess Royal*, indicating fifty-three men had been flogged 2141 lashes, or over forty lashes per man. Williams hoped the navy would "make some stringent changes in the matter of flogging."[16] Subsequently in a letter to the *Times*, "An Employer of Labour" deplored the "harsh and fatuous conduct" of Admiral William Bowles and other "incompetent" officers in this "so-called mutiny." The episode was an example of the failure to recognize "better educated, more intelligent men now" in the navy, claimed the anonymous writer.[17] In this case the Admiralty reacted quite differently. It severely censured the commanding officer of *Princess Royal*, Captain Baillie, and the ship's officers and police. In addition it pardoned, released, reimbursed, and granted leave to all of the accused. In the aftermath, Admiral Bowles, who was the convening authority, and Captain Baillie became embroiled with the Admiralty in recriminations resulting in the captain being "discharged to the shore" and the admiral resigning, leaving with the request that "a real and efficient Police force" be established aboard all ships "to prevent insubordination and desertion."[18]

The third episode was among the later series of incidents and was particularly alarming because the Royal Marines aboard the ship, H.M.S. *Edgar*, participated. The Admiralty rushed the marine commander, General Wesley, to Portsmouth where *Edgar* was located, to intervene and investigate. He ordered twenty courts-martial and had the detachment broken up and transferred.

It required an explosive situation such as this to force the Admiralty into unaccustomed and decisive action, most of which was incorporated into the comprehensive Naval Discipline Act of 1860. Leave policy was liberalized, the use of corporal punishment was significantly limited, monthly pay was instituted, eligibility for good conduct pay was reduced from five to three years, and a formally organized Ship's Police was introduced, "a superior class of persons to perform duties of Master-at-Arms and Ship's Corporal," paradoxically, something called for by the departing Admiral Bowles.[19] Under circumstances such as these in the past, the expected Admiralty response would have been quite the opposite: leave cancelled, corporal punishment increased, pay withheld, good conduct pay cancelled, etc. Commodore Dunlop, senior officer at Woolwich, apparently was disappointed because of Admiralty permissiveness. He later lamented that

> 1859 was the decisive year. . . . if the voice of the Admiralty had been heard throughout the Fleet in sterner tones in 1859, little more would have been necessary, now I feel certain that much more severe measures must be adopted in order to maintain the discipline of the Fleet.[20]

The reforms of 1859-60, significant as they were in the

overall view, failed to end the disturbances. Although the crisis situation passed and did not recur, isolated incidents erupted during the decade of the 1860s, notably aboard H.M.S. *Ringdove, Liverpool,* and *Leander.* A "disgruntled" crew threw gun parts overboard "in the presence of the enemy" (China) from H.M.S. *Ringdove* on the China Station in 1863. Courts-martial handed down stiff imprisonment sentences to fifteen seamen, but these were remitted by the Admiralty, an indication of justification.[21] "Cans and vinegar beakers were thrown at officers" and shouts of "leave" and "work up until twelve o'clock at night" exemplified the outbreak on *Liverpool* in 1863. A dozen men received minor punishments, but more leave was granted, again an act of appeasement.[22]

Four sources presented contradictory accounts of the events occurring aboard H.M.S. *Leander* on 9 November 1865. The ship's log described an incident in which the crew refused to muster until after the marines had been armed "ten to twelve minutes" later. The *Digest* entry delineated circumstances under which the men remained below "a considerable time." Able Seaman Tilling presented a more detailed account in his journal, claiming forty-five minutes elapsed during which time the men yelled "money and leave!" No leave had been granted for nine months, and some men had not been ashore for two years. At lunch time representatives from each mess had gone to the commodore who was aboard asking for leave according to regulations. He refused to see them during his meal. Tilling observed, "This was the signal for us to show we would not be trifled with any longer." Much is made at the courts-martial of the unshipping of a ladder at this time, and responsibility was never determined. The commodore, now obviously alarmed, commenced a sequence of panicky steps to restore order. "Clear the Lower Decks" was piped with no results; two officers were ordered below to rouse out the crew, again to no avail; then the marines were formed and armed. The men finally mustered, and the commodore asked them to state their grievances. Again Tilling: "but no one was so foolish as to fall in the trap he was laying for them." Charges brought at the courts-martial specified not only participation in, but also failure to suppress, mutiny and designated thirteen defendants including the master-at-arms, ship's corporal, and boatswain. Sentences consisted of acquittals (four), imprisonments, disratings, and degradings, the latter being a new punishment placing the accused in an inferior class for conduct with a consequent loss of privileges. Seaman Robert Hounsell was sentenced to two years' imprisonment at hard labor and forty-eight lashes, the only serious punishment not remitted later. In its review, the Admiralty lamented that there was

> no well-founded cause for complaint.... Having carefully read the minutes of the Courts-Martial.... it appeared...that the most guilty had escaped detection....
>
> My Lords are surprised and pained.... Ship's Commanding Officer to be informed that My Lords find no excuse for such disgraceful conduct.... In consideration of Good Conduct imprisonment of the first five to be remitted. Marines praised for their steady and good character.

Immediately prior to the incident, *Leander* had been singled out because of a "remarkably small number of convictions" reported in the Quarterly Returns. Later in the year a note in the *Digests* stated that the ship's company was "ashamed of its conduct." One week after the incident, formal leave was granted.[23]

With the single exception of the outbreak aboard H.M.S. *Marlborough*, the Admiralty's response to these events had been unprecedented. Recognition of extenuation and justifiability was admitted not only in the remission and mitigation of punishments and the unusually precipitate actions but also in the nature of the reforms subsequently instituted. All indications lend support to the thesis that the authorities because of fear and a sense of vulnerability to public pressures overreacted to the disturbances so as to prevent recurrance of, at least, an embarrassing and, at most, a dangerous imbroglio.

## B. Lack of Leave and Desertion

Geographic distribution of the fleet, the variety of its tasks, the tediousness and boredom, the attitude of the Admiralty and ships' officers toward the bluejacket, anachronistic policies of recruitment, the absence of guidelines on granting leave and liberty ashore, and the drastic fluctuation in the annual manning level all contributed to an alarming problem of desertion in the Royal Navy during the nineteenth century, as illustrated by chart 5 and table 6 in the appendix. Lack of leave was the principal complaint during the disturbances of 1859-60, and a high rate of desertion plagued the authorities throughout most of the century. It is statistically probable that our typical bluejacket would have "gone over the hill" at least once during his career.

Naval ships of the British fleet were organized into squadrons or stations[24] and distributed all over the world, individual units being assigned for a commission from three to five years. The ship's operations were directed by the squadron or station commander-in-chief and included independent activities such as searching for illegal slave ships or protecting commerce from Oriental pirates. Too frequently the crews received no liberty or leave in foreign ports, or even, on occasion, in domestic ports.

The Admiralty provided no policy or guidelines concerning liberty (i.e., short periods of time, one or two days) or leave (up to several weeks' time) during commissions; in 1846, the opportunity for paid leave of six weeks between commissions was offered; in 1850, that was increased to eight weeks and the time counted for pension. This did not attract the seaman: in the first year 3195 men were paid-off, only 474

# REFORM IN THE ROYAL NAVY

took leave, and only 291 of those returned. The mistrust with which the Admiralty held the bluejacket was obviously reciprocated.

Lack of trust was the basis for lack of leave. The practice of requiring all hands to remain aboard for long periods was a holdover from the days when a large number of the crew comprised "pressed" men, Quota-men, and even those serving as an alternative to criminal sentence. In consequence the ship effectively became a prison, and volunteers were allowed no freedom to insure retention of the others. Yet frequently so many men absconded that ships were prevented from conducting vital operations.

After the disturbances of 1859, the Admiralty response was accommodating. In April 1860, new regulations provided guidelines and authority to commanding officers and to commanders-in-chief to grant monthly leave (a maximum of forty-eight hours and four days, respectively). "The first experiments were watched in an agony of suspense by senior officers."[25]

Further, in 1866, the last year of the Somerset regime, leave policy and disciplinary performance were linked and standardized. Each crew was divided into three classes for leave, the first class consisting of those with outstanding records who were given maximum opportunities to go ashore, and the third class consisting of those designated as unreliable who were restricted. Provision for mobility between classes offered an incentive to move toward first class.[26]

Despite all of these earlier reforms it was not until 1890 that leave ceased to be defined as a privilege and became a right for the bluejacket. A directive ordered commanding officers to grant designated amounts of leave to all men of good character.[27]

There existed a much larger and related problem, absence over leave or desertion, there being a distinction. Legal definition of the difference between the two offenses caused confusion at this time. Before 1860, expert opinion emphasized length of time, over twenty-one days,[28] as the distinguishing factor; absence over leave in excess of that time must ensue before a man could be officially declared a deserter and have "R" (for Run) placed beside his name on the ship's muster list and before certain legal procedures and recovery processes could be set in motion. The Naval Discipline Act of 1860 defined desertion differently: "intention to desert" must be proved, and time no longer was a determinant. The law officer, the legal advisor, elaborated in response to a query in 1862 that "the moment the man shows intention to remain away he is a deserter—even if his leave has not yet expired."[29]

Confusion over the distinction between desertion and absence over leave appeared in record keeping as well, as indicated in table 4.[30]

Table 4. Desertions and Absences

| Year | Information from standard and traditional sources | Information from Annual Report of Crime and Punishment | |
|---|---|---|---|
| | Desertions per month | Desertions per month | Absences without leave per month |
| 1857 | 271 | not computed | |
| 1858 | 157 | not computed | |
| 1859 | 195 | not computed | |
| 1860 | 232 | not computed | |
| 1861 | not available | not computed | |
| 1862 | 156 | 64 | 3400 |
| 1863 | not available | 44 | 3488 |
| 1864 | not available | 30 | 3077 |
| 1865 | 111 | 25 | 2826 |

Men deserted from the Royal Navy at appalling rates, and the lesser offense, "breaking leave," was reported on many stations as the most persistent. Table 6 in the appendix provides an illustration. The incidence was approximately 40,000 per year, a figure close to the total number of men in the naval service. Admittedly only about 2000-2500 consisted of those formally charged with desertion and many others fled more than once during the year, but the former were permanent losses and in the years around 1859 many had received the bounty.[31] The *Times* observed that this situation was "a severe reckoning which shows the causes for desertion more tempting than the inducements to remain." The Governor of Lewes Prison, exclusively for naval prisoners, reported at the end of 1864 that "Desertion and Absence without Leave continued to be the prevailing offenses for which men are imprisoned."[32]

The bluejacket who fled, either temporarily or with the intention to remain away permanently, was in jeopardy during his absence and upon return. Punitively he could be imprisoned and he

> forfeited all Pay, Head Money, Bounty, Salvage, Prize Money, and Allowances that have been earned by him, and all Annuities, Pensions, Gratuities, Medals, and Decorations that may have been granted to him and also all Clothes and Effects which he may have left on Board the Ship. . . . [33]

Other punishment consisted of "mulcts" of pay, the amount based upon the length of time absent, and liability from future wages for all expenses incurred in apprehension including rewards and cost of transportation under guard back to the ship. The damaging designation "R" remained on the official muster list until after the man had resumed duty for three years with character evaluations of "very good." The authorities faced a dilemma. Obviously these harsh punishments were having little or no preventive influence. One admiral expressed concern that summary measures failed to reduce the incidence, and the Admiralty concurred.

> . . . My Lords consider that it would be unwise to endeavor to stop the too common offence of leave breaking by resorting to greater severity than the rules laid

down. My Lords have no intention of limiting the power of the Commander-in-Chief to order a Court-Martial whenever thought necessary.[34]

In 1866, an interim designation "R-2" was provided as a moderating measure because the authorities believed strict adherence to the use of "R" "encouraged desertion (instead of the less serious absent without leave) and was prejudicial to men having no intention to desert."[35]

At the same time the Admiralty perservered in other ways in an effort to reduce the losses. Incorrigible leave breakers in Home waters were transferred to the China Station. In addition to new regulations and standardized punishments, Whitehall instituted extensive and costly arrangements to seek out, apprehend, and return deserters, including inauguration of a Naval Police ashore to patrol the port areas, the offering of generous rewards (three pounds), utilization of advertisements containing descriptions in the *Police Gazette* and *Hue and Cry*, and even distribution of photographs to the police. Every ship maintained a *Description Book and Open List* containing "an accurate description of every Person in the ship, except the Commissioned and Subordinate Officers." Legislation provided means for prosecuting those who aided deserters in any way, including a fine of thirty pounds which magistrates hesitated to administer because it was deemed excessive, but the Admiralty refused to consider reduction.[36]

If punishment was severe and chances of being apprehended good, what compelled the bluejacket to abscond? Some reasons have been presented above: to collect the bounty for rejoining under an assumed name, to escape from virtual imprisonment, or to avoid cruel punishment. Repeal of the navigation laws created attractive prospects in England's merchant service, and contemporaries asserted that a seaman could find higher pay, better conditions, and less stringent discipline there. Recent scholarship has raised questions about these claims, however.[37] Foreign navies and merchant services, especially the American and on occasion the Confederate, attracted numerous deserters. The *Digests* reflected serious concern over this particular efflux, Halifax, Nova Scotia, being the most notorious for its "great temptations." Another lure, gold, became so attractive in New Zealand, and to some extent in California, during our period that the Admiralty forbade the fleet to call at any New Zealand port and officially denounced local residents for encouraging men to desert. In a "confidential Circular" of 9 July 1861, Admiral Sir Alexander Milne, commander-in-chief of the North American and West Indian Squadron, traced the problem to the "abusive and bullying language used by the officers to the men, in some cases telling the men to go and not show their faces again." Finally, there were mundane, perennial, and romantic reasons such as family problems and marriage or avoiding or escaping such attachments.[38]

Efforts to relieve the problem in this case achieved limited success. During a visit to New York and Boston in 1863 by the North American Squadron, Admiral Milne reported "great inducements were held out to the crews to desert but the men resisted all temptations."[39] However, in 1872, expressing concern over the issue, the First Lord, G. J. Goschen, demanded a new monthly report, "Returns of Deserters," and reduced the time interval for reporting each incident to the police from ten to two days.[40]

The situation ultimately improved. The bluejacket demonstrated that he could be trusted to return to his ship on time if treated reasonably and with an attitude of mutual respect. As with other problems the Admiralty recognized the existence of an improving caliber of seaman by magnanimously increasing privileges.

## C. Problems of Leadership: The Naval Officer, 1850-80

The social issues of the Royal Navy recounted up to this

point have centered upon the bluejacket and the lower deck. The more formal quarterdeck, traditional symbol and source of authority for the naval officer, also was the object of reform efforts, primarily to diminish the possibility of the officer's capricious and arbitrary behavior. Change has been a theme of this study, yet change was most difficult to accept among the officers, and they were required to alter their attitudes and outlooks most of all. The hierarchical structure and class stratification of Victorian society perpetuated the status quo, and this caste orientation was prevalent within the navy, reinforced by judicial and organizational institutions and traditions. Professor Peter Karsten has conducted intensive research on naval officers of the United States Navy between 1840 and 1920; his conclusions obviously do not apply to the Royal Navy, but there were important links and similarities that cannot be overlooked, and no equivalent study exists of officers in England. The corps of American naval officers, Karsten concluded, formed "a strikingly homogeneous socio-professional group, with a remarkably stable pattern of thought and behavior.... my findings reveal racism, authoritarianism, warmongering, navalism and a number of other unattractive qualities...."[41]

Recruitment for officers in the Royal Navy was exclusively from the wealthy classes, although commissions and promotions were not purchased as in the army. Naval cadets, the name for those young men in training destined for commissions, came from the class of "gentlemenly birth." There was no mobility from enlisted to officer status; Admiral Sir Alexander Milne probably represented the dominant position: "as regards promotion from the forecastle to the quarterdeck, I have no desire to see any but a gentleman by birth decorated in a Post Captain's uniform."[42]

The Royal Navy before 1850 had had a brilliant history with much of the credit for past achievements going to an extraordinary group of naval officers, a virtual cult having been created around the most famous of them, Lord Nelson.

Naval officers of the nineteenth century were expected to carry on this glorious tradition, but few opportunities arose to continue the exploits of the past.

During the period 1850 to 1880, most individual naval officers exhibited competence, diligence, and adequate leadership characteristics, some few being especially successful by living up to the standards set by those remarkable predecessors. Unfortunately another few created serious difficulties for the navy because of their laziness, inertia, and inconstancy. Here again the existence of the mediocre and incompetent officer cannot be isolated from other issues; indeed, this group exacerbated almost all of the other problems from despotic and sadistic punishment practices to the high rate of desertion. Sir Francis Burdett was thinking along these lines in a House of Commons debate on flogging in the navy when he called for abolition of summary punishment since that would reduce opportunity for caprice.[43] A naval officer enjoyed unusual judicial powers, being "judge and jury." In a review of primary sources, William R. Hunt has concluded that "so many accounts indicated that flogging was carried out at the whim of paranoic officers."[44]

We have seen above that the Royal Navy experienced problems because of insufficient numbers of enlisted men; among the officers the numbers were excessive, and in long periods of peace the build-up became cumulative. "Seniority promotion clogged the List" of eligible officers, there being no provision for retirement or purging the excess. "The situation worsened after 1835.... The most alarming weaknesses existed in the British naval officer class." By 1850 when there were midshipmen over sixty and captains unpromoted for sixty years, senility, infirmity, and years ashore without experience created a situation dangerous to national security. Sir William Laird Clowes and others stressed the consequences of superannuation:

> During the war with Russia, the Navy, all things consid-

ered, disappointed the expectations of the country, and it may well be that its comparative failure to effect brilliant results may be traced in some degree to the excessive age of many of the Flag-officers and Captains. . . . [45]

There was concern as well about the effect upon the navy internally. The enthusiasm and initiative of the young and ambitious would be quashed and frustrated. Those officers not utilized actively were assigned to "half-pay," a kind of limbo status. Some relief was achieved when a few lieutenants were released in 1851 and again in 1864, but not until 1870 when the Navy List of officers was divided into "Active" and "Retired" were the problems of excessive numbers and clogged promotion zones brought under control.

More important than these conflicts of internal interest within the officer class was the crisis in leadership and the obscurantism among naval officers. In 1797 the mutineers demonstrated their feelings about a large number of officers by expelling them, and the Admiralty accepted the fact of repudiation by not restoring them. At the Nore, officers had been tarred and feathered. There had been little change or improvement in the caliber of naval officers since that time. Among the indictments there was particular complaint about midshipmen, especially because of their irresponsibility and cavalier attitudes.[46]

Little rapport, no empathy, and insufficient sympathy were exhibited by officers in relations with the men. The entire naval ethic perpetuated a barrier between them; the officers flouted an attitude of superiority, and the men were to remain in their place. The rigidly stratified organization strictly prohibited fraternizing[47] and insured no mobility from enlisted to officer status. An extreme attitude was exemplified in a supercilious pamphlet in 1841, *An Epitome, Historical and Statistical Description of the Royal Naval Service* by E. Miles "with assistance of Lieutenant Lawford Miles, R.N.," and dedicated to the Queen. The author dealt only with class superiority.[48]

# REFORM IN THE ROYAL NAVY

Efforts to solve the problem of leadership were made from above, i.e., the authorities at Whitehall. The naval officer had been reluctant to change, but he was forced to do so. Beginning about 1850 and accelerated during the Somerset administration, pressure was exerted utilizing every device: warning, insult, public exposure, peer pressure, reprimand, inspection, and punishment. The aim was to end tyrannical and brutal practices and capricious and arbitrary actions. There evolved a kind of hierarchy of punishment for officers from warning to imprisonment, although never including corporal punishment.[49] As will be seen in the next section, the Admiralty became especially alarmed at the increased incidence of alcoholism among officers and altered the principal method of dealing with it from a private, confidential, accommodating approach to a public, punitive, humiliating process.

Officers did continue to enjoy many privileges and much favoritism. Examples can be cited of reducing, remitting, and pardoning judicial sentences. One critic claimed officers in the nineteenth century had little to fear from the most extreme abuses.[50] In another instance, the Admiralty explained, "every matter concerning an officer is considered on its own merits."[51] In most personal financial matters officers were sheltered by a policy of "hands-off." Many on half-pay lived abroad to avoid creditors.[52] Distraught parents demanding a young officer support the child of their unwed daughter received no satisfaction. "My Lords cannot interfere, the Law is open to them." And the Admiralty refused to intervene in a bigamy case.[53]

Nothing so direct as punitive and intimidating measures against officers was possible in normal relationships from below, i.e., the bluejacket, but the resort to defiance, an abnormal alternative, did occur. Many of the disturbances of 1859-60 implied a lack of confidence in the officers, and in most cases the Admiralty admitted the deficiency by remission and appeasement. Moreover, the articulate seaman did not hesitate to candidly express his appraisals. Able Seaman

Tilling, irate at just having seen a flogging, questioned why officers were exempt. "If it teaches a lesson to men," he exclaimed, "why not an officer? What is good for the goose is surely good for the gander." He was a consistent critic of midshipmen ("fair weather workers") and officers, and even the Admiralty admitted that the mutiny aboard his ship, *Leander,* was due to the incompetence of officers. An anonymous seaman complained of the hypocrisy: ". . . why should those officers who are notorious swearers . . . read prayers and bring discredit on religion?" Another noted that naval officers were bad influences upon young boys, and still another singled out the chaplains who did not "mingle with the common sailors."[54]

During this period a variety of other incidents involving the behavior of officers occurred. One was arrested and discharged to half-pay for duelling;[55] Midshipman Lord Charles Beresford and several young officers of *Clio* stole the coat of arms of the minister of the United States in Honolulu;[56] a Naval Cadet lost one year's seniority for joining the filibuster expedition of Garibaldi in southern Italy;[57] and, most delightful of all, Mr. Hawtrey was arrested by the Northern occupation authorities in New Orleans and subsequently reprimanded by his commander-in-chief "for singing the Southern National Air in the streets."[58]

## D. Alcoholism: Lower Deck and Quarterdeck

The one problem existing in the Royal Navy which indiscriminately cut across the dichotomy between the lower deck and the quarterdeck was alcoholism. Intemperance was no respecter of rank, class, or status, nor was the problem confined to the navy, or even to the armed services. To say that alcoholism in the services cut across traditional barriers is not to say that officers and men caroused and fraternized, for they decidedly did not. It was as much a problem with one as the other. Excessive intoxication was a more serious problem in the army. Consumption of alcohol reached its high point in the United Kingdom in 1876, the per capita consumption being about three times more than at present. (See table 5.)

Table 5. Consumption of Alcoholic Beverages for the United Kingdom[59]
(Per capita per year in gallons)

| Year | Alcoholic Spirits | Beer | Wine |
|---|---|---|---|
| 1850 | 1.05 | 19 | |
| 1860 | 0.80 | 25 | |
| 1876 | 1.4 | 34 | .53 |
| 1885 | | 28 | |
| 1898 | | 30 | |
| 1913 | | 29 | |
| 1920 | 0.34 | 20 | |

Table 6 in the appendix presents a comparative indication of punishment for drunkenness and is convincing proof that the problem was critical.

The enormity and seriousness of alcoholism and its debilitating impact on the navy alarmed observers at the time. Sir John Henry Briggs, longtime chief clerk of the Admiralty and its historian in the nineteenth century, noted: "From time immemorial the crime of drunkenness has, unhappily, been one of the predominating vices of the naval service."[60] Dame Agnes Weston concluded after decades of working closely with the temperance movement among seamen that "Drink has always been the seaman's snare—the cause, as many a commanding officer has stated, of nearly all the crime in the service."[61] Admiral Lord Charles Beresford recalled that ". . . drunkenness was the fashion then [c. 1860], just as sobriety is, happily, the fashion now [1914]." On occasion it was actually dangerous for officers "to go on the lower deck, which was given up to licence," he claimed.[62] Ashore the problem was worse. Seamen, naval and merchant, were notorious for debauchery and intoxication, enough to be stereotyped:

> The real fact must not be disguised, that the life and habits of the common sailor render him the most unfeeling, unprincipled being on earth . . ., constantly drunk when ashore . . . he returns to the ship diseased both in body and mind.[63]

Time has not caused any change in opinion. Professor Michael Lewis singled out "love of strong drink as most typical of the 'old seaman'; he drank from habit, and as the principal if not the only pleasure that normally came his way."[64] A. J. Pack in a note in *Mariner's Mirror* summed up the consequences of the problem. Excessive drinking exerted

> . . . an anaesthetising effect on the senses and also had disastrous effects on health. Liver complaints, dysentery, fevers and debilitation leading to scurvy . . . and many unnecessary accidents occurred because of it. The rum was the cause of excessive intoxication which then resulted in excessive punishment—a vicious circle.[65]

The drinking of alcoholic beverages and the problem of drunkenness in the navy were not confined to times when the officers and men were ashore. Alcohol was readily available in the form of the daily rum ration issued to all hands since 1655 and only just abolished in 1970. The practice originated on the Jamaican expedition of Admiral Sir William Penn, but the personality most identified with it was the eighteenth-century Admiral Edward Vernon. When commander-in-chief of the West Indian Squadron he became alarmed at "the swinish vice of drunkenness" and instituted measures to control and standardize the issue by mixing one quart of water with each half-pint of rum. The diluted ration, consisting of a half-pint per day, was divided into a forenoon and afternoon allotment and became known as "grog" after the grosgrain boatcloak habitually worn by the admiral.[66]

Two gills a day, a half-pint, composed the ration until 1825 when it was halved and halved again (to one-eighth pint) in 1850 when, to compensate, the food ration was increased. In related efforts the Admiralty initiated a series of reforms emphasizing alternatives to drinking alcohol from providing tea and cocoa to recreational facilities and educational opportunities. The option of money-equivalent to the grog issue was offered until abolition in 1970. None of these measures achieved significant diminution of drunkenness during our period.[67]

The consequences of excessive consumption of alcohol included health, professional, and criminal problems, and in the navy these often overlapped. The designation "d.ts.," delirium tremens, and "chronic disease of the liver" recurred in the *Digests* as explanations for inability to perform duties or to function satisfactorily. Drunkenness was itself a punitive charge, and offenses such as insubordination, striking a superior officer, and other forms of violence were often linked with intoxication.

At the enlisted level the punitive measures related to drunkenness were changed from corporal punishment to "stopping grog" or local confinement, a moderating step and in line with the trend established for all disciplinary practices on the lower deck. Beyond this the authorities demonstrated insight by instructing commanders to protect the inebriated man from creating more serious problems for himself. The comprehensive Circular Order No. 131 of 7 October 1853, dealing with reform of discipline, admonished commanding officers that

> Altercation with a drunken man is in all cases to be avoided; nor is a person under the influence of liquor to be placed in a situation which may cause further excitement and thereby lead to acts of unconscious violence and insubordination.[68]

For officers the shift was more dramatic and unique. The former method of dealing with an officer guilty of excessive drinking was a quiet, "respectable" withdrawal to half-pay with no punitive connotations, or resignation without due process, an administrative procedure. In the early 1860s, this routine was abandoned and the Admiralty demanded a court-martial, providing a sample format of the charges for "habitual intemperance." In 1869, Commander Swinburne, H.M.S. *Cruiser*, resigned because of alcoholism, and his commander-in-chief was censured for permitting it. "He ought to be made a public example of," the Admiralty exclaimed. The punishments from this formal, public, and humiliating process included transfer to undesirable duty (the master of a steam tug was placed in charge of a pitch boat), reduction to the lowest rate of half-pay, expulsion, and reduction of pay "as Their Lordships may think fit." These were calculated to be particularly embarrassing for the nineteenth-century naval officer involved in the keen competition for recognition and promotion. In addition, bureaucratic devices such as a monthly report of each officer's alcohol consumption and placing maximum limits upon wine bills were instituted. Midshipmen were allowed a bill of fifteen shillings a month.[69]

In Great Britain a series of temperance campaigns became increasingly prevalent after 1830, and several attempts at investigation and limiting legislation proved unsuccessful, largely because of obstruction from various "interests." Outside Parliament the temperance societies sponsored pamphlets, journals, periodicals, speakers, demonstrations, and pledges of varying degrees of abstinence.[70] The navy and its constituents became a major target of the temperance movement.

The prominent name in temperance campaigns with the navy, and incidently the merchant service, was Dame Agnes Weston who began her own movement by combining Evangelical Christianity, temperance, and establishment of seaman hostels, first in Bath, then more extensively in Portsmouth and Devonport between 1850 and 1885. In 1868, she and several naval officers formed the Royal Navy Temperance Society, a subsidiary of the National Temperance League. Within ten years there were over two hundred branches aboard navy ships with 8,000 "pledged abstainers." Her activities were expanded to include Sailor's Rests providing a variety of services ashore. Among the results credited to Miss Weston was relief from the problem of crimps, unscrupulous landlords who exploited the seaman.

None of these efforts inside or outside the navy appeared to exert any significant impact until after our period. Gradually the problem of alcoholism diminished in the navy and elsewhere, the decline being "greatly accelerated" during World War I, and the diminution was "not necessarily due to the temperance movement." There were a number of factors: internally, the reduced rum ration, the influx of a higher caliber of personnel, planned recreational programs, and a policy of generous leave, with much credit being given to Admiral Lord Fisher when he was commander-in-chief of the Mediterranean Squadron in the 1890s; externally, cheaper and more accessible nonintoxicating drinks, less respectable and less convenient public drinking, and fear of health damage.[71]

A critic of the Admiralty has accused it of perpetuating the rum ration "as a means of doping the men into enduring their conditions," and even worse, of substituting drunkenness for reform of those conditions.[72] There may have been some basis for this attack before 1850, but after then the Admiralty confronted the problem and improved the conditions, and furthermore, no evidence can be found that any officer or official encouraged intoxication. Indeed, the sources support the contrary. In an observation on the occasion of the announcement of abolition of the grog issue, Lawrence Phillips summed up:

> The spirit was issued in quantity to give the seaman relief from his comfortless existence, when life at sea was harsh and violent. With improvement in conditions at sea, the

rum issue was reduced. In today's Navy the continuance of the rum ration cannot be justified.[73]

Nostalgia prevails. Seaman James Toggle lamented after forty years on the lower deck that

> everything gets worse and worse. . . . When I first went to sea we used to have our quart of grog a day; now they serve out tea. It may do all very well in peace but it won't do in war. Only let them Yankees get hold of you, they'll l'arn you it.[74]

# V

# Other Problems and Issues

## A. Offenses of Sexuality

The climate of opinion at mid-century relating to sexuality was very "Victorian," i.e., characterized by secretiveness, misconceptions, prudery, hypocrisy, euphemisms, and the double standard. References to this particular subject were scarce, unreliable, consciously obscured, and confusing. A contemporary critic, Dr. William Acton, was frustrated in his efforts to "ventilate the question." Attempts at reform instituted by the Admiralty concentrated on consequences, not causes. In the same vein, acceptable methods of regulation and attempts to reduce the incidence of offenses centered upon the female, the "prostitute," a term not defined. The age of consent remained at twelve until 1875 when it was raised to thirteen. Brothel keepers enjoyed virtual legal immunity until 1885. Attempts at regulation were looked upon as typically "continental" and therefore evil, or as interference with the right of private property and therefore profanation.[1]

During the period from 1850 to 1880 the main problem confronting the Admiralty under this category was the high incidence of venereal disease within the armed services, the situation being more serious in the army than in the navy. The eighteenth-century practice of fining the infected seaman fifteen shillings, which went to the surgeon, had proved a failure because too many concealed the disease to avoid expense. Since 1795, treatment had been free. Meanwhile the rate of infection consistently increased so that by the 1850s authorities were ready to resort to extraordinary measures. Contemporary records indicated that officials were largely concerned about the expense and loss of man-hours of those infected.

Medical experts expressed concern in the *Lancet*, a medical journal, in 1846.[2] The incidence of infection in the army was 250 per 1000 men, over two times more than in the French army (and ten times what it would be in the British Expeditionary Force during World War I). About 1860 the base at Malta experienced a virtual epidemic, and the naval ports of Plymouth and Portsmouth were declared "infected areas."[3]

In 1862, a joint War Office-Admiralty departmental committee investigated the problem and recommended providing medical treatment to prostitutes on a voluntary basis. This was implemented, the departments subsidizing foreign and domestic "lock wards" in hospitals.[4] The results were disappointing, and these efforts were deemed insufficient.

Meanwhile some success was being achieved at Malta, the credit going to Admiral Sir William Fanshawe Martin, commander-in-chief, Mediterranean Squadron, and General Sir Henry Storks, commander of the base. Their rigorous program involved regular medical inspection and stringent supervision of prostitutes. Admiral Martin suggested alternatives— e.g., recreational and barracks facilities ashore—but these were ignored in Whitehall.[5]

In 1864 officials of the service departments drew up legislation which, from their perspective, would achieve the objective of reduction of the incidence of venereal diseases among soldiers and sailors. It provided for the regulation of prostitutes, but in restricted areas. A "Bill for the Prevention of Contagious Diseases at Certain Naval and Military Stations" was shuttled—some said smuggled[6]—through Parliament without debate. The provisions were to apply for three years, but this measure was soon deemed inadequate, and in 1866 "An Act for the Better Prevention of Contagious Diseases at Certain Naval and Military Stations . . . to deal with such notorious common prostitutes as either are diseased or from their mode of life are likely to be so," was passed. In 1868 an effort to extend the provisions of the act to the general public failed, but in 1869 the act was strengthened and expanded to other areas of predominant interest to the armed services.[7] The name "Contagious Diseases Act" was adopted directly from a series of contemporary bills dealing with cattle plague and sheep infections, distinctions being made by tacking on such parenthetical phrases as "Contagious Diseases (Animals) Act," or "Contagious Diseases (Women) Act," or "Contagious Diseases (Not Concerned with Animals) Act."

Operation of the Contagious Diseases Acts of 1864, 1866, and 1869 was as follows: within a five—later ten—mile radius[8] of eleven[9]—later eighteen[10]—"protected districts," the locations of naval and military facilities, women designated as prostitutes were required to undergo medical examination periodically, in practice about every fortnight, and, if found venereally infected, to submit to treatment in a hospital "lock ward" for up to three—later nine—months. Special constables recruited from the Metropolitan Police and performing their duties in plain clothes were authorized to designate prostitutes. Brothel keepers who harbored diseased prostitutes were subject to punishment. To appease those critics who complained about no reclamation provisions the acts called for moral and religious instruction by a chaplain during the time the diseased woman was confined. All costs, including expenses for maintenance of the lock wards, surgeons, nurses or matrons, special constables, and chaplains were shared on a use basis by the War Office and the Admiralty, which were responsible for administering the acts. The terms "prostitute" and "solicitation" were not defined, though "Contagious Disease," "police" and "justice" (i.e., judge) were. The special constables, called "morals police" (*police de moeurs*) on the continent, enjoyed broad discretionary powers. In their testimony before investigatory bodies they emphasized the need for cooperation with certain local persons, in particular, brothel keepers. One policeman explained his criterion for designation:

In all military centres nearly every woman of the lower and lower middle classes who may happen to possess personal attractions is of a loose character.[11]

Within the protected districts medical examinations for all designated women were compulsory. Arrangements for time and place were made by the constables and visiting surgeons. Each examination required about two minutes. The speculum was utilized for the inspection, and there were complaints about the process being painful. A chronological history of inspections and treatment was maintained on a form, the Register of Common Women. At first certificates of "cleanliness" were given out, but that procedure was soon abandoned for obvious reasons and certification was retained by the police.[12]

Those designated women not submitting voluntarily were brought before local magistrates by the constables. At the legal proceeding the burden of proof was upon the accused. Continued defiance meant imprisonment, the length of time increasing with each offense.

Treatment for venereal diseases generally consisted of the external or internal application of mercury, as illustrated by a contemporary maxim: "One night with Venus and a lifetime with mercury." The treatment has been assessed as "imprecise and clumsy," and mercury often caused serious side effects.[13]

Extension of the acts to the general public failed in Great Britain, but the provisions for state regulation of vice were implemented in a number of British colonies in the late 1860s: Hong Kong, Ceylon, India, Barbados, Jamaica, Gibraltar, Trinidad, and some self-governing dominions.[14]

In the Admiralty records at the Public Record Office is a letter dated 4 March 1864, from Henry Mortimer Roydon to Sir Samuel Morton Peto, Liberal M.P. for Finsbury and a railroad building tycoon,[15] containing astute and perceptive observations about the acts.

The whole subject from beginning to end is beset with

the gravest difficulties, but the object sought to be attained is one of paramount importance in its political, social, and essentially in its financial point of view as to justify extreme measures if they can be devised without encroaching upon the civil rights of these unfortunate women and without proving positively oppressive and unjust.[16]

He warned that the special police could abuse their powers. For the women "these proceedings would be an invasion of their civil rights and personal liberty." He called for the prosecution of men known to be infecting clean women, and he speculated that this could apply to officers "and thereby interfere with discipline."[17]

Implementation of the provisions occurred quietly and with little reaction at first. The special constables were recruited from experienced Metropolitan Police officers. From the perspective of the service departments success was beyond expectations, for their statistics demonstrated a progressive decrease in the number of cases of venereal disease, as shown in table 6.[18]

Table 6. Incidence of Venereal Disease in the Navy

| Year | per 1000 men |
|---|---|
| 1850 | 70 |
| 1856 | 168 |
| 1862 | 125 (Army-291) |
| 1863 | 104 |
| (Contagious Diseases Act passed) | |
| 1868 | 53 |
| 1874 | 48 |
| (Contagious Diseases Act enforcement lapsed) | |
| 1882 | 183 |
| 1883 | 316 |
| 1905 | 49 |
| 1913 | 22 |

In areas where the acts did not apply the Admiralty adjusted. For example, in 1881 in Hull, a high incidence of venereal disease caused the authorities to transfer all the young men aboard H.M.S. *Repulse*, stationed there, and to replace them with older men.[19]

At about the time the first signs of dissent against the acts became evident, in 1868, the Admiralty instigated a procedure not aimed at the female. Circular Order No. 25 of 2 June 1868, "Concealment and Spread of Venereal Disease by Seamen of the Royal Navy," required all unmarried seamen under age thirty-five to submit to medical inspection of genitalia prior to proceeding on leave.[20] The Admiralty never gave in to demands to stop pay during the time a man was under treatment for venereal disease, though the army did. The inspection policy soon lapsed.

Debate in the House of Commons on the act of 1866 pointed to some of the issues subsequently raised in the campaign for repeal. The member for Oxfordshire called it "a very queer bill on a very queer subject. . . . Its endeavour was to remove all the penalties which a higher power had imposed upon sin without the punishment." The member for Tower Hamlets described it as "simply a Bill for keeping public women at public expense for the gratification of our soldiers and sailors."[21]

Public debates and campaigns utilizing various media had been mobilized over the issues of impressment and corporal punishment. Beginning in the late 1860s, a similar but more intensive and sensational movement concentrated upon the Contagious Diseases Acts. In this case it lasted almost two decades, from 1868 to 1886, and those fighting against the acts, "the repealers," achieved their aim.

Repealers argued that the acts constituted state recognition and control of prostitution, that they violated personal and civil rights of females, that they were discriminatory against women and permitted immunity to men who were responsible for spreading the disease, that arbitrary and tyrannical power was held by the special constables, and that the process of inspection was unfair, often crudely manipulated, and painful to undergo.

Opposition developed in 1868 and was joined a year later by Mrs. Josephine Butler, the "beautiful, histrionic, charismatic" wife of an Oxford don, George Butler. The National Association and the Ladies National Association for the Repeal of the Contagious Diseases Acts were formed and a journal, *The Shield,* was established. The campaign was waged throughout the 1870s, greatly assisted in 1874 by the addition of Sir James Stansfeld, a former cabinet minister and Junior Naval Lord. Eventually the repealers published 520 books and pamphlets, held 900 public meetings, and acquired 2.6 million signatures on 17,300 petitions to Parliament. Mrs. Butler personally spoke at a large number of meetings, toured the country, and visited brothels and lock wards. In one speech, entitled "Social Purity," she condemned

> this unnatural, this bastard law . . . , this masterpiece of tyranny and immorality. . . . The act proclaimed the doctrine of the necessity of vice for man, and of the impossibility of self-restraint.[22]

She felt "good men have been duped and deceived" by the acts, because they believed the thrust of them was to "save little girls, to stop solicitation in the street, to put down bad houses, or to rescue women." On the contrary, the acts "force girls up to the horrible examination house," where a policeman "registers her name on a list of those doomed by these Acts to serve sin under State superintendence."[23]

Other repealers included John Stuart Mill, Francis William Newman, William Logan, W. T. Stead, and Sheldon Amos. Comment varied: the acts were called "un-British" and "Safe-Harlot-Providing"; "no woman was safe from arrest in the designated areas"; "strumpets now call themselves 'Queen's women'"; "There can be no right of men to destroy a certain number of women making them the victims of their lusts in order that those they marry may be virtuous"; and "we have entered into a partnership with the brothels . . . to clean them up."[24]

In 1870 General Sir Henry Storks, the commander at Malta who had been instrumental in reducing the incidence of venereal disease, returned home and entered the Liberal government as Under Secretary to the Minister of War, precipitating the need to stand for election. He entered the by-election of the seat vacated by the death of a Liberal member at Colchester, one of the specified areas. Josephine Butler and the Ladies National Association opposed Storks in a vigorous and violent campaign. Storks, who had advocated extension of the provision of the acts to soldiers' wives, was defeated. The repealers attempted this tactic several more times.

Defeat at the polls was political language which was much better understood than pamphlets, petitions, and demonstrations, especially when women were participating. In 1871 the government appointed a Royal Commission (William Massey, chairman) to study the situation. Mrs. Butler appeared before it and stressed a consistent theme: apply the acts equally to men and women. The Royal Commission was not impressed.

> We may at once dispose of this recommendation so far as it is founded on the principle of putting both parties to the act of fornication on the same footing by the obvious but not less conclusive reply that there is no comparison to be made between prostitutes and the men who consort with them. With the one sex, the offenses are committed as a matter of gain, with the other it is an irregular indulgence of a natural impulse.[25]

Proponents of the acts did not remain passive. In 1866 the Association for the Control of Prostitution by Government Regulation, a continental lobby, established headquarters in England, and the next year the Association for the Promotion of the Extension of the Contagious Disease Act (1866) to the Civil Population of the United Kingdom was formed, comprised mostly of medical men. They received active assistance from the government departments, e.g., the Admiralty occasionally printed and distributed copies of speeches by supporting members of Parliament.[26]

The Contagious Diseases Acts were necessary, proponents claimed, because prostitution was recognized as a permanent feature of society and needed to be controlled, because diseases threatened public health, because statistics proved the acts accomplished their goal, and because prostitutes were rehabilitated during treatment. Supporters refused to debate or discuss the issues in public and preferred to lobby through members of Parliament and utilize the written media. Efforts were made to expand the provisions to large urban areas, especially London. Such a measure was defeated in 1868. Prominent backers for the acts included the Royal Colleges of Physicians and Surgeons, brothel-keepers, army and navy authorities, most bishops, and most Tory M.Ps. Personalities actively involved were Dr. Lyon Playfair, M.P., Dr. William Acton, Henry Mayhew, and Captain Lord Charles Beresford. Of the media, *Lancet* and the *Saturday Review* were consistent supporters.[27]

In the written and oral debates over the Contagious Diseases Acts, both sides used statistics to support relative positions. No doubt the incidence of venereal disease decreased among soldiers and sailors and the number of prostitutes diminished within the specified areas, but this latter number probably increased just outside those boundaries. The acts only applied to about one percent of the population. Sir John Simon, Superintendent-General of Health, initiated a formal investigation by means of empirical social research to test some of the claims of proponents pressuring for extension of the acts. In his published *Eleventh Report*, his findings effectively repudiated the arguments of those who would expand the provisions. For example, Simon's statistics proved that the rate of venereal disease in the poverty areas of London was seven percent, not twenty to thirty-three percent as proponents claimed; that inherited syphillis in children was one and a half percent, not twenty percent. He advised against extending the acts to the civil population.[28]

The repealers soon acquired martyrs who greatly assisted their campaign. Several women refused to submit to inspection; others interfered with the police, and still others in confinement broke windows and damaged property within the lock wards. All were prosecuted; some imprisoned.[29] One sure way to avoid treatment was to become pregnant. The records contained numerous entries of discharges of uncured patients for that reason.[30] Two instances of the ultimate martyrdom, suicide to avoid inspection, occurred. Mrs. Percy, an actress and dancer from Aldershot, and probably not a prostitute, and Elizabeth Holt of Plymouth both drowned themselves.[31]

The Royal Commission of 1871 had been hostile to the repealers; in 1882, a more sympathetic Liberal government appointed a Select Committee, this one including Sir James Stansfeld as a member. Mrs. Butler and a representative from the Salvation Army, which opposed the acts, testified. Reluctantly the government gave in to the pressures of public opinion which had become stronger in opposition. Enforcement was eased about 1880; the acts were suspended in 1883, and formally repealed in 1886. An effort was made to continue the inspections and treatment on a voluntary basis, but to no avail.[32]

The effect was an immediate and dramatic increase in venereal disease among soldiers and sailors.[33] The Admiralty was distressed; the reports from the field were all the same: "High ratio of disease," "increase in syphilis since suspension of compulsory inspection," "enormous increase of VD," and "extraordinary increase."[34] Eventually the incidence declined so that by 1914 the situation was stabilized. The incidence of venereal disease followed the same trend as the incidence of desertion, drunkenness, and corporal punishment in the late nineteenth century. A number of factors contributed to the moderating of these problems. Lieutenant Commander Joseph Montague Kenworthy, a former M.P., cites "better education, more facilities for recreation and sport, more leave and a different outlook on life."[35] Others credit the later reforms of Admiral Lord John Fisher and the higher caliber of personnel.[36]

The subject of sexuality was avoided as much as possible in official matters. A facade was constructed. The regulations forbade women aboard ship and there was no opportunity for leave or liberty. It would logically follow that there was no need for female companionship except every five years between commissions.

At the realistic level, however, the regulations were obviously ignored and violated, a situation universally supported by the sources. The following random selections prove the point:

> The ship filled with prostitutes at every port, by permission of the commanding officer. Not many years ago (it was since 1840) the Captain of a frigate at a West Indian port (Barbados) gave an order to the First Lieutenant, that every man and boy was to have a black woman on board, and the order was carried out. . . . [37]

Admiral C. B. Penrose, writing in 1824, answered a critic who accused the navy of permitting "certain immoral practices." Allowing "women of bad character" aboard was an ancient custom "always forbidden either by general or particular instructions but always allowed . . . but as a necessary or rather unavoidable evil. . . . To keep the seamen contented on board was the main reason."[38] Seaman Samuel Leech recalled "boatloads of defiled and defiling women aboard," especially on Sunday, "a day of sensuality," and at Christmas, a day of "debauch."[39] In his comprehensive surveys of diaries and journals of the lower deck, Henry W. F. Baynham concluded that women still came aboard in large numbers in the nineteenth century.[40] In a discussion of the question in the medical journal, *Lancet*, in 1853, the rationale was reviewed:

> ... If prostitution does and will exist in civil life amongst *celibats*, to hope or believe that soldiers and sailors, healthy, vigorous men, will refrain from promiscuous sexual intercourse (for the majority are not allowed the chances of any other) would be a dream of Utopia.[41]

It can thus be seen that behind the facade, accommodation and indulgence prevailed. The bluejacket was permitted heterosexual outlets not officially acknowledged.

However, Admiralty reform measures ultimately affected this aspect of life on the lower deck. In a circular letter of 9 September 1869, women were again ordered to be excluded and they became increasingly difficult to hide aboard modern ships. Their presence was little noted subsequently.[42]

In the case of homosexuality, the facade became a barrier. The extreme difficulty of researching this subject is exacerbated by the multiplicity of terms employed to describe a wide spectrum of acts, presumably immoral and not involving women. The *Digests* of this period contained such phrases as

> ... perpetration of lewd acts ... gross indecency ... scandalous and unclean conduct ... indecent assault ... sodomy ... indecent acts to Boys ... an unnatural offence ... uncleaness [sic][43] ... nasty acts ... disgraceful conduct ... scandalous action ... conduct unbecoming [admittedly generally referring to some crime committed by an officer involving money or theft] ... filthy conduct ... indecent liberties ... improper conduct ...

Rarely were there accurate descriptions such as "an act of indecency by exposing himself when drunk," "voiding his urine in the steerage of the ship," or "beastiality with animals" (livestock carried aboard).⁴⁴ Obstructionism, circumspection of clerks, apparent feelings of repulsion, innocuous terms used to describe base acts, terms of depravity used to describe harmless acts (such as cursing), variation of judgment of what was considered "immoral," and attempts to whitewash, all contributed to the difficulty of accumulating reliable and authoritative evidence.⁴⁵

The Admiralty consciously contributed to the obscurantism. Courts-martial were conducted for crimes of homosexuality, there being several celebrated ones during our period, but a Court of Enquiry, an administrative process not open to the public, was preferred; otherwise "the publication of the details would have a bad effect on the fleet." Summary punishment could be awarded from such proceedings.⁴⁶

Conditions on the lower deck were conducive to homosexual contact: cruises lasting several years away from domestic ports, the lack of leave ashore, crowded circumstances which precluded privacy, the proximity of old men and boys, and the decreasing availability of women aboard ship. Nevertheless, intimacies between males were looked upon as especially demoralizing and were held to be anathema in all armed services. Homosexual acts were treated with maximum seriousness and punished with extreme severity. In the early days "keel-raking" was awarded with the added feature of firing a gun while the accused was underwater "as well to astonish him the more . . . as to give warning to all others to look out and beware."⁴⁷ The severity had been since reduced. The 1862 edition of Thring's *Treatise* defined the most serious offense, sodomy, as "carnal knowledge" of man or beast and recommended punishment of penal servitude for life or not less than three years.⁴⁸

Externally, seamen and boys were the objects of paying and practising homosexuals, especially around London, and professional male prostitutes, called "sailors' whores," catered to naval and merchant seamen just paid-off.⁴⁹

Some perceptive officers suggested ways to face the issues

of sexuality by alternative approaches and attacking the causes. Examples included construction of barracks, recreational facilities, and Sailors' Homes ashore, provision for increased conjugal opportunities, restrictions upon males, and improved sanitation arrangements. Some of these measures, in the category of habitability, were considered by Whitehall.

## B. Habitability and "Indulgences"

As part of what had now become a comprehensive reform program, the Admiralty improved habitability, the overall conditions and environment on the lower deck. This included a variety of measures relating to health, victualing, food, pay and allowances, education, and recreation.

Health and medical arrangements during this period "improved astonishingly," equivalent to the "Great Sanitary Awakening" in the civil sector.[50] Naval medical officers had enjoyed a high reputation throughout the century, many coming from the Scottish universities where the training was superior.[51] One of them, Sir William Burnett, made a significant contribution to advances in health and in statistics with his *Statistical Reports on the Health of the Navy* which was begun in 1830 and computed annually after 1856.

In 1866, Admiral Sir Alexander Milne chaired a study on medical officers and their services. Many had complained of being discriminated against by the executive officers. Florence Nightingale inspired a study and reform of naval hospitals in 1868, and there was a formal investigation into the matter of ventilation in warships. Metal ships created more internal condensation, dampness and discomfort thus making the bluejacket more susceptible to tuberculosis.[52]

In 1856, the Admiralty accepted a formal naval uniform and two years later authorized its issue to every incoming Continuous Service man. Health experts had recommended this for a century, the rationale being less exposure to louse-borne diseases such as typhus, improved personal cleanliness, and, incidentally, another step toward uniformity.[53] An anonymous seaman in 1877 complained bitterly about the uniforms: "... ungainly in appearance, ... uncomfortable, ... injurious to the health, in exposing the chest, and hindering the circulation of blood by means of its tightness around the hips, ... and too costly." The hat was "ungainly" and difficult to store. The Admiralty did modify the neck of the frock by adding flannel to protect the throat.[54] Another measure was free distribution to all hands of "mess traps," a compact kit of eating and drinking utensils comprising tin kettles and dishes, but no knives and forks until 1897, such implements "regarded as being prejudicial to discipline and manliness."[55] Free bedding was issued to all Continuous Service men in 1859. Providing necessities such as utensils and uniforms was itself a significant financial relief for the bluejacket. This eliminated a burdensome debt previously incurred by all upon induction.[56] It was during this period that the first toilets and washing basins were installed, but these first facilities were quite crude. Admiral Lord Charles Beresford recalled that "sanitary appliances" were located "right forward in the bows" and could not always be used. As a result the lower decks, especially in rough weather, were "no better than cesspools."[57]

Innovation also occurred in the area of victualing or supply. By definition "victualing" applied only to food, but in reality the purser, called the paymaster after 1852, dealt with clothing (called "slops"), bedding, utensils, incidentals such as tobacco, and with money. By whatever name, the shipboard administrator of these items was the object of much criticism and complaint from the seamen who, with apparent unanimity, believed him to be corrupt and insensitive.

One of the measures to ease the crisis of 1859 was an increased food allowance involving more and better food "with the view of improving the conditions of the petty officers, seamen and marines of the fleet." Yet even after the increase, the navy meat ration compared unfavorably with other services:

| | |
|---|---|
| Royal Navy | 5 lb. 4 oz. per week |
| U.S. Navy | 7 lb. per week |
| Merchant Service | 8 lb. 12 oz. per week |

The daily bread ration was slightly higher in the navy, and a pound of tobacco was allotted per month.[58]

Improvement in the quality and variety of food was accomplished by canning, a process introduced earlier in the century but accepted for use on a large scale during our period. First came canned or preserved beef, called officially "soup and bouilli," and inevitably the seaman created his own terms for it: "bully beef," "two buckets of water and one onion" or "Fanny Adams," after a celebrated case of a girl who disappeared. Next came vegetables. Australia became the chief supplier of canned foods. This advance has been appraised as "the most beneficial step in the nineteenth-century victualling" by Professor Christopher Lloyd.[59] In 1870, a departmental committee concluded that ship's cooks were generally incompetent, and shortly afterward a School of Cookery, with emphasis on correct preparation of food, was established at Portsmouth.[60] There was still an anonymous denunciation of cooks several years later.[61] Like the paymaster, this ship's service man was little appreciated. Sam Noble, A.B., complained about the food in the late 1870s. He singled out salt beef (called "salt 'oss") and said he found some "marked with a date before Trafalgar," from which he carved a model frigate.[62]

Perennial problems and scandals with private contractors and suppliers to the navy relate to our theme only in that the bluejacket was the consumer of spoiled and poisonous food.[63]

This variety of approaches to the problems of health, food, and sanitation achieved obvious and dramatic success as illustrated in table 7.[64]

## Table 7. Deaths in the Navy

| Table of Mortality Rates in the Royal Navy | | Annual Ratio of Deaths (all causes) per 1000 men in the Royal Navy | |
|---|---|---|---|
| Year | Rate | Year | Rate |
| 1780 | 1 in 8 died | 1834 | 20.4 |
| 1810 | 1 in 30 | 1856 | 15.5 |
| 1830 | 1 in 72 | 1857 | 22.0 |
| 1885 | 1 in 112 | 1858 | 25.8 |
| 1895 | 1 in 143 | 1859 | 16.7 |
| 1905 | 1 in 256 | 1862 | 15.3 |
| 1913 | 1 in 309 | 1865 | 11.3 |
| | | 1868 | 8.9 |
| | | 1871 | 8.5 |
| | | 1875 | 8.8 |
| | | 1885 | 7.0 |
| | | 1895 | 6.6 |
| | | 1905 | 3.9 |
| | | 1910 | 3.1 |
| | | 1936 | 2.0 |

One inducement of universal importance which could make the difference between attracting good or bad quality men was the amount of pay. This and time of payment had been issues creating difficulties for centuries—traditionally the excessively low wages had been scandalously late. An interim ticket system only created more hardship for the seaman and his family. Low wages had been the principal grievance of the mutineers in 1797. Wages of the naval seaman, real and actual, generally increased during the century. There has been major disagreement among economic and social historians about the overall trends of real wages (and the "condition of England"), especially for the first half of the century, but there is more general agreement that conditions during the second half improved. Certainly actual wages increased as shown in table 8.

Table 8. Wages for Seamen[65]

| Year | Average Pay Per Month Ordinary Seaman | Able Seaman |
|---|---|---|
| 14th century | 9s | |
| 1440 | 6s | |
| 1480 | 6s | |
| 1546 | 6s 8d | |
| 1588 | 10s | |
| 1620 | 14s | |
| 1631 | 15s | |
| 1653 | 19s | 24s |
| 1797 | 23s 6d | 29s 6d |
| 1806 | 25s 6d | 33s 6d |
| 1844 | 26s | 34s |
| 1852 | 33s 7d | 41s 4d |
| 1862 | 38s 9d | 49s 1d |

Those in occupations of critical need or involving high professional competence were paid quantum amounts over and above their seamen peers. Engineers of enlisted status, i.e., stokers, received higher wages, forty-six shillings before and fifty-four shillings six pence after 1846. Those seamen extensively trained in gunnery received three pence per day additional pay, and divers enjoyed extra remuneration.

Supplementary and non-substantive pay included an incentive to improve discipline, the Good Conduct Badge and Pay, commenced by Admiral Milne in 1849. The concept came from successful army use. All seamen with character evaluations of "very good" for five consecutive years received an extra three pence per day for each award up to three. The length of time was later reduced to three years. However, two traditional opportunities for extra remuneraton, prize and head money for captured ships and slaves respectively, diminished before and during our period, both having at one time been inducements for recruiting.[66]

Admiral Sir William Fanshawe Martin recommended weekly payment of wages for ships in port for extended periods. The clerks complained, but the policy proved beneficial.

The allotment provision, i.e., the option of permitting the bluejacket to designate a person to collect part of his pay monthly, had begun in 1757. There were restrictions upon whom might be designated, but some were subsequently removed, for example, after 1833 a seaman could legally specify illegitimate children. In 1858 procedures for pay and allotments were streamlined and rationalized, removing the basis for most complaints. The result was prompt payment monthly.[67]

So far discussion has dealt with health and physical wellbeing. More consideration for other aspects of habitability and environment generated by the impact of various problems and public pressures caused the Admiralty to find ways to make life in the navy more attractive and meaningful. An obligation was recognized to raise the "moral and intellectual standard" of the seamen, "contributing, as far as possible, to the relief of that monotony which is more or less inseparable from their profession."[68]

Educational reforms in the nineteenth century were depicted as efforts to "elevate," "uplift," or raise character, and this was the thrust of the approach in the navy. "Inducements to self-instruction" such as establishment of Reading Rooms aboard ship, expansion of ship's libraries, a requirement that every petty officer must be capable of reading and writing, encouragement of subscriptions to journals and newspapers, Bible classes, and lectures by officers comprised the approaches. Beginning in 1862, at a cost of 250 pounds each, the Admiralty supplied "Magic Lanterns, Slides and Lectures" to large ships.[69] More formally, in 1861 the position of schoolmaster aboard ship was upgraded to commissioned status, the salary was raised, and a university degree required. Many chaplains, who already had the degrees, shifted to this new professional branch. Their functions involved basic education and their main pupils were boys and midshipmen. Three years later a director of Naval Education took over coordination of the branch. All of this was an adjunct to the new training curriculum of the Continuous Service system. At the officer level more specialized courses in gunnery, navigation, and engineering evolved into a school aboard H.M.S. *Britannia* and ultimately into the Royal Naval College.[70]

Recreation was recognized as a need for the higher caliber seaman, and steps were taken to provide more both afloat and ashore, the purpose being to relieve tedium and raise morale. Entertainment, generally spontaneous, had been a feature of shipboard life. Some favorites were male dancers, bands and concerts, amateur theatrical performances, and especially "nigger parties" when seamen would black themselves and dance and sing. Much of this occurred on holidays, and the festivities were always concluded with the National Anthem. Athletic events were held ashore, and, during our period, athletic grounds for cricket and skittles and even a gymnasium (at Portsmouth) were constructed. Recreation became more organized; games were purchased, and space aboard ship was permanently set aside for them. All of these were limited efforts, but they were indicative of a new attitude and sensitivity coming to the fore at Whitehall.[71]

The term "indulgences" described proffered privileges and additional services aboard ship. Allowing the opportunity for purchase of a pint of beer evolved into setting up canteens aboard ship where a seaman could not only purchase beer but also coffee, tea, and small delicacies.[72] An early experiment aboard H.M.S. *Raleigh*, Captain Tryon commanding, was directly associated with the temperance campaign. Daily at four bells (in the middle of each watch), all hands were piped for coffee, the lamp room having been modified to accommodate a facility offering "coffee, sugar, jam, potatoes, cheese, preserved lobster, salmon, sardines, etc. . . . Coffee was one and a half pence per pint." *Raleigh* gained the "soubriquet of the Coffee Ship," and similar, equally successful attempts were achieved aboard H.M.S. *Indus* and *Cambridge*, the latter making a sixty pound profit in a year, selling about eighty pints of coffee per day.[73]

The work of Dame Agnes Weston prompted Whitehall to respond to the need for services ashore for the seaman on leave and liberty, although in one area, accommodations, little was accomplished. Construction of barracks ashore for occasional use by seamen and to replace the notorious hulks where men were quartered in grossly unsanitary conditions was recommended numerous times, but the Admiralty, pleading lack of funds, made only token efforts. Miss Weston had provided a safe deposit system, adaptable to a savings bank, as part of the services of her Sailors' Rests. It was one way to foil the crimps. The Admiralty instituted such a system aboard naval ships with an arrangement to transfer funds to the Dockyard Bank when ashore.[74]

Finally, the Admiralty gave the privilege of free postage to all seamen. All of these endeavors contributed to the improvement of conditions and the environment on the lower deck.

## C. The Peculiar Role of Religion *vis-a-vis* Discipline

The juxtaposition of religion and discipline involved intriguing and provocative connotations in the history of the Royal Navy and even closer connections in the Royal Marines. The two subjects were constantly linked—one supported the other; one depended upon the other. A regulation of 1623 required attendance at divine service or be "knocked on the head with a bucket of water and fined 6d."[75] Article I of the Articles of War of 1660, 1749, and of the Naval Discipline Acts required "all Officers in Command" to "cause the Public Worship of Almighty God according to the Liturgy of the Church of England."[76] The first three numbered paragraphs in the chapter on discipline in the *Queen's Regulations and Admiralty Instructions* dealt with mandatory Divine Services on Sunday and Morning Prayers on weekdays.[77] Paragraph Four enjoined the captain, not the chaplain, to discountenance and suppress all cursing and swearing, drunkenness, gaming, rioting and quarrelling; all dissolute and disorderly practices, and, in general, everything tending to the dispargement of religion, or to the promotion of vice and immorality.[78]

In 1879, a Commander Johnson and the officers of H.M.S. *Rover* objected to compulsory attendance at Divine Service. The Admiralty disapproved, explaining "that this subject is not one of religious toleration but entirely related to naval discipline." Johnson replied by expressing his regrets for absence.[79]

Prominent though unofficial opinion supported this stance. The Duke of Wellington defined religion as "the greatest support and aid to military discipline and order."[80] In the chapter on discipline in his four-volume *History of Merchant Shipping*, W. S. Lindsay includes only two points: dress regulations for officers and instructions to "keep up the worship of Almighty God every Sunday."[81]

The Church of England enjoyed a state monopoly over religion in the nineteenth century, and this superior position carried over to the navy. A naval chaplain, an appointment regularized by Samuel Pepys in the seventeenth century, served aboard all major warships. All appointments were approved by the Bishop of London. The Chaplain acquired warrant status in the eighteenth century and commissioned status in 1843, though never "ranked," then or now.[82]

In addition to the exclusiveness of chaplain appointees, the Church of England enjoyed a monopoly on all services, there being niggardly provision for dissenters or Roman Catholics. Compulsory attendance created captive audiences and all sorts of practices and devices of administrative privilege prevailed. Certificates of application for an allotment could only be verified by "a Minister of the Church of England" and a request for exception received a negative response. Alteration of the seaman's initial designation of religious denomination was permitted only to men of good character, a technique which not only ostentatiously demonstrated tolerance, but also manipulated discipline.[83] An extreme example of the monopolistic and dogmatic stance of the Church of England took place in 1857. A thirteen-year-old Scottish boy attended his first compulsory divine service and refused to bow when the name of Jesus was mentioned. He was placed in irons and given thirty-six lashes. The next Sunday he again refused, but the Ship's Corporal caned him on the back of the neck, causing an involuntary, reflexive bow. Apparently this sufficed for all concerned.[84]

Meager provisions were made for selected dissenting denominations (Presbyterian and Wesleyan) and more grudgingly, Roman Catholics. Prayer books, hymnals, and bibles were supplied by the Admiralty on a per capita basis to the approved denominations, and subsidies (ten shillings for each service) were paid to pastors and priests who conducted dissenting and Catholic services ashore which seamen attended.[85]

Occasional tolerance did not apply when conflicts arose between authority and religion, between the captain and the chaplain. In case after case the Admiralty refused for any reason to jeopardize the power of the commanding officer aboard ship, not for established religion, not for any chaplain, and certainly not for dissenters or Catholics. When disputes arose the Admiralty, without exception, upheld the commander; the Board explained that it could not "sanction any interference with the authority of officers, or with the discipline of the ships, on the ground of religious persuasion." In a clash over the content of a sermon, a chaplain was dismissed to half-pay on the grounds that no one could "subvert" the authority of the commanding officer.[86]

The authority-religion dichotomy evoked the most intolerance and virtual paranoia among naval officials when related to Roman Catholicism. On this matter Victorian prejudices, anti-Catholic and anti-Irish, combined, being further exacerbated during our period by Fenianism. Fenianism, prominent in the 1850s and 1860s, was an extreme Irish nationalist movement with close ties to American sympathizers. The Irish question always aroused concern at the Admiralty; Fenianism evoked alarm. It apparently made no difference that the movement was eventually denounced by the Catholic Church. Several incidents involving enlisted personnel, especially in the mid-1860s when the Fenian crisis was at its height, demonstrated the oversensitivity prevalent at Whitehall.[87]

D. Peripheral Issues

*1. Seaman Organizations.* The third quarter of the nineteenth century was one of rising consciousness and confidence for organized labor and the trades union movement in Great Britain, but this did not apply to the service department personnel. The Admiralty took a dim view of any attempt at organizing by enlisted men, the response to Fenianism being an example of the reaction. Combinations smacked of conspiracy, political activity, or even mutiny. The regulations were explicit: they forbade any meeting or session not chaired by the commanding officer or chaplain. For example, newspaper accounts of a gathering of petty officers at Portsmouth reacting to a circular of 1877 requiring the wearing of the naval uniform off duty when traveling evoked sharp response at Whitehall. There were other instances of similar alarm.[88]

Those few groups which did form legally evolved into charitable or educational associations or evangelical-temperance leagues. Clearly the bluejacket acquired no vehicle to air his grievances, no pressure group to articulate his complaints, no spokesman, and no lobby. Certainly the officers were not sensitive to his plight. This situation undoubtedly contributed to the disturbances of 1859.

By contrast the Admiralty was generally indulgent and

supportive of various religious and quasi-religious humanitarian movements such as Evangelicals, odd strands of Methodists, temperance associations, Bible societies, and cooperatives administered by or for naval personnel. Magnanimous missions to seamen by these institutions provided improved accommodations ashore, wholesome recreation and entertainment, "moral uplifting" in a systemic way, and protection against the notorious crimpage system. Some accomplishments included conversion of antiquated warships donated by the navy into floating chapels, the Bethel Flag or Chaplain's pennant, a journal, *The Seaman's Magazine,* Bible Society activities comparable to what the Y.M.C.A. or U.S.O. offer today, the Royal Portsmouth Sailor's Home with beds for 150, and cooperative societies with a membership by 1900 of a hundred thousand seamen. These private eleemosynary efforts for the benefit of navy and merchant seamen exemplified similar philanthropic endeavors on a larger scale conducted in the civil sector of Victorian society.[89]

*2. Pensions.* The final stage in the career of our typical bluejacket was retirement with its monetary award, the pension. This had been instituted in 1831, and requirements for eligibility were set at twenty-one years service in the Royal Navy if no out-of-service time exceeded five years and if service occurred between the ages of ten and fifty years. Under the hire-and-discharge system these qualifications were obviously unrealistic because few seamen had served so consistently with the navy, and few could receive the pension. The advent of Continuous Service meant a more reasonable arrangement for eligibility and made fulfillment more productive for the man; he simply must complete his second engagement. This was another incentive making Continuous Service more attractive. Once this recruitment system was established, more men were able to utilize this inducement accruing benefit to themselves and to the navy.[90]

# VI

# Reform and Transition: The Naval Discipline Acts

Describing the environment existing on the lower deck subject by subject and phase by phase in a qualitative manner creates impressions of isolation, compartmentalization, and disorganization and, still, the story is incomplete. The multiplicity of aspects influencing the career of a typical bluejacket of the Royal Navy from recruitment to pension during the third quarter of the nineteenth century has been presented, but the legislative basis for reform has thus far been omitted. There has also been no adequate opportunity to introduce important persons and to elaborate upon individual contributions to reform. Decisions and directives were made in the name of the government or the Board of the Admiralty, impersonal institutions, but individual leaders influenced those actions to one degree or another.

There remains a series of measures formulated by the Admiralty which are more difficult to categorize because they dealt with a conglomeration of issues and problems which were approached in a collective manner. In particular, these included two significant Circular Orders promulgated in the 1850s and the series of Naval Discipline Acts passed by Parliament in the 1860s. These represented the culmination of the policy of humanitarian and administrative reform responsive to outside pressures and designed to adapt the Royal Navy to changing circumstances. Moreover, these measures were related and interconnected. The Naval Discipline Acts incorporated policies introduced in the circulars.

The harbinger, Circular Order No. 131 of 7 October 1853, entitled "Minor Punishments and Seaman's Certificates" and promulgated only six months after Continuous Service was introduced, was the product of the then Junior Lord of the Admiralty, Captain Alexander Milne.[1] First, on the matter of certificates, the circular called for a more thorough character evaluation process, including consultation between commanding, junior, and petty officers prior to completing these periodic appraisals which accompanied the seaman during his career, divulging to all who saw his records a chronological assessment of his character and performance. The Admiralty was laying the groundwork for more extensive use of these evaluations. The minor or summary punishment section ordered policies incorporating more extensive and more direct supervision of discipline and, at first glance, gave the appearance of contradiction. Specifically, authorization to punish summarily, since 1848 the sole prerogative of the commanding officer, could now be delegated to the officer next in line, the commander or first lieutenant, and to no other. All punishments awarded must be recorded in the Defaulter's Book, later to be reflected in the Quarterly Punishment Returns which went to the Admiralty. The circular contained extensive and elaborate instructions, guidelines, and advice on local punishment practices: suggestions for reducing drunkenness, hints on how to treat a potentially violent intoxicated man to protect him from further trouble, and a plea for moderation and leniency, especially for first and second offenses. Finally, there was a formal list of summary punishments "hereby authorized," increasing in severity from number one through sixteen.[2] The purpose of the new regulations was "establishing for the future a more uniform system . . . to encourage and promote the comfort of the well-conducted men."

The power to punish, apparently broadened by this circular, was, in fact, restricted and limited since violations could now be more readily discovered. Petty and junior officers who had previously followed the practice of instantaneous punishment, always illegal, now became more vulnerable to detection. The Admiralty was laying the foundation for comprehensive reform of punishment policies and looked upon this circular as a salient and fundamental treatise. Subsequently, especially during the early 1860s, it would be supplemented and ruthlessly enforced.[3] The *Times* considered this directive important enough to print an extensive summary.[4]

The second of the two circulars, No. 396 of 10 December 1859, opened the campaign which, within a decade, effectively eliminated corporal punishment in the navy. This directive provided for dividing all enlisted men into two classes for conduct. Character evaluations below "good" meant assignment to the Second Class; "good" and above to the First Class. The circular prohibited corporal punishment for men in the first class for conduct, with the usual exceptions, and then only after court-martial. Rules for mobility from first to second class, between evaluations, specified the requirement of a formal warrant, the act itself composing a type of punishment called "degrading"; from second to first required one year of good conduct, later reduced to six months. The circular further restricted use of corporal punishment to eight designated offenses[5] committed by men in the second class. A covering letter to commanders-in-chief warned:

> My Lords desire you will further impress upon all officers in command that although men in the Second Class must still be considered as liable to punishment for those grave offences only which are enumerated in the Circular Order, it is by no means their Lordships' intention that such offences, in all instances, are to be visited by this degrading punishment, which is never to be resorted to except under such circumstances as, upon the most mature reflection, may render a severe example indispensable for the maintenance of proper discipline.[6]

Separation of the men into classes based upon conduct exemplified another method by which the Admiralty maintained close scrutiny over punishment practices. The stated goal for each ship was two or three percent of the crew in the second class, and special praise went to those few ships attaining that standard, an exceptional and positive approach among the many negative censures, denunciations, and abusive attacks found in the *Digests*. The overall averages were higher: in 1862, men in the second class made up 11.8 percent; in 1863, 12 percent.[7] Nevertheless, as early as eight months after implementation, Admiral Lord Clarence Paget informed the House of Commons of success.[8]

These two significant reform steps coincided with French invasion scares and with the two manning study reports in the 1850s. Promulgation of the latter circular, late in the critical year of 1859, placed it among the series of measures implemented by the Admiralty to relieve discontent.

Simultaneously preparation began on the first of a series of Naval Discipline Acts which were to incorporate all of the changes recently introduced. Not since 1749 had the Admiralty accumulated regulations into a compact legislative package. The preamble contained the rationale:

> An Act for Amending and Consolidating the Laws relating to the Governing of Her Majesty's Ships, Vessels and Forces by Sea; to Naval Courts-Martial; to the Prevention of Desertion; and to the Preservation of Discipline in Her Majesty's Navy. (23 and 24 Victoria Cap. 123).[9]

The discipline act was more than a replacement for the old Articles of War, and yet, it did not supersede *Queen's Regulations*. It contained the new schedule of authorized punishments and alterations of existing guidelines, e.g., reducing the number of offenses calling for death from twenty-two to seventeen and compulsory death from ten to two (treason and murder).

Another was a new obligation to suppress mutiny, obviously a direct result of recent disturbances. Two major changes relating to courts-martial, seating of lieutenants and requiring the presence of a judge-advocate, facilitated that judicial process.

The debate over the act in Parliament brought out other motivations. The Duke of Somerset, First Lord of the Admiralty, introduced the bill in the House of Lords on 29 June 1860. At second reading he explained that no comprehensive discipline bill had been enacted for a hundred years, though there had been changes "of the law and the progress of public opinion." Before the more conservative house he stressed that discipline was not being relaxed. The Admiralty was "not prepared to give up corporal punishment—confinement would be the only substitute." During the debate before the committee of the whole, the Duke confessed that one purpose of the more moderate policy on corporal punishment concerned the attraction of merchant seamen. "They are at present deterred by corporal punishment," he said. Admiral Lord Clarence Paget, Secretary of the Admiralty, steered the bill through the House of Commons on a different tack, apologizing for what might appear to be "Draconic" punishments but urging consideration that the navy dealt with "the very dregs of society" which meant punishment must be "swift, certain and severe." He stressed the innovative features such as greater ease in constituting courts-martial and more effective definition of desertion involving proof of intent. In the debate William Williams lamented that flogging had not been abolished as was recently accomplished in France and the United States and that the commanding officer retained excessive authority over punishment. Sir Charles Napier noted that, in the light of recent disturbances, discipline required improvement. The act passed 23 August 1860, and received the Royal Assent five days later.[10]

The second bill of the series, that of 1861, provided for minor modifications to the penalties for mutiny, brought the policies concerning penal servitude in line with recent changes of civil criminal procedures, and cleared up some confusion about awarding cumulative punishments not provided for in the original act.[11] Subsequent acts in 1864 and 1866 and the amendment of 1865 all passed without debate, and the changes were minor: e.g., commanders-in-chief and port senior officers were authorized to issue warrants to apprehend stragglers, petty officers and seamen were protected from arrest for debt, another alteration was made in the minimum penal servitude sentence limitation, and the number of days of solitary confinement was changed to fourteen.[12]

The consecutive Naval Discipline Acts had altered provisions concerning penal servitude to reflect civil legislative changes. The instability resulted from a curious phenomenon, a dramatic increase in the incidence of robberies with violence, called garroting, in 1862. Contemporaries linked the situation to lack of severity in penal practices and institution of a "ticket-of-leave system." So the minimum penal servitude sentence was increased and increased again.[13]

In the last hundred years, historians have treated the final act, that of 1866, as salient, but the tenor of entries in the *Digests* and discussion, or lack of it, at the time suggested no great significance. These acts had virtually become annual affairs by that time, and several proposals were presented for further changes after 1866. Admiral Sir William Fanshawe Martin recommended that men concealing venereal disease should forfeit pay and that measures were needed to prevent illegal sale of seamen's clothing ashore, but the First Lord, H. T. L. Corry, believed these to be unnecessary. The fact that a new First Lord no longer advocated legislation as a means to reflect innovations constituted a change of policy. The previous Board had explained "that it is better to repeal existing acts and bring in a New rather than introduce amended acts."[14] In the mid-1870s, William Hickman and others recommended further legislation and in one instance the Board considered a proposal "discourteous." Amendments were made later, but nothing equivalent to the change in the 1860s recurred.[15]

As has been demonstrated, the period of most intensive reform effort began in 1859 and continued through the mid-1860s. This coincided with the administration of the Duke of Somerset. As if to assess progress late in that regime, a letter went out to all commanders in the navy requesting an overall evaluation of the policies up to 1865. W. G. Romaine, who signed the request, reviewed the intent and methodologies of the recent reform and stressed the significant transition ushered in by the Naval Discipline Act.

> . . . it classified and defined the punishments to be awarded, and this limited the power of Commanding Officers to award punishments under the general head, according to the manners and customs used at sea. As a consequenee [sic] of this change, Courts-Martial were, in many cases, necessarily substituted for the sole authority of the Commanding Officer, and to facilitate the holding of such Courts, their composition was altered, by making officers of a lower rank competent Members; at the same time greater latitude has been given to Commanders-in-Chief for the discharge of worthless and incorrigible characters, and great care has been taken to establish such regulations as were necessary to give full effect to the Act.
>
> Among those regulations none are more important than those which have for their object the establishment of an uniform practice in awarding minor punishments, and in recording offences.

Romaine continued by describing additional measures: publication of statistical reports on crime and punishment, "thus, Commanding Officers can judge their own ships as superior or inferior to others in conduct," various measures to encourage the "well-disposed" such as leave in an amount "formerly unknown in the Service," and institution of records and forms to facilitate supervision over discipline. The responses were generally supportive, but there was criticism of the report on crime and punishment and of excessive paper work.[16]

Subsequently an official history summed up the reform measures of the 1860s.

> ... the severities of the old act [1749] were further modified and alternative punishments were introduced for all but two of the remaining crimes. In 1860 an Act which may be considered as the first edition of the present [1950] Naval Discipline Act was passed. It was followed by later editions in 1861 and 1864, the last-named Act being repealed in 1866 by the Act which, with minor amendments, is in force today. This legislation retained the principal features of the 1749 Act but modified the severity of some of the punishments to conform to the civil law.[17]

So far this presentation has concentrated upon problems and issues and has neglected lengthy appraisals of persons, their contributions and responsibilities, though the approach has not intended to be merely subjective. A number of officials at Whitehall, senior naval officers, and bureaucrats contributed significantly toward the transformation in the conditions and welfare of the bluejacket between 1850 and 1880.

The First Lord of the Admiralty at the time when the decisions for comprehensive reform were made, 1859-66, was the Duke of Somerset, prior to 1855, Lord St. Maur, but it is difficult to determine his role. There appears to be general agreement that he was "a remarkable administrator" with "ability, sound judgment and impartiality."[18] His biographers noted "shrewdness and administrative capacity"[19] and a recent appraisal declared, "His tenure at the Admiralty must surely be reckoned one of the most successful periods in British naval history."[20] His personal interests dealt principally with technical developments and suppression of the slave trade and he "did pride himself on substituting a well-defined code of naval disciplinary laws in place of the previous vague and uncertain authority."[21] Other than the discipline acts, little mention was made about personnel matters and the conditions on the lower deck. Somerset received insufficient recognition for any of his achievements because he was overshadowed by Lord Palmerston and William Gladstone and because he was in the House of Lords.

If the primary impetus was not at the very top, then the Naval Lords must be considered, and a variety of significant accomplishment can be found at that level. Admiral Sir William Fanshawe Martin has been most identified with personnel matters during our period. Early in 1860 he became commander-in-chief of the Mediterranean Squadron. His flagship was H.M.S. *Marlborough*, scene of a major disturbance only a few months previously. The fleet was based at Malta where the incidence of venereal disease was appalling and drunkenness was rife. Large contingents of the crews were disgruntled bounty men. The achievements of Admiral Martin have been universally praised. He personally went ashore apprehending drunks and "rowdies," ordering them to return to individual commanding officers over whom he exerted tight control. At this point his response was anomalous. Instead of demanding maximum reprisals, he insisted upon moderation and humanitarian treatment. This was the crux of Admiral Martin's accomplishment and success. Sir John Knox Laughton, at Malta at the time and later Professor of Modern History, King's College, London, credited Admiral Martin with breaking up the old system of "rowdyism" and "turning the problems of personnel around."[22] The *Dictionary of National Biography* elaborated:

> by tact, by care, by unremitting attention, and by judicious severity he brought the fleet into that admirable

order which is still referred to in the navy as one of the glories of the past.[23]

Admiral Martin next came to Whitehall as a Naval Lord, continued his reform of discipline "almost amounting to a revolution," and "converted the senior officers" to his program. He was compared to Lord St. Vincent and acclaimed as "the greatest flag officer of the nineteenth century."[24] He concentrated much effort on the training of boys and implemented a model program of construction of barracks ashore in hopes of replacing the notorious hulks. Mention has previously been made of his initiatives in instituting weekly payment of wages. Unfortunately, about 1870 he and the First Lord, Hugh Childers, clashed over the organizational structure of the Board of the Admiralty, and Admiral Martin was dismissed. He remained a rather vociferous critic from outside for several years.[25]

Admiral Sir Maurice Berkeley, also a Naval Lord, was primarily a reformer of recruiting and manning. As did Admiral Sir Charles Napier, Berkeley personally experienced an acute shortage of personnel as a commanding officer in the Mediterranean during the crisis there in 1840. Between 1846 and 1859 at Whitehall he was responsible for manning and greatly influenced the significant recruiting measures of the 1850s.[26]

Admiral Sir Alexander Milne's contributions overlapped virtually the entire period of this study. He has been primarily linked with unraveling the intricacies of dockyard administration and naval stores contracts, but he also made contributions in the area of personnel matters. He introduced incentive or Good Conduct pay and badges, professional supplements for gunners, and stressed uniform policies of punishment.[27]

Among the bureaucrats, two stand out: William Hickman and W. G. Romaine, both of whom concentrated their expertise on legal matters and review of statistical information. Both were noted authorities on court-martial procedure and on the whole subject of discipline.[28]

Other officials at the Admiralty deserve mention: Sir James Graham and Captain Robert Harris were especially identified with education; Admiral Sir F. W. Grey, Senior Naval Lord under the Duke of Somerset, was instrumental in personnel reforms; Sir John Pakington pressured action to reduce the incidence of venereal disease; and, completely outside the Admiralty, William S. Lindsay, M.P. and shipping executive, pamphleteered against official incompetence and was instrumental in rebuilding the bridges between the merchant service and the navy.[29]

Collectively these persons and their contributions, along with those of many others during the period from 1850 to 1880, transformed life on the lower deck and established a cadre of seamen who possessed the professional capabilities and the incentives to serve a modern navy.

This was a critical phase in the history of the Royal Navy in a number of areas. The period of coasting along on past glories and unchallenged dominance came to an end. Methods of construction, design, propulsion, and firepower which had been unchanged for centuries suddenly became obsolete. Tactically and strategically a jolt was experienced in the Baltic and Black Sea campaigns of the Russian War. In 1859, another type of shock forced the Admiralty to re-appraise personnel policies. It was then that a new consciousness and sensitivity to the needs of its enlisted constituency began to pervade Whitehall. Urged on by public and parliamentary pressures, the authorities revised administrative procedures and reorganized lines of authority and responsibility. The measures instituted consisted of tentative steps, trial-and-error, experiments, heavy-handed intimidation, and some failures, but a pattern of reform can be delineated and defined, and the indicators, with minor exceptions, pointed toward success and progress.

The result was a more acceptable image of the navy from the perspectives of the potential recruit, his parents, the senior petty officer, the commanding officer, the merchant seaman, the back bencher, the newspaper editor, the pamphleteer, and the general public. It had been these latter external groups who had convinced a reluctant Admiralty that problems did exist and that changes must be made not only in the interest of national security, a traditional basis, but also for the sake of individual dignity and retention of a more dedicated and qualified bluejacket.

# Appendix

CHART 1. NUMBER OF MEN BORNE IN THE ROYAL NAVY, 1830-75[1]

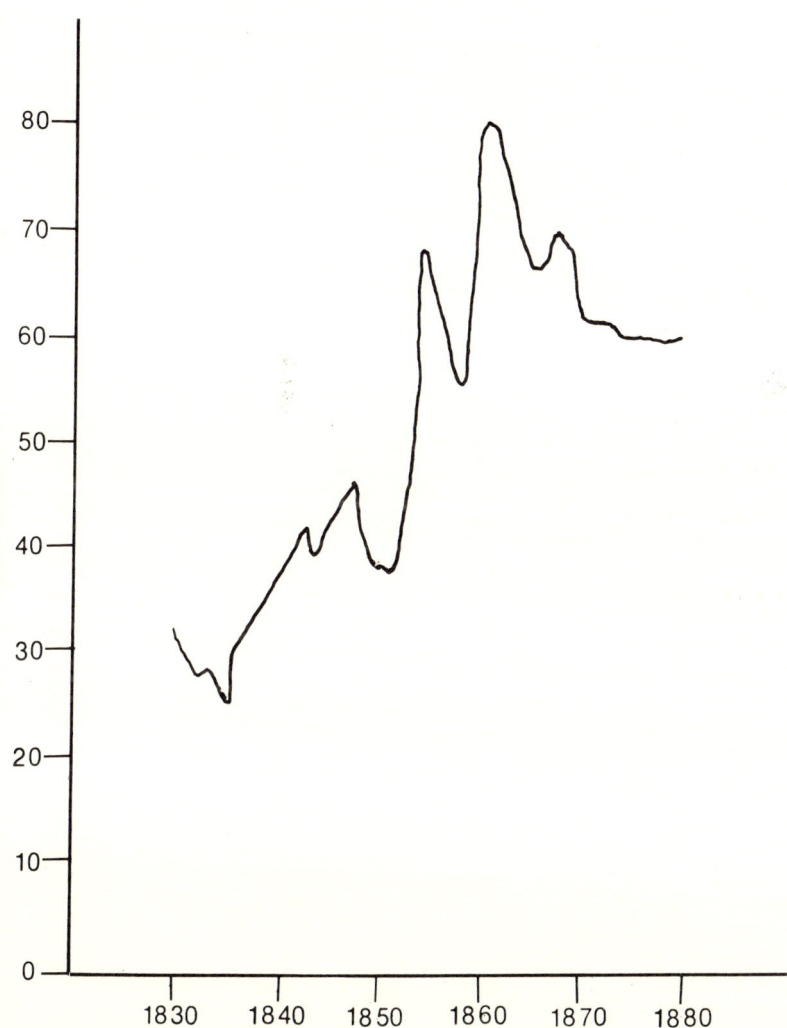

CHART 2. NUMBER OF MEN FLOGGED IN THE ROYAL NAVY, 1830-65[2]

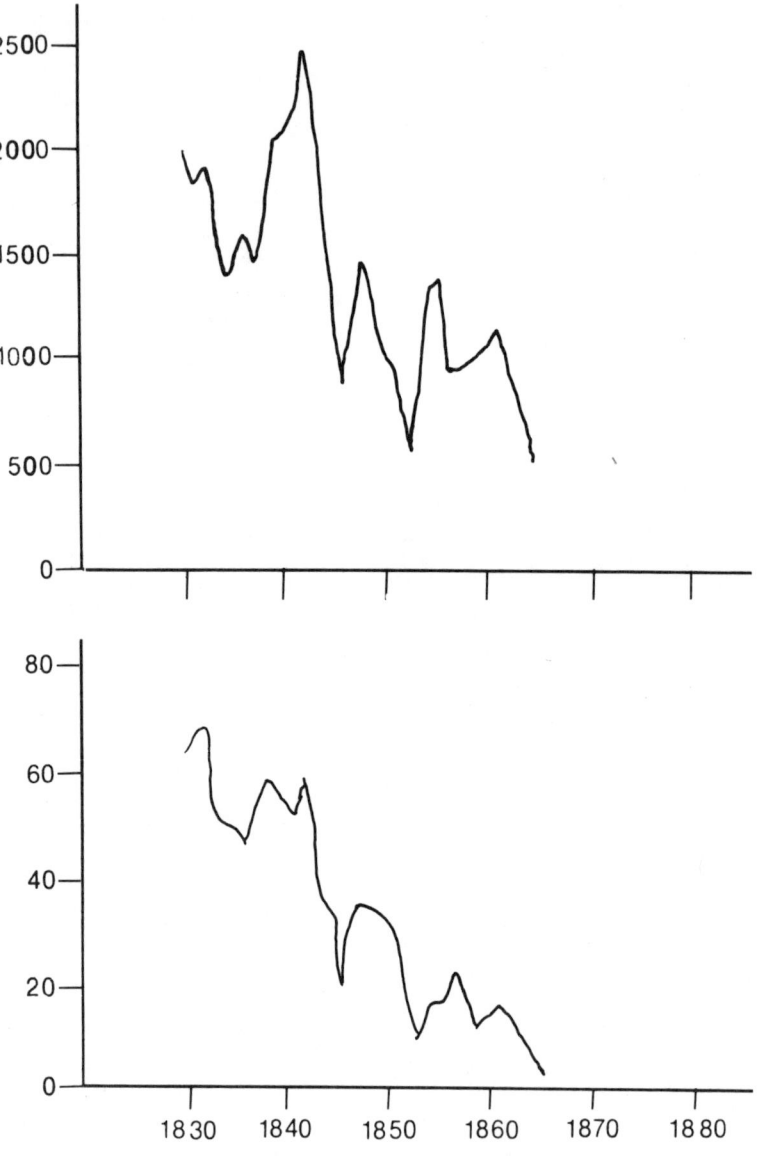

CHART 3. FLOGGINGS PER 1000 MEN IN THE ROYAL NAVY, 1830-65[3]

# REFORM IN THE ROYAL NAVY 129

CHART 4. AVERAGE NUMBER OF LASHES PER FLOGGING IN THE ROYAL NAVY, 1830-65[4]

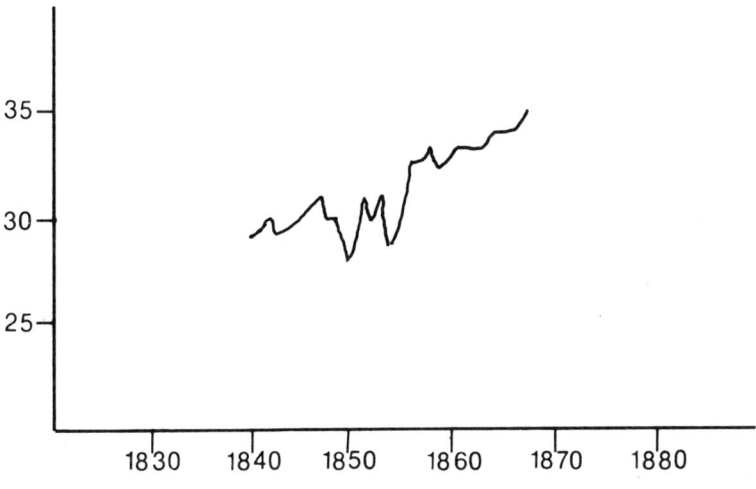

CHART 5. TREND INDICATED BY THE AVERAGE NUMBER OF DESERTIONS PER MONTH IN THE ROYAL NAVY, 1800-70[5]

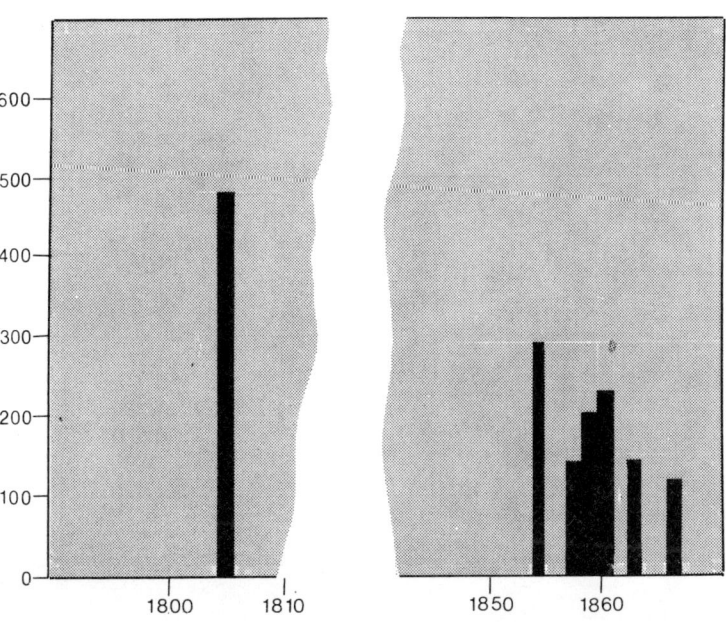

6. TABLE OF OFFENSES NOT REQUIRING COURTS-MARTIAL IN
THE ROYAL NAVY, 1862-65[6]

| Year | Total Offenses | Theft | Drunkenness | Disobedience |
|---|---|---|---|---|
| 1862 | 102,392 | 677 | 10,375 | 6064 |
| 1863 | 109,638 | 620 | 10,142 | 7873 |
| 1864 | 104,599 | 509 | 10,027 | 7769 |
| 1865 | 93,736 | 534 | 9,553 | 7454 |

| Year | Desertion | Absent Without Leave | Mutiny | Indecency | Minor |
|---|---|---|---|---|---|
| 1862 | 774 | 40,800 | 0 | 53 | 43,648 |
| 1863 | 531 | 41,860 | 15 | 45 | 48,552 |
| 1864 | 366 | 36,932 | 0 | 35 | 48,961 |
| 1865 | 306 | 33,915 | 0 | 43 | 41,931 |

# Notes

## Notes to the Preface

1. Sir William Laird Clowes, *The Royal Navy, A History*, 7 vols. (London: Low and Marston, 1897-1903); Christopher John Bartlett, *Great Britain and Sea Power, 1815-1853* (New York: Oxford University Press, 1963); Michael Arthur Lewis, *A Social History of the Navy, 1793-1814* (London: Allen & Unwin, 1960) and *The Navy in Transition, 1814-64* (London: Hodder & Stoughton, 1965); Charles Christopher Lloyd, *The British Seaman, 1200-1860* (London: Collins, 1968); Geoffrey Jules Marcus, *The Age of Nelson*, Vol. 2 of *A Naval History of England* (London: Allen & Unwin, 1971); Robert Greenhalgh Albion, *Forests and Sea Power* (Hamden, Conn.: Archon, 1965); Peter Kemp, *The British Sailor* (London: Dent, 1970); Gerald Sanford Graham, *Great Britain in the Indian Ocean* (London: Oxford University Press, 1967), *Sea Power and British North America, 1783-1820* (Cambridge: Harvard University Press, 1941), and Graham and R. A. Humphreys, eds., *The Navy and South America, 1807-23* (London: Navy Records Society, 1962); Roger Charles Anderson, *Naval Wars of the Baltic, 1522-1850* (London: n.p., 1910) and *Naval Wars in the Levant, 1559-1853* (Liverpool: University of Liverpool Press, 1952); Arthur J. Marder, *The Anatomy of British Sea Power* (New York: Knopf, 1940); Sir John Henry Briggs, *Naval Administrations* (London: S. Low, 1897).

A perusal of the historiography of the Royal Navy of the nineteenth century leaves the researcher confused and bewildered. A recent survey is entitled, "The Condition of the Fleets," and, as usual, "fleets" is stressed. The writer, Ruddock F. Mackay, calls for "more studies of technical development," yet only two lines in eight pages are devoted to social history, and nothing is included about personnel or "conditions" on the lower deck. Essay in Robin Higham, ed., *A Guide to the Sources of British Military History* (London: Routledge and Kegan, Paul, 1971), pp. 238-45.

Established histories of the Royal Navy are equally unbalanced and deficient. Sir William Laird Clowes, editor and primary contributor of the definitive study of seven volumes, the last two of which deal with the nineteenth century, alludes to change on the lower deck. The bluejacket "became clean, neat, orderly, self-respecting, scientific, and with few exceptions, sober." He apologizes for giving "a mere bald catalogue" of legislative and administrative reform. He notes certain health improvements and the Contagious Diseases Acts, but provides little information on personnel. The major emphasis is on technical, engineering, and gunnery subjects. Clowes, *Royal Navy*, 7: 73 and Sir William Laird Clowes in Henry Duff Traill and James Saumarez Mann, eds., *Social England* (London: Cassell, 1897), 4: 585.

2. [John Bechervaise], "By the Old Quarter Master," *A Farewell to My Old Shipmates* (Portsea: Woodward, 1847), pp. 6-8.
3. Charles Christopher Lloyd in a review of Peter Kemp's *The British Sailor* in *Mariner's Mirror* (August 1971), p. 356.
4. Others have cited the need for a social history of the lower deck during this period. Henry W. F. Baynham, author of compilations of autobiographical writings of seamen, recalled:

> To my knowledge the only recent work on this subject is R. Taylor's article in the *Mariner's Mirror* (1958-59), "On Manning the Royal Navy, 1852-62," though even this views the problem more from the administrative than the personnel level.

Baynham, "A Seaman in H.M.S. *Leander*, 1863-66," *Mariner's Mirror* 51 (1965): 343 and *Before the Mast* (London: Hutchins, 1972), pp. 9-10.
Another reviewer of Peter Kemp's *The British Sailor*, and Kemp himself for that matter, call for further study. The subject "offers an attractive field for young scholars, especially those interested in a quantitative and sociological approach." *Times Literary Supplement*, 7 May 1971, p. 545.
5. Standard accounts of the Naval Discipline Acts create misconceptions and secondary sources perpetuate stereotyped interpretations. For example, the final act of the series, that of 1866, is singled out as the panacea which provided for abolition of flogging, innovative humanitarian practices, comprehensive improvement of conditions, increased wages, additional leave, and, best of all, an improved caliber of seaman. A few accounts cite one more of the five acts, and the others are ignored. Admittedly, the act of 1866 did remain basic and fundamental for almost a hundred years and is subsequently referred to by name and date as the salient piece of discipline legislation, but since all are quite similar, the innovative statute would be the first chronologically, the act of 1860. The reformist trend commences within the Admiralty as early as 1853.
Some examples of the confusion will prove the point. The standard legal guide for the late nineteenth century, *A Treatise on the Criminal Law of the Navy* by Theodore Thring, Barrister of Middle Temple, refers to the Naval Discipline Act of 1866 as "the foundation . . . (in itself to a great extent a reprint of the Acts of 1861 and 1864)." He omits reference to any of the reforms of the 1850s, the first act of 1860, and the amendment of 1865. Professor Christopher Lloyd ignores the early acts. The Articles of War of 1749, he says, "continued in force with few alterations until 1866." More recently, Lieutenant Commander Peter Kemp, sometime Admiralty librarian, has completed a general survey of social history and falls into the trap of acknowledging only two acts, again those of 1861 and 1866. Admiral G. A. Ballard in G. M. Young's *Early Victorian England* appreciates the significance of the act of 1860 but ignores subsequent ones. F. H. Dean in another bibliographical essay in Higham, *Guide to Sources*, pp. 621-31, vaguely sums up that "various subsequent Acts were passed between 1749 and 1866." Finally, even contemporaries contribute to the confusion. That

colorful and notorious naval officer-parliamentarian, Admiral Lord Charles Beresford, a junior officer during this period, recalls the act of 1861 and the "new" Naval Discipline Act of 1866. Theodore Thring and C. E. Gifford, Thring's *Criminal Law of the Navy*, 2nd ed. (London: Stevens, 1877), pp. iii, 177-79; Lloyd, *British Seaman*, p. 239; G. M. Young, *Early Victorian England*, 2 vols., 2nd ed. (New York: Oxford University Press, 1951), 1: 329-31; Lord Charles Beresford, *The Memoirs of Admiral Lord Charles Beresford*, 2 vols. (Boston: Little, Brown, 1914), 1: 17-18.

The Naval Discipline Act of 1866 remained the basic discipline legislation for the navy until repealed in 1957. In structure the 1957 act is the same as the 1866 act. It contains forty-four Articles of War—several additional articles concern modern features such as "dangerous flying" which were not provided for previously. Traditional phraseology is maintained. The navy successfully alienated itself from a trend which was prevalent in the post-World War II British Army and Air Force and American armed services: consolidation of judicial codes. There were amendments to the Naval Discipline Act of 1866 in 1884, 1890, two in 1915, 1917, 1922, 1938, and 1941. Great Britain, Admiralty, *Committee to Consider the Administration of Justice Under the Naval Discipline Act* (House of Commons), Vol. 1, Command 8094, pp. 9-13. Great Britain, Admiralty, *Admiralty Memorandum on Naval Court-Martial Procedure*, BR 11/1958, pp. 111-71; Robert S. Pasley, "A Comparative Study of Military Justice Reforms in Britain and America," *Vanderbilt Law Review* 6 (1953): 307-28; Byron A. Wiley, "Non-judicial Punishment in the Royal Navy," *U. S. Naval Institute Proceedings* 93 (July 1967): 139-41.

## Notes for Chapter I

1. Charles Christopher Lloyd, *The Navy and the Slave Trade: The Suppression of the African Slave Trade in the 19th Century* (New York: Longmans, Green, 1949); William Ernest Frank Ward, *The Royal Navy and the Slavers* (London: Allen & Unwin, 1969); Oliver Ransford, *The Slave Trade* (London: John Murray, 1971); W. E. Burghardt DuBois, *The Suppression of the African Slave-Trade to the U. S. of A., 1638-1870* (New York: Schocken, 1969), pp. 131-50, 168-200; Daniel Pratt Mannix and Malcolm Cowley, *Black Cargoes* (New York: Viking, 1965); Howard Temperley, *British Antislavery, 1833-70* (London: Longmans, 1972), pp. 168-83; Philip Howard Colomb, *Slave-catching in the Indian Ocean* (New York: Negro University Press, 1969); Kenneth Bourne, *The Foreign Policy of Victorian England, 1830-1902* (New York: Oxford University Press, 1970), pp. 48-49; Patrick Richardson, *Empire and Slavery* (New York: Harper and Row, 1968), pp. 14-21, 111-24; Marder *Anatomy*, pp. 10-23; Anthony Preston and John Major, *Send a Gunboat!* (London: Longmans, Green, 1967), pp. 3-7; Arthur Howard W. Robinson, *Marine Cartography in*

*Britain* (Leicester: University Press, 1961); Sir John Edgell, *Sea Surveys* (London: Her Majesty's Stationery Office, 1965); Clowes, *Royal Navy*, 6: vii; 7: vi-vii; Cyril Northcote Parkinson, *Britain in the Far East* (Singapore: D. Moore, 1955); Christopher Lloyd, *Search for the Niger* (London: Collins, 1973), and "Dr. Baikie and the Niger," *History Today* (October 1971): 740-46; James Morris, "The Royal Navy," *U.S. Naval Institute Proceedings* 98 (March 1972): 64-68; Baynham, *Before the Mast*, pp. 81-99; Gerald Sanford Graham, "By Steam to India," *History Today* 14 (May 1964): 301-12.

2. James Morris, "A View of the Royal Navy," *Encounter* 40 (March 1973): 15-27; George C. Perry and Nicholas Mason, *The Victorians* (New York: Viking, 1974), pp. 146-53; Stanley Bonnett, *The Price of Admiralty* (London: Robert Hale, 1968); Michael Lewis, "An Eye-Witness at Petropaulovski, 1854," *Mariner's Mirror* 49 (November 1963): 265-72; Colin F. Baxter, "Admiralty Problems during the Second Palmerston Administration, 1859-65," Ph.D. dissertation, University of Georgia, 1965; Ernest A. Gray, "The Stone Frigates of Sebastopol: The Navy's Role on Land and Sea in the Crimean Campaign," *History Today* 19 (June 1969): 388-96; Mrs. Tom Kelly, *From the Fleet in the Fifties* (London: Hurst & Blackett, 1902), pp. vii-ix.

The standard account of the Crimean War is Arthur William Kinglake's, *The Invasion of the Crimea*, 6 vols. (London: 1863-80). Also see David Bonner-Smith and A. C. Dewar, eds., *Russian War*, 3 vols. (London: Navy Records Society, 1943); Philip Warner, *The Crimean War* (London: Weidenfeld & Nicolson, 1972); Bowen Stilon Mends, *Life of Admiral Sir W. R. Mends, 1812-97* (London: Murray, 1899).

3. Peter Padfield, *Aim Straight* (London: Hodder and Stoughton, 1966), p. 23.

4. Outstanding examples are Sir John Colomb; his brother, Philip; Fred T. Jane; Sir Julian S. Corbett; Admiral Sir Herbert Richmond; Sir John Knox Laughton; the journalist, William Thomas Stead; and the American Captain (later Admiral), Alfred T. Mahan. D. M. Schurman, *The Education of a Navy* (Chicago: University of Chicago Press, 1965), p. 3; William C. Brian Tunstall, *Realities of Naval History* (London: Allen & Unwin, 1936), pp. 202-203; Sir John Knox Laughton, *Studies in Naval History—Biographies* (London: Longmans, 1887), pp. 4-9 and "The National Study of Naval History," *Transactions of the Royal Historical Society*, n.s., 12 (1898): 81-94; Marder, *Anatomy*, pp. 44-48 and *Fear God and Dread Nought*, 3 vols. (London: Cape, 1952-59); Clowes, *Royal Navy*, 2: vii-x; 7: 81; Sir William Scarlett Jameson, *The Fleet that Jack Built* (New York: Harcourt, Brace, 1962); [William H. Ragan], *Admiralty Administration*, 2nd ed. (London: Longmans, Green, 1861), pp. v-vii.

5. [Ragan], *Admiralty Administration*, pp. v-viii.

6. Great Britain, Parliament, *British Sessional Papers* (House of Commons), (New York: Readex Microprint, 1966), Vol. 5 (1860): 1; L. G. Carr Laughton, "The Preamble to the Articles of War," *Mariner's Mirror* 7 (March 1921): 82-86.

7. Phillip Appleman, William A. Madden, and Michael Wolff, eds., *1859: Entering an Age of Crisis* (Bloomington: Indiana University Press, 1969); Jacques Barzun, *Darwin, Marx, Wagner: Critique of a Heritage* (Garden City, N.Y.: Doubleday Anchor, 1958); James B. Conacher, *The Aberdeen Coalition, 1852-55* (London: Cambridge University Press, 1968) and *The Peelites and the Party System, 1846-52* (London: David & Charles, 1972); Robert E. Zegger, "Victorians in Arms: The French Invasion Scare of 1859-60," *History Today* 23 (October 1973): 705-11. For a contrary view relating to the Royal Navy see R. Mackay in Higham, *Guide to Sources*, pp. 238-45. He sees 1854 as a turning point, but, inevitably, for reasons of engineering and mechanical advances.

There are several accounts of Victorian England which bracket the year 1859, each for different reasons and from various perspectives. Ernest L. Woodward, *The Age of Reform, 1815-70* (New York: Oxford University Press, 1938); George S. R. Kitson Clark, *The Making of Victorian England* (Cambridge, Harvard University Press, 1962); Asa Briggs, *The Age of Improvement* (New York: McKay, 1962) and *Victorian People* (New York: Harper and Row, 1963). He selects 1851-67. W. L. Burn, *The Age of Equipoise* (New York: Norton, 1964); Geoffrey Best, *Mid-Victorian Britain, 1851-75* (London: Weidenfeld & Nicolson, 1971); Derek Beales, *From Castlereagh to Gladstone, 1815-1885* (New York: Norton, 1969); D. F. MacDonald, *The Age of Transition* (New York: St. Martins Press, 1967).

8. The *Times*, 9 May 1859; *Annual Register*, 1859, p. 556; Appleman, *1859*, pp. 163-94; Woodward, *Age of Reform*, pp. 178-80; Francis Wrigley Hirst, *The Six Panics, and other Essays* (London: Methuen, 1913), pp. 20-27; Bourne, *Foreign Policy*, pp. 100-103.

9. David Roberts, *Victorian Origins of the British Welfare State* (New Haven: Yale University Press, 1960; reprinted Hamden, Conn., Archon Books, 1969), pp. 93-95, 318-22.

The controversy over the nineteenth-century "revolution in government" is an expansive one. Oliver MacDonagh, "The Nineteenth Century Revolution in Government: A Reappraisal," *Historical Joural* 1 (1958): 52-67 and *A Pattern of Government Growth, 1800-60* (London. MacGibbon, 1961); Henry Parris, "The Nineteenth-Century Revolution in Government: A Re-Appraisal Reappraised," *Historical Journal* 3 (1960): 17-37 and *Constitutional Bureaucracy* (New York: Kelley, 1969); Burn, *Equipoise*, pp. 7-17, 132-33, 158-60; Emmeline Waley Cohen, *Growth of the British Civil Service* (New York: Norton, 1940), pp. 17-21; Geoffrey R. Elton, *Modern Historians on British History, 1485-1945* (Ithaca, N.Y.: Cornell University Press, 1970), pp. 121-22; Woodward, *Age of Reform*, p. 93, n.; Lucy Brown, *The Board of Trade and the Free Trade Movement, 1830-42* (Oxford: Clarendon Press, 1958); Valerie Cromwell, "Interpretations of Nineteenth Century Administration: An Analysis," *Victorian Studies* 9 (March 1966): 245-55; William O. Aydelotte, "The Conservative and Radical Interpretations of Early Victorian Social Legislation," *Victorian Studies* 11 (December 1967): 225-36; David Roberts, "Jeremy Bentham and the Victorian Administrative State," *Victorian Studies* 2 (March 1959): 193-210; Royston J.

Lambert, *Sir John Simon, 1816-1904* (London: MacGibbon, 1963); Maurice Wright, *Treasury Control of the Civil Service, 1854-74* (Oxford: Clarendon Press, 1969); Gillian Sutherland, ed., *Studies in the Growth of Nineteenth-Century Government* (Boston: Routledge and Paul, 1972).

David Roberts emphasizes newly created central agencies with authority to regulate and influenced by Benthamite and Evangelical converts. Though not "newly created," the Admiralty adapted and adopted many of the techniques which had proved successful elsewhere.

10. Woodward, *Age of Reform*, p. 172; Henry Brooks Adams, *The Education of Henry Adams* (Cambridge, Mass.: Riverside Press, 1947), p. 193. The statement by Professor Kitson Clark is quoted in Burn, *Equipoise*, p. 304. Baxter, "Admiralty Problems"; Best, *Mid-Victorian Britain*, pp. 282-86; Donald Southgate, *"The Most English Minister"* (New York: St. Martins Press, 1966); Robert Blake, *The Conservative Party from Peel to Churchill* (London: Constable, 1970), pp. 488-91; Appleman, *1859*, pp. 116-25; Wilbur Devereux Jones, *Lord Derby and Victorian Conservatism* (Athens, Ga.: University of Georgia Press, 1966).

11. Flogging was effectively reduced to negligible proportions—later to be suspended—during the regimes of Lords Palmerston and Russell, yet each had previously supported the practice of corporal punishment. Lord Palmerston especially had consistently supported the practice in debates in the House of Commons earlier in the century. Great Britain, Parliament, *Hansard's Parliamentary Debates*, 1st ser., Vol. 31 (21 June 1815), p. 936; 2nd ser., Vol. 10 (15 March 1824), p. 1038; 2nd ser., Vol. 16 (13 February 1827), p. 679; M. W. Patterson, *Sir Francis Burdett and His Times, 1770-1844* (London: Macmillan, 1931), 1: 285; Jasper Ridley, *Lord Palmerston* (New York: Dutton, 1970), pp. 47-52, 87.

12. William Ashworth, "Economic Aspects of Late Victorian Naval Administration," *Economic History Review*, 2nd ser., 22 (December 1969): 491-505; Bartlett, *Great Britain and Sea Power*, pp. 103-16; Marder, *Anatomy*, pp. 119-22; Hirst, *Six Panics;* Woodward, *Age of Reform;* Conacher, *Aberdeen Coalition*, pp. 58-69; C. J. Bartlett in Kenneth Bourne and D. C. Watt, *Studies in International History* (Hamden, Conn.: Archon, 1967), p. 189.

13. Kemp, *British Sailor*, p. xiii.

14. Charles M. Clode, *The Administration of Justice Under Military and Martial Law*, 2nd ed. (London: John Murray, 1874), pp. 38-39; Michael Arthur Lewis, *The Navy of Britain* (London: Allen & Unwin, 1948), pp. 318-19; George Ernest Manwaring and Bonamy Dobree, *The Floating Republic* (New York: Harcourt, Brace, 1935), p. 37; Samuel Leech, *Thirty Years from Home* (London: H. Collins, 1851), p. 22.

15. Lewis, *Navy of Britain*, pp. 92-93.

16. Robert D. Foulke, "Life in the Dying World of Sail, 1870-1910," *Journal of British Studies* 3 (November 1963): 105-36; Henry Norton Sulivan, *The Life and Letters of Admiral Sir Bartholomew James Sulivan, 1810-90* (London: J. Murray, 1896), pp. 58-111; Beresford, *Memoirs*, 1: 19;

Cecil Scott Forester, ed., *The Adventures of John Wetherell* (New York: Doubleday, 1954); Philip Howard Colomb, *The Memoirs of Admiral Sir Astley Cooper Key* (London: Metheun, 1898); Ann Parry, *The Admirals Fremantle* (London: Chatto & Windus, 1971); Sir Albert H. Markham, *The Life of Sir Clements R. Markham* (London: John Murray, 1917); Padfield, *Aim Straight*; Admiral Sir Percy Scott, *Fifty Years in the Royal Navy* (London: Murray, 1919); Henry W. F. Baynham, *From the Lower Decks* (London: Hutchinson, 1969); Leech, *Thirty Years*; Patrick Riley, *Memories of a Bluejacket* (London: Sampson Low, 1931); Frederick Jackson Bell, *Room to Swing a Cat* (New York: Longmans, Green, 1938); Baynman, *Before the Mast* and "Seaman from *Leander*."

17. Bartlett, *Great Britain and Sea Power*, p. 49.

An incredible series of changes and innovations occurred during our period: types of propulsion (steam), devices for propulsion (screw propellor), material of construction, armor protection, guns, shells (shape and content), the torpedo, the torpedo boat, the torpedo boat destroyer, the submarine, use of the ram, water-tight subdivision, and new design techniques (the experimental model). Oscar Parkes, *British Battleships* (London: Seeley, 1958), pp. 1-143; Edward H. H. Archibald, *The Wooden Fighting Ships in the Royal Navy, A.D, 897-1860 (London: Blandford, 1968)* and *The Metal Fighting Ship in the Royal Navy 1860-1970* (London: Blandford, 1971); Donald MacIntyre and Basil W. Bathe, *The Man of War* (London: Methuen, 1969); Christopher Lloyd, "The Torpedo," *History Today* 6 (August 1956): 552-55; R. W. Yates, ed., "From Wooden Walls to Dreadnoughts in a Lifetime," *Mariner's Mirror* 48 (November 1962): 291-303.

18. Sulivan, *Life and Letters*, pp. 58, 111.

19. Louis Blanc, *Letters on England*, 2 vols. (London: 1866-67), 2: 55; Christine Bolt, *Victorian Attitudes to Race* (London: Routledge & Paul, 1971), pp. xi-xiii; Appleman, *1859*, p. 116; Samuel Edward Finer, *The Life and Times of Sir Edwin Chadwick* (London: Methuen, 1952), pp. 6-43; Marder, *Anatomy*, pp. 44-64.

20. Best, *Mid-Victorian Britain*, pp. 224-27.

Asa Briggs in "Crimean Centenary," *Virginia Quarterly Review* 30 (1954): 542-44, claims it was the Crimean War which gave impetus to the power of the press. Burn in *Equipoise*, pp. 237-38, reviews the impact:

> Although they used the pen and the printing press instead of the pistol and the rope they constituted, in some sort, a vigilante movement . . .; making nuisances of themselves, occasionally making heroes of themselves; meddling with, thwarting, sometimes assisting the processes of administration; an important, perhaps necessary and beneficial, feature of the contemporary scene.

21. Appleman, *1859*, p. 215.

22. Jay Luvaas, *The Education of an Army* (Chicago: University of Chicago Press, 1964), p. 98; Bartlett, *Great Britain and Sea Power*, p. 315. The latter was edited by Dr. William Howard Russell, who was praised by Sir William Laird Clowes as "singularly able and outspoken" and his journal "pertinaciously exposed many naval abuses and procured the granting of many naval reforms." Clowes, *Royal Navy*, 7: 81.

23. Rear Admiral S. R. Franklin, U.S.N., cited in Leech, *Thirty Years*, p. 5; for a contrary view that Melville had little influence, see Charles Robert Anderson, *Melville in the South Seas* (New York: Columbia University Press, 1939).

Charles Napier Robinson and John Leyland, *The British Tar in Fact and Fiction* (New York: Harper, 1909); Frederick Marryat, *Works*, 5 vols. (Hartford: Andrus, 1849). *Peter Simple* was the most popular; the *King's Own* depicted the mutinies of 1797; *Mr. Midshipman Easy* and *Frank Mildmay* were others. Captain Marryat served under one of the most popular of the early nineteenth century officers, Admiral Lord Cochrane, who appears in several works. Christopher Lloyd, *Captain Marryat and the Old Navy* (London: Longmans, 1939); Oliver Warner, *Captain Marryat* (London: Constable, 1953); Cyril Northcote Parkinson, *Portsmouth Point* (Liverpool: Hodder & Stoughton, 1948).

Didacticism was typical of much Victorian fiction. P. J. Keating, *The Working Classes in Victorian Fiction* (New York: Barnes & Noble, 1971), pp. 4-5.

24. Sir Leslie Stephen and Sir Sidney Lee, eds., *Dictionary of National Biography*, 21 vols. (London: Oxford University Press, 1937-38), 4: 94-95; Leslie Gardiner, *The British Admiralty* (London: Blackwood, 1968), p. 275; Great Britain, Admiralty, *Queen's Regulations and Admiralty Instructions for the Government of Her Majesty's Naval Service*, 1862, p. 106. The regulations in this edition were much more precise and commanding than a similar prohibition in the edition of 1844. *Queen's Regulations*, 1844, p. 96; Arvel B. Erickson, *The Public Career of Sir James Graham* (Cleveland: Western Reserve University Press, 1952), p. 332; Great Britain, Public Record Office, *Admiralty Courts-Martial Records*, 2/1562 of 1853.

25. William Schaw Lindsay, *History of Merchant Shipping and Ancient Commerce*, 4 vols. (London: Sampson, Low, 1874-76); Captain A. Course, *The Merchant Navy* (London: Muller, 1963); R. J. Cornewall-Jones, *The British Merchant Service* (London: Low, Marston, 1898); Sir Henry Evan Auguste Cotton, *East Indiamen* (London: Batchworth, 1949); Stephen Jones, "Blood Red Roses: The Supply of Merchant Seamen in the Nineteenth Century," *Mariner's Mirror* 58 (November 1972): 429-42.

26. Hilary Jenkinson in J. H. Collingridge, et al., *Catalogue of an Exhibition of Naval Records at the Public Record Office* (London: His Majesty's Stationery Office, 1950), p. 5.

27. In the Channel Squadron, for example, convictions diminished "from 3485/1000 of average mean force borne in 1863 to 2588/1000 in 1865, a difference of about 90% in favor of 1865." The *Report on Crime and Punishment* for the year 1864 indicated significant reduction in flogging:

| Year | Ratio of Men Flogged |
|---|---|
| 1862 | 1 in 54 |
| 1863 | 1 in 65 |
| 1864 | 1 in 84 |

Great Britain, Public Record Office, *Admiralty Digests*, IND 12585 of 1866;

IND 12597 of 1867; IND 12598 of 1867; IND 12602 of 1867; IND 18285 of 1880; Great Britain, Public Record Office, *Admiralty In-Letters* (Adm 1), Adm 1/5774 of 1866.

28. Kemp, *British Sailor;* H. Baynham, *Before the Mast* and "Seaman in *Leander,*" p. 343.

## Notes for Chapter II

1. Lindesay Brine, "The Best Method of Providing an Efficient Force of Officers and Men for the Navy, Including the Reserves." *Journal of the Royal United Service Institution* 26 (1882): 197; Roy Taylor, "Manning the Royal Navy: the Reform of the Recruiting System, 1847-61." M.A. thesis, Birkbeck College, London, 1853, p. 27; H. I. Vansittart Neale, "Manning the Navy—Seamen," *Naval Library Pamphlets* 3 (February 1883): 253-56; Hans Busk, *The Navies of the World* (New York: Routledge, Warnes, 1859), pp. 35-39; [Ragan], *Admiralty Administration,* pp. 29-30, 87-88, 120-22; James Reddie, "On Manning the Navy," *Journal of the Royal United Service Institution* 11 (1867): 328; T. A. Brassey, "Manning the Navy," *Brassey's Naval Annual* (1886): 104.

2. Frank Charles Bowen, *History of the Royal Naval Reserve* (London: Lloyds, 1926), pp. 3-4; William Schaw Lindsay, *Manning the Royal Navy and the Mercantile Marine* (London: Pewtress, 1877), pp. 5-81; Cristopher Lloyd, "The Press Gang and the Law," *History Today* 17 (October 1967): 683-90; Norman McCord, "The Impress Service in Northeast England during the Napoleonic War," *Mariner's Mirror* 54 (May 1968): 163-80; James Stewart, "The Press-Gangs of the Royal Navy," *U.S. Naval Institute Proceedings* 86 (October 1960): 81-87.

3. Captain Frederick Chamier favored impressment in didactic novels in the 1830s. It was, he claimed, the only way to man the fleet. Robinson, *British Tar,* pp. 331-32. The Earl of Hardwicke, chairman of the Royal Commission on Manning the Navy of 1858, favored revival. Bowen, *Royal Naval Reserve,* p. 4.

4. Quoted from Kemp, *British Sailor,* p. 104.

5. J. R. Hutchinson, *The Press-Gang Afloat and Ashore* (London: E. Nash, 1913), pp. 17-18. Professor Christopher Lloyd claims and the reader will probably agree that Hutchinson exaggerates and presents a false picture of the incidence of impressment. Lloyd, *British Seaman,* p. 13.

6. Frederick Marryat, *Suggestions for the Abolition of the Present State of Impressment in the Naval Service* (London: Richardson, 1822), pp. 1-47. The pamphlet "caused some flutter in naval circles, and is said to have drawn down on him the ill will of the Duke of Clarence, afterwards King William IV." *Dictionary of National Biography,* 12: 1086-88; 14: 42.

7. [Thomas Hodgskin], "The Abolition of Impressment: Review Article," *Edinburgh Review* 4 (1824): 161-79.
8. Anselm John Griffiths, *Impressment Fully Considered* (London: Norie, 1826), pp. 45-55.
9. G. H. Gardner, "On the Formation of Reserves of Officers and Seamen for the Royal Navy, and the Evils and Inadequacy of Impressment to Provide the Same," *Journal of the Royal United Service Institution* 15 (1871): 601-603.
10. In 1840 during a crisis in the eastern Mediterranean involving Mehemet Ali, the British fleet under Admiral Napier found itself critically short-handed.
11. In addition there was a problem about cooperation with the French and their reluctance to do so, and even accusations that Admiral Napier indulged "too liberal and long continued potations of Scotch whiskey." Admiral Napier's biographer claimed he was "sacrificed ... to cover the sins of others. ... and, but for the altered spirit of the times, he might probably have shared the fate of the unfortunate Admiral Byng." E. Elers Napier, *Life and Correspondence of Admiral Sir Charles Napier*, 2 vols. (London: Hurst & Blackett, 1862), 2: 329; Lloyd, *British Seaman*, p. 280; Sir Herbert William Richmond, "Sir James Graham's Reforms in Administration and Command at the Admiralty." *Naval Policy and National Strength* (London: Longmans, Green, 1928), p. 247.
12. Robinson, *British Tar*, pp. 309-22; *Hansard*, 2nd ser., Vol. 11 (10 June 1824), pp. 1171-86; 3rd ser., Vol. 20 (15 August 1833), p. 646; 3rd ser., Vol. 150 (28 May 1858), p. 1060; *British Sessional Papers*, Vol. 5 (1860), p. 1; Gardner, "Formation," pp. 601-603; Bowen, *Royal Naval Reserve*, pp. 3-4; Lloyd, "Press-Gang," pp. 683-85; Neale, *Manning*, pp. 253-56; Lindsay, *Manning Royal Navy*, pp. 28-29; Erickson, *Sir James Graham*, pp. 337-69; Sir Walter Runciman, *The Shellback's Progress in the Nineteenth Century* (London: Walter Scott, 1904), p. 148; Taylor, "Manning," M.A., pp. x, 1-10, 134-39 and "Manning the Royal Navy: the Reform of the Recruiting System, 1852-62," *Mariner's Mirror* 44 (November 1958): 303-307; Lewis, *Navy of Britain*, pp. 307-22 and *Navy in Transition*, pp. 185-91; Bartlett, *Great Britain and Sea Power*, p. 47; Brian James Bond, "The Introduction and Operation of Short Service and Localisation in the British Army, 1868-92," M.A. thesis, King's College, London, 1962, p. 36; P. Jones, "British Army," pp. 121-26; Baynham, *From Lower Decks*, pp. 13, 87-97; Sir Frederick William Grey, *Suggestions for Improving the Character of our Merchant Seamen and for Providing an Efficient Naval Reserve* (London: n.p., 1873).
13. Peter Daggett Karsten, *The Naval Aristocracy* (Riverside, N.J.: Free Press, 1971), pp. 78-79. It was obviously ignored, but there was a legislative requirement that sixty-seven percent must be native-born Americans.
14. Lloyd, *British Seaman*, p. 281.
15. Brine, "Best Method," p. 184; Bartlett, *Great Britain and Sea Power*, p. 47; R. Taylor, "Reform of the Recruiting System," pp. 303-307; Lewis, *Navy in Transition*, pp. 185-91.

16. Oddly enough the army was shifting from long-term to short-term service at this time. Bond, "Introduction and Operation," p. 36.
17. Reddie, "On Manning," p. 357.
18. There had been a French invasion scare in 1844 stemming from statements from a variety of sources—King Louis Philippe's son, the Duke de Joinville, and the Duke of Wellington, among others—that steam-powered ships might cross the Channel anytime. The incident is reminiscent of Prime Minister Stanley Baldwin's later ominous prediction, "The bomber will always get through." Bartlett, *Great Britain and Sea Power*, pp. 168-69; Bourne, *Foreign Policy*, pp. 54-55, 61.
19. There is dispute over the results of the offer of the bounty. Estimates vary from 3,000 to 11,000 but the weight of evidence favors the former. R. Taylor, "Manning," pp. 182-88.
20. Erickson, *Public Career*, pp. 337-69; R. Taylor, "Manning," and "Reform of the Recruiting System," pp. 307-308; Runciman, *Shellback*, p. 148; Baxter, "Admiralty Problems," pp. 115-16; Sir Frederick William Grey, *On the Organization of the Navy* (London: n.p., 1860), pp. 6-8; Gardner, "Formation of Reserves," pp. 617-19; Reddie, "On Manning," pp. 279-363; Great Britain, Orders-in-Council, *The Orders in Council and Some of the Acts of Parliament for the Regulation of the Naval Service*, 5 vols. (London: Her Majesty's Stationery Office, 1856-88), 1: 525; *Encyclopedia Brittannica*, 9th ed. (New York: Allen, 1890) 17: 295; Adm 1/5997 Pro H 568 of 1866.
21. Busk, *Navies*, p. 186; Kelly, *From the Fleet*, pp. 76-107, 272-77.
22. They were, in addition to the Earl of Hardwick, Edward Cardwell, Sir James Elphinstone, W. S. Lindsay, Commodore John Sheperd (who had served on the Manning Committee of 1852), Vice Admiral William Fanshawe Martin, First Naval Lord, and Richard Green.
23. Frank Charles Bowen, *His Majesty's Coastguard* (London: Hutchinson, 1928) and *Royal Naval Reserve*, pp. 3-23; Lloyd, *British Seaman*, pp. 180-82; Lewis, *Navy of Britain*, pp. 234-35; Lindsay, *Manning*, pp. 5-81; Busk, *Navies*, pp. 35-39; James Lennox Kerr and Wilfred Granville, *The R.N.V.R.* (London: Harrap, 1957), pp. 18-20; Baynham, *From the Lower Decks*, pp. 13-14; [Ragan], *Admiralty Administration*, pp. 85-97; Taylor, "Manning," pp. 182-88; Gardner, "Formation of Reserves," pp. 617-20; Bartlett, *Great Britain and Sea Power*, pp. 304-17; Gardiner, *British Admiralty*, pp. 270-71; *Dictionary of National Biography*, 7: 328-32 and 9: 663-65; *Hansard*, 3rd ser., Vol. 26 (17 March 1825), pp. 1120-32.
24. Bowen, *Royal Naval Reserve*, pp. 4-37; R. Taylor, "Manning," pp. 229-65; Kerr, *R.N.V.R.*, pp. 18-21; Lewis, *Navy of Britain*, pp. 234-35, 305-306 and *Navy In Transition*, pp. 190-91; Charles Douglas-Home, *Britain's Reserve Forces* (London: Royal United Service Institution, 1970), p. 26; [Ragan], *Admiralty Administration*, pp. 97-102; Gardner, "Formation of Reserves," pp. 601-22; Lord Thomas Brassey, *The British Navy*, 5 vols. (London: Longmans, 1882-83), see Vol. 4, *Dockyards, Reserves, Training, Pensions;* Brassey, "Manning," pp. 104-106 and "Our Reserves of Seamen," (London: Longmans, 1872), pp. 1-48; Thomas Gray, *Under the Red Ensign*

(London: Simpkin, Marshall, 1878), pp. 67-72; Traill, *Social England*, 6: 598; W. F. Caborne, "The Royal Naval Reserve," *Journal of the Royal United Service Institution* 33 (January 1889): 41-43.

25. Bartlett, *Great Britain and Sea Power*, pp. 203-10; Beresford, *Memoirs*, 1: 6-9; Taylor, "Manning," p. 13; Leech, *Thirty Years*, pp. 22-23; *Admiralty Digest*, IND 18091 of 1871. The seamen called the engineers "chimney sweeps."

26. S. W. C. Pack, *Britannia at Dartmouth* (London: Redman, 1966), pp. 24-30; Edward Phillips Statham, *The Story of the Britannia* (London: n.p., 1904), pp. 55-70; Robert T. Young, *The House that Jack Built* (Aldershot: Gale and Polden, 1955), pp. 1-29; Leech, *Thirty Years*, pp. 22-23; C. D. Waters, "Recruiting to the Regular Forces," *Journal of the Royal United Service Institution* 102 (1957): 55-60; Baynham, *From the Lower Decks*, pp. 157-60; Adm 12/1088 of 1882; Adm 12/1105 of 1883.

27. Lewis, *Navy in Transition*, pp. 190-91; Reddie, "On Manning," pp. 309-25; J. McD. Moody, "Recruiting for Her Majesty's Service," *Journal of the Royal United Service Institution* 29 (1885): 581-97; Taylor, "Manning," pp. 192-200; Baynham, *From the Lower Decks*, p. 120; Stewart, "Press-Gangs," pp. 81-87.

## Notes for Chapter III

1. In the eighteenth century it was "unaccountably lost," there presumably being only one copy, and was later found among the personal papers of a deceased Admiralty clerk in 1874. Great Britain, Admiralty, *Black Book of the Admiralty*, 4 vols. (London: Longmans, 1871-76.)

2. The reason given for alterations was "to remedy some defects which were of fatal consequence in conducting the preceding War" of Austrian Succession. The "defects" concerned actions, or inactions, of commanders in touch with the enemy, and, as to be expected, the provisions dealing with personnel were made more severe. Some articles called for the death penalty exclusively. It was one of these, Article XIII, under which Admiral John Byng was charged in 1757 and when he was found guilty of failure to pursue the enemy, he was executed.

3. Clode, *Administration of Justice*, pp. 41-42; Thring, *Criminal Law*, 1861 ed., pp. 18-19; James Snedeker, *A Brief History of Courts-Martial* (Annapolis: U. S. Naval Institute, 1954), pp. 27-41; Lloyd, *British Seaman*, pp. 23-25; Kemp, *British Sailor*, pp. 5, 90; David Hannay, *Naval Courts-Martial* (London: Cambridge University Press, 1914), pp. xl-xliv; Gardiner, *British Admiralty*, pp. 35-36, 84-94; S. W. C. Pack, *Admiral Lord Anson* (London: Cassell, 1960), pp. 163-71; *Admiralty Memorandum*, BR11, p. 1; *Queen's Regulations*, 1844, 1862, 1967 eds.; *Committee to Consider the Administration of Justice under the Naval Discipline Act*, 1: 308.

4. Thring, *Criminal Law*, 1861 ed., pp. 18-19.
5. The legal profession was equally suspicious. A barrister writing in *Temple Bar* in 1862 denounced courts-martial as farces.

It is high time that this amateur playing at trials should have an end, and that these pranks, which are about as legal as the doings of the sham judges and notaries who come on in the Opera, should be repressed.

George Augustus Sala, ed., "Tried by Court Martial," *Temple Bar* 5 (July 1862): 280-86.

6. The following were salient features of naval courts-martial in the nineteenth century: commanders-in-chief of squadrons or stations acted as convening authorities and appointed the president of the court, who was always the senior member by rank. Constitution of a court (after 1860) required the presence of at least three ships, and lieutenants might serve. Rules of evidence and legal procedures such as no self-incrimination and no leading questions were similar to those of civil cases. Voting on the finding by the court was by secret ballot, all members being required to vote as a military duty. Automatic review of the findings by the legal experts at the Admiralty followed. Queen's Bench was available to the accused on appeal for cause, but this was seldom utilized and of doubtful benefit since the sentence, if not capital, was immediately executed. The accused could object to certain members in his court-martial without stating cause. A three-year statute of limitations applied. Finding for a lesser included offense was available in a case where no decision could be reached on the more serious charge. After the finding, evidence on previous convictions was admissable prior to sentencing.

The requirement that all ranking officers sit led to complications and unfortunate consequences in extreme cases. For example, four admirals and thirty-six captains sat on a court-martial in the Downs for a minor offense, and often not enough ships were present, which meant lengthy delays or summary punishment for serious offenses.

A Marine sergeant in 1870 thanked the court for permitting him to use professional assistance in a trial for enlisting militiamen. The trial lasted five days and the sergeant was found guilty and reduced to the ranks.

*Queen's Regulations*, 1844, 1862, 1967 eds.; Great Britain, Public Record Office, *Admiralty Courts-Martial Records*, various; Adm 1/5779 of 1861; Adm 1/5782 of 1861; Adm 1/5914 of 1864; Adm 1/5808 of 1862; Adm 1/6041 of 1862-74; Adm 1/5863 of 1868; Adm 1/6042 of 1866; Adm 1/6043 of 1867-68; Adm 1/6135 of 1869; Adm 1/6162 and 6163 of 1870; *Admiralty Digest*, IND 12470 of 1859; Snedeker, *Brief History*, pp. 45-47; Clode, *Administration of Justice*, pp. 120-55; Gardiner, *British Admiralty*, pp. 52-53, 124-25; Roberts, *Victorian Origins*, p. 299; Roy Frank Johnson, *The Royal George* (London: Charles Knight, 1971), p. 121; Owen Rutter, ed., *The Court-Martial of the Bounty Mutineers* (London: Hudge, 1931), pp. 47-50; A. G. Gardiner, *Life of Sir William Harcourt*, 2 vols. (London: Constable, 1923), 1: 154-55; Kemp, *British Sailor*, p. 10; Sala, "Tried by Court-Martial," pp. 180-86; Higham, *Guide to Sources*, p. 619; Thring, *Criminal Law*, 1861 and 1877 eds.

7. Bowen, *His Majesty's Coastguard*, pp. 128-29, 212-13, 264.
8. William Andrews, *Old-Time Punishments* (London: W. Andrews & Co., 1890) and *Bygone Punishments* (London: W. Andrews & Co., 1899).
9. Examples of older forms included the Defaulter's Book containing a record of every offense and punishment awarded to every enlisted man aboard. It was the guide for filling out Quarterly Punishment Returns. The Record of Conduct Book, Certificate of Conduct of Officers Book, Liberty Book, and Absentee Book were others. New or revised in the early 1860s were the Abstract and Schedule of Punishments, the Daily Record of Offenses and Punishments, and the Inspection Form, the latter insuring that all punishment records were fully examined by higher authority. Adm 1/5796 of 1862; Adm 1/5863 of 1863; T. P. Gillespie, "The Plymouth Port Orders of 1858," *Mariner's Mirror* 46 (February 1960):66.
10. Adm 1/5790 of 1862; *Admiralty Digest*, IND 12519 of 1862; Adm 1/6062 of 1868; Sir Cyprian Bridge, *Some Recollections* (London: Murray, 1919), p. 159.
11. Adm 1/5997 of 1866. The following is an extract from the Returns of Crime and Punishment in the Navy for 1862 which was submitted to the House of Commons and effectively became public knowledge. One can easily determine, though admittedly a biased view, how ships and commanding officers rate relatively in the matter of corporal punishment.

| Name of Ship | Number of Quarterly Returns | Number Flogged | Number of Lashes | Number of Men Liable to Corporal Punishment |
| --- | --- | --- | --- | --- |
| *Aboukir* | 3 | 3 | 108 | 800 |
| *Acorn* | 4 | 0 | 0 | 116 |
| *Adventure* | 3 | 2 | 336 | 93 |
| *Agamemnon* | 4 | 13 | 470 | 828 |
| *Ajax* | 4 | 3 | 60 | 314 |
| *Algerine* | 4 | 5 | 204 | 34 |
| *Algiers* | 4 | 11 | 217 | 818 |
| *Bacchante* | 4 | 20 | 816 | 526 |
| *Cameleon* | 4 | 7 | 228 | 155 |
| *Coquette* | 8 | 3 | 96 | 78 |
| *Cornwallis* | 4 | 6 | 168 | 320 |

. . . .

Specific offenses are also listed. Adm 1/5862 of 1863.
12. *Admiralty Digest*, 1859-65, passim.
13. Ibid., 1850-80, passim.
14. Adm 1/5749 of 1862.
15. Adm 1/5779 of 1861; *Admiralty Digest*, IND 12502 of 1861.
16. *Admiralty Digest*, IND 12506 of 1861; Scott, *Fifty Years*, pp. 7-8.
17. *Hansard*, 3rd ser., vol. 170 (20 April 1863), pp. 381-90; 3rd ser., vol. 170 (19 May 1863), pp. 1969-94.
18. To an officer censures and reprimands were deemed punishment as, of course, were dismissals and discharges.

19. Adm 1/5974 of 1866; Bennett, *Charlie B*, p. 23; Scott, *Fifty Years*, pp. v-ix, 1-7; John George Cox, ed., *Cox and the Ju Ju Coast* (Jersey: Ellison, 1968), pp. 71-73; Kemp, *British Sailor*, p. 210; Baynham, *Before the Mast*, pp. 140-41, 164-70; J. Moody, "Recruiting," pp. 587-97.
20. Adm 1/5997 Pro H of 1866, p. 324.
21. Roy Taylor, "Reform of the Recruiting System," p. 52.
22. Adm 1/5862 of 1863; Adm 1/5973 of 1866; Adm 1/5997 Pro H 568 of 1866; *Admiralty Digest*, IND 18034 of 1868; IND 18071 of 1870; *Hansard*, 3rd ser., Vol. 89 (18 March 1846), pp. 196-99; J. H. Briggs, *Naval Administration*, p. 146; William Hickman, *A Treatise on the Law and Practice of Naval Courts-Martial* (London: Murray, 1851) and ed., *Reports and Opinions of Officers on the Acts of Parliament and Admiralty Regulations for Maintaining Discipline and Good Order in the Fleet, Passed and Issued since the Year 1860* (London: Harrison, 1867).
23. *Holy Bible*, II Corinthians, Chapter XI, verses 24-25.
24. Dudley Pope, *The Black Ship* (Philadelphia: Lippincott, 1964), pp. 332-33.
25. Unfortunately, these sources are of little further assistance. They have an incredible sameness, are invariably self-centered, and contain only detailed information on the wind direction and force, barometer and weather, sails in use, and other extraneous data. Victor A. Montagu, *A Middy's Recollections, 1853-60* (London: Black, 1898), pp. 68-69; Great Britain, National Maritime Museum, *Journals and Diaries, Logs*. Log NE3, MS-9569; Log NE7, 54-MS-016; Log NR20, 53-MS-034/11; Log NR21, 53-MS-134/12.
26. Scott Claver, *Under the Lash* (London: Torchstream, 1954), p. 198; Clode, *Administration*, p. 33. Joseph Collinson, "Hon. Secretary, Criminal Law and Prison Committee, Humanitarian League," claimed in a pamphlet in 1905 that 1836 was the decisive year. This is not supported by the facts (despite the title of the pamphlet). *Facts about Flogging*, Revised ed. (London: Fifield, 1905), pp. 4-13.
27. Claver, *Under the Lash*, pp. 17-20, 29-30, 215; Lloyd, *British Seaman*, pp. 201, 239-40 and *Captain Marryat*, p. 131; Kemp, *British Sailor*, p. 59; Baynham, *From the Lower Decks*, p. 111; Dudley Pope, *Black Ship*, pp. 332-33; Scott, *Fifty Years*, p. 13; Leech, *Thirty Years*, pp. 29-37; Samuel Noble, *Sam Noble, Able Seaman 'Tween Decks in the Seventies* (New York: Stokes, 1925), p. 52; Markham, *Life of Sir Clements R. Markham*, pp. 40-42; Robinson, *British Tar*, pp. 314-18; Geoffrey Penn, *"Up Funnel, Down Screw"* (London: Hollis & Carter, 1955), pp. 56-59; Charles Frederick Walker, *Young Gentlemen* (London: Longmans, Green, 1938), p. 145; Sir Thomas J. Spence Lyne, *Something About a Sailor* (London: Jarrolds, 1940), p. 22; Woodward, *Age of Reform*, p. 267; [Tom Holman], *Life in the Royal Navy*, 3rd ed. (London: Sampson Low, 1892), pp. 5-7; Lionel Yexley [James Wood], *The Inner Life of the Navy* (London: Pitman, 1908), pp. 10-14; Padfield, *Aim Straight*, p. 20; L. Gardiner, *British Admiralty*, pp. 124-25, 141, 155-57; Wilson, "Discipline," p. 96; Riley, *Memories*, pp. 139-40; Hickman, *Treatise*, p. 22; A. S. White, "Flogging in the Army,"

*Journal of the Society for Army Historical Research* 20 (Summer 1941): 114; Clifford Elliot Walton, *History of the British Standing Army*, 3 vols. (London: Harrison, 1894), 3: 553-78; Harold D. Langley, *Social Reform in the United States Navy* (Chicago: University of Illinois Press, 1967), pp. 132-48; Karsten, *Naval Aristocracy*, pp. 85-86; *Admiralty Memorandum*, BR11, pp. 2-3.

The official court-martial sentence for "flogging round the fleet" read:

> To be punished by receiving ____ lashes on his bare back, with a cat-of-nine-tails, alongside such of His Majesty's ships at such time and in such portions as the Commander-in-Chief shall think fit to direct.

Edgar K. Thompson explains that it ended in the Royal Navy in the 1790s, but continued to be used in other navies. "Note on Keelhauling," *Mariner's Mirror* 58 (May 1972): 171-72.

In the army it was deemed degrading for a soldier to execute the punishment of flogging, so the practice evolved to use the nonmilitary drummer. In army practice a drummer was relieved after twenty-five lashes.

A yellow-journalism, cheap-paperback approach compares the English "cat" as a "close rival" to the Russian contribution to corporal punishment, "the horrible knout." George Ryley Scott, *The History of Corporal Punishment* (London: Torchstream Books, 1948), p. 70.

There exists a dearth of scholarly studies on this subject; too many approaches being similar to that of G. R. Scott, which is strictly sensationalism. Even Scott Claver's study is not exhaustive and scholarly. Worst of all is *The History of the Rod and Other Corporal Punishments* by Gilbert Oakley, "D. Psy." (?), which is unworthy of further comment. (London: Walton Press, 1964).

28. The following are examples: Able Seaman Tilling aboard H.M.S. *Leander* in the 1860s recorded several:

> "4 April 1864. At 7:30 A.M. a grating was lashed to the main rigging. Williams receiving part of Court-Martial sentence for desertion: [absent 132 days] took his four dozen without murmur. He writhed and trembled very much but after three dozen he felt no pain.... Baynes and Dunn also desertion: [absent 56 days each] cried out very much, the prisoners ... went below under the sentry's charge. No such thing as dressing their backs was ever thought of."

Tilling himself was punished for mutinous language.

> "26 January 1866. Ralph gave me the first dozen and sheeted it home too. Then the Master left-handed boatswain's mate and then Tyzill. I was to have got 48 but the Commodore let me off one dozen."

Baynham, "Seaman on *Leander*," p. 348.

In 1860 Charles Buxton, M.P., presented a vivid account before the House of Commons, in this case an army punishment:

> The Commanding Officer instructed the men administering the punishment, ... You will do your duty, ... give a stroke, draw the tails of the cat through the fingers of the left hand, to rid them of slush, flesh, or blood. ... I felt an astounding sensation between the shoulders, which went to the toenails in one direction, my fingernails in another, and stung me to the heart as if a knife had gone through my body. ... The time between each stroke seemed so long as to be agonizing, and yet the next came too soon. ...

*Hansard*, 3rd ser., Vol. 96 (16 February 1860), pp. 1175-76.

Also see the *Times*, 5 September 1834, p. 3b; Hickman, *Treatise*, p. 22; John Nicol, *The Life and Adventures of John Nicol, Mariner* (New York: Farrar & Rinehart, 1936), pp. 54, 100; Kenneth Gilbert Balmain Dewar, *The Navy from Within* (London: Gollancz, 1939), pp. 14-16; Baynham, *From the Lower Decks*, pp. 111-12; Leech, *Thirty Years*, pp. 29-37.

29. In 1810 William Cobbett was fined a thousand pounds and served two years in Newgate Prison for printing an attack on the practice of flogging in the army. The "seditious libel" was in the *Political Register*, June 1809, covering an account of an army mutiny at Ely put down by German Legion Cavalry. The five leaders of the mutiny received 500 lashes each. The account read as follows:

> Five hundred lashes each! Aye, that is right! Flog them! Flog! Flog! Flog! They deserve a flogging at every meal time. Lash them daily! Lash them daily! What! Shall the rascals dare to mutiny? ... Lash them! Lash them! Lash them! They deserve it, oh, yes! They merit a double-tailed cat! Base dogs! ...

Asa Briggs, *William Cobbett* (New York: Oxford University Press, 1967), pp. 34-37; Woodward, *Age of Reform*, p. 22, n; Claver, *Under the Lash*, p. 26.

30. Sir Francis Burdett recalled that while he was in the Tower in 1810 for political reasons he witnessed the flogging of a thirty-year veteran who was seventy years old. Sir Francis was a consistent agitator against flogging until 1837. Patterson, *Sir Francis Burdett*, 1: 285; *Dictionary of National Biography*, 3: 296-98; Claver, *Under the Lash*, pp. 24-25.

31. J. H. Briggs, *Naval Administrations*, pp. 61-65; Vivian Stuart, *The Beloved Little Admiral* (London: Hale, 1967), p. 132. Hume led the radical debate on "abuses," one of which was flogging, in the "Reformed Parliament of 1833," which caused a record sitting of 1270 hours in the House of Commons. Simon Maccoby, *English Radicalism*, 6 vols. (London: Allen & Unwin, 1935-61), 3: 88-89, n; Philip D. Jones, "The British Army in the Age of Reform, 1830-54." Ph.D. dissertation, Duke University, 1968.

32. The commission, composed of James Archibald Lord Wharncliffe as chairman, three generals, and three civilians, studied punishment methods in the army in 1835-36. Seventy-one witnesses with various perspectives were called: French officers, army generals, prison officials, parsons, privates,

recruits, surgeons, and the past and current army commanders-in-chief, the Duke of Wellington and General Lord Hill, respectively. The question of abolition was not seriously considered, the emphasis being placed on a search for an alternative punishment. Most of the witnesses were sympathetic to continuation, and no satisfactory alternatives were recommended. The report concluded that as long as current recruiting practices continued, there was no substitute. The inherent characteristics of recruitment meant the British soldier was inferior to the continental conscript, and as a consequence, the strictest discipline measures were required. Flogging was limited, depending on the type of courts-martial: 200 lashes from a general, 150 from a district or garrison, 100 from a regimental court-martial. Corporal punishment was recommended as necessary under these limitations. Ensign Cornelius O'Donoghue called the report "a sop to stop the yelpers." The *Times*, 19 March 1836, p. 5b; Claver, *Under the Lash*, pp. 202-56; H. De Watteville, *The British Soldier* (New York: Putnams, 1955), p. 147; Cornelius O'Donoghue, "Corporal Punishment Commission, Defects in Military Education, and Promotion from the Ranks." *Fraser's Magazine* 13 (May 1836): 645-56.

33. Thring, *Treatise*, p. 251; Colomb, *Memoirs*, pp. 20-21, 77, 419; Sir William Fanshawe Martin, *Memorandum on Corporal Punishment* (Portsmouth: Griffin, 1881), pp. 5-17; Sir Charles Vinicombe Penrose, *Observations on Corporal Punishment* (London: Bodmin, 1824), pp. iii, 1-65.

Captain A. J. Griffiths wrote in 1826 supportive of naval discipline and corporal punishment. Seamen were drawn from the lowest and most criminal elements, he claimed, and alternative forms of punishment could not work aboard a warship where 600 of these "worthless characters" lived together. "... the overzealous philanthropists—the hue and cry men, expect they are to be governed with a feather." The problem had not been solved ashore by alternative methods. "Crime is increasing despite gallows, transportation, treadmill, the stocks, prison, and work houses." Griffiths, *Impressment*, pp. 33-44. The chapter title: "Erroneous Opinions of the Discipline or Punishments in the Navy are the Causes of the Disgust."

More vociferous and opinionated was the two-volume, privately published (London: Colburn, 1826; Philadelphia: n.p., 1835) *Naval Sketch-book* by "An Officer of Rank." The anonymous author was, in fact, Commander (later Captain—in 1833) William Nugent Glascock, who, while on half-pay, had written:

> several volumes of naval novels, ... reminiscences ..., which, as novels, are stupid enough, and in their historical parts have little value, but are occasionally interesting as social sketches of naval life in the early part of the century.

As in the case of Captain Griffiths, he vehemently attacked those who advocated abolition of corporal punishment, e.g., radicals like Joseph Hume, one of the "parliamentary pigmies." Reliance upon corporal punishment, he concluded firmly, could "decide our existence as a nation." *Dictionary of National Biography,* 7: 1297-98. The subtitle of *Naval Sketch-book* deserves full reproduction: "... or, the Service Afloat and Ashore with Characteristic Reminiscences, Fragments, and Opinions on Professional, Colonial and Political Subjects, interspersed with copious Notes, Biographical, Historical, Critical and Illustrative." [William Nugent Glascock], *Naval Sketch-book,* 2: 2-15.

In 1858 Captain Archibald Sinclair, R.N., wrote a book defending corporal punishment, *Discipline, etc., c. 1815.* He asserted that flogging was necessary to maintain discipline, that it was definitely not degrading, and that truly reflective seamen recognized the need for its continuance. Robinson, *British Tar,* pp. 323-24.

Major-General Charles J. Napier, the future conqueror of Scinde, wrote a pamphlet in 1837 denouncing the use of flogging. "It does more harm than good." It created permanent scars and it hardened its victims. Claver, *Under the Lash,* pp. 196-97; DeWatteville, *British Soldier,* p. 147.

34. Burn, *Equipoise,* pp. 227-28.

35. The *Times,* 2 September 1834, p. 6b; 30 September 1834, p. 3e; 30 October 1834, p. 3c; 22 February 1836, p. 4f; 24 February 1836, p. 6f; 16 July 1843, p. 8d; 20 July 1843; 24 July 1843, p. 3d; 1 August 1843, p. 8c; 4 August 1843, p. 7a; 8 January 1855, p. 5f; 24 January 1855, p. 10c. Lloyd, *Captain Marryat,* p. 132; Hirst, *Six Panics,* p. 17. In 1854 the names of 84 of 199 naval ships awarding no corporal punishment for six months were printed.

36. E.g., see *Tait's Edinburgh Magazine* 1 (August 1832): 635-36; n.s., 1 (1834): 316-19; "A Cautious (and therefore a true) Friend to the Sea-Service," (pseud.), "Corporal Punishment in the Mercantile Marine," *Nautical Magazine* (1843): 367; *Fraser's Magazine* (February 1865): 154-65; Archibald Forbes, "Flogging in the Army," *Nineteenth Century* 6 (October 1879): 604-14.

*Tait's Edinburgh Magazine* in 1832 contained an article with extensive background information on a celebrated incident of flogging in the army. Joseph Hume had informed the House of Commons of the incident involving the flogging of Private Somerville of the Scots Greys for refusing to mount an unruly horse. Public meetings of protest were held. Apparently there was much more to the Private Somerville case. During the reform bill crisis in 1832 an anonymous letter appeared in the *Weekly Despatch* confessing that some soldiers had "sent their names to the roll of the Birmingham Political Union." Private Somerville was suspected of writing the letter. In the letter was the statement:

> I made no such public avowal of my opinion, for I knew it to be an infringement of military law.... We knew we would protect property in the event of a clash. But against the liberties of our countrymen we would have never, never, never raised an arm! The Duke of Wellington

may assure himself that military government shall never be again set up in this country.

Two days later Private Somerville was ordered to ride "an unbroken horse," tried and failed, ordered to try again, refused, and was confined. He was interrogated by Major Wyndham, the regimental commander, about the letter and admitted authorship. "Five minutes later!" he was court-martialed for disobedience and sentenced to 100 lashes. Two hours later he was flogged before the regiment. Major Wyndham addressed the regiment, as was customary, but he confined his remarks to "the libel of which Somerville had confessed himself the author." The next day a private who refused to obey an order was sentenced to twenty-four hours' imprisonment. *Tait's Edinburgh Magazine* 1 (August 1832): 635-36; Patterson, *Sir Francis Burdett*, 2: 606-607.

Sir Robert Peel, a later prime minister, cited this case and warned of the dangers of soldiers and officers becoming partisans and members of political clubs. As a consequence of their responsibilities they cannot enjoy all the rights of a citizen, he said. In 1835 all officers and men were ordered to disassociate themselves from assemblies. Nothing in what Peel said sanctioned the devious method of "punishing" Somerville. Adm 12/1074 of 1881.

37. Luvaas, *Education of an Army*, p. 98.

38. "Old Officer," (pseud.), "A Chapter on Flogging," *Tait's Edinburgh Magazine*, n.s., 1 (1834): 316-19.

39. William Howitt, "Military Flogging," *The People's Journal* 2 (1847): 78-79.

40. Forbes, "Flogging in the Army," pp. 604-14. Forbes claimed the French army had "never been in the field since universal service was established." He apparently overlooked the campaigns between 1793 and 1815!

41. *Annual Register* (London: Baldwin & Cradock, 1849), pp. 97-98.

42. Lloyd, *Captain Marryat*, pp. 128-32; F. Marryat, *Works*, 5 vols.; Robinson, *British Tar*, pp. 331-41, 383.

Captain Chamier was a reactionary, claiming seamen should not be educated for they were not capable of understanding. "Let them alone; they are used to coporal punishment; they think less of the disgrace than the pain."

Herman Melville denounced corporal punishment as "opposed to the essential dignity of man" and "as religiously, morally, and immutably *wrong.*" Three chapter titles are: XXXVI. "Some of the Evil Effects of Flogging"; XXV. "Flogging Not Lawful"; XXVI. "Flogging Not Necessary." Melville, *White-Jacket* (Boston: Page, 1892).

43. Piers Compton, *Cardigan of Balaclava* (London: Hale, 1972), pp. 99-102; The *Times*, 22 February 1836, p. 4f; 24 February 1836, p. 6f; *Annual Register*, 1849, pp. 97-98.

44. *Queen's Regulations*, 1844 ed., p. 90; 1862 ed., pp. 223-25; *Admiralty Digests*, IND 12538 of 1862; Bartlett, *Great Britain and Sea Power*, p. 312;

Lloyd, *British Seaman,* pp. 231-32; Claver, *Under the Lash,* p. 198; J. H. Briggs, *Naval Administrations,* p. 4.
  45. One gets the impression that this exchange was prearranged.
  46. *Hansard,* 3rd ser., vol. 208 (28 July 1871), pp. 392-94.
  47. Great Britain, Home Office, *Corporal Punishment Report* (London: Her Majesty's Stationery Office, n.d.), p. 4.
  48. Taylor, "Reform of Recruiting," p. 52; White, "Flogging," p. 115; Claver, *Under the Lash,* p. 32; L. Gardiner, *British Admiralty,* p. 273; Sir Leon Radzinowicz, *A History of English Criminal Law and Administration from 1750,* 4 vols. (New York: Macmillan Co., 1948-68), 1: 313; Lloyd, *British Seaman,* p. 273; Baynham, *From the Lower Decks,* pp. 113-14; Higham, *Guide to Sources,* pp. 619-22; Dewar, *The Navy from Within,* pp. 14-15; Penn, *"Up Funnel,"* p. 72; Lyne, *Something About a Sailor,* pp. 23-24; Walker, *Young Gentlemen,* pp. 141-43; Pack, *Britannia,* pp. 31-37; *Admiralty Digest,* IND 18097 of 1871, IND 18099 of 1871, IND 18138 of 1873, and IND 18280 of 1880; Adm 1/6068 of 1868; Adm 12/1039 of 1879; Adm 116/183 Case F47; *Hansard,* 3rd ser., Vol. 187 (3 June 1867), p. 1490 and 3rd ser., Vol. 187 (25 July 1867), pp. 82-83; Richard Eder, "Caning in British Schools," New York *Times,* 15 October 1972, p. A3.

  Sub-lieutenant John George Cox of *Fly* relates an incident in 1869 off the West African coast, the "Ju-Ju Coast." A merchant captain brought three seamen aboard, two to see the surgeon and "one to get flogged"—a "Krooman," i.e., a Negro seaman. The commanding officer refused to permit the flogging. John George Cox, ed., *Cox and the Ju Ju Coast* (Jersey, Ellison, 1968), p. 42.

  Admiral Sir Percy Scott recalled that:

> The birch was used freely. It was administered publicly with great ceremony, and was the only punishment that incorrigible boys did not like. No idea of disgrace was attached to it, but it hurt. How stupid it is to talk of doing away with the birch at our public schools! [in 1919]

Admiral Scott was a prominent member of the "Fish Pond," later reformers identified with Admiral Lord Fisher. Scott, *Fifty Years,* p. 4.

  Lionel Yexley as a boy trainee recalled, ". . . I felt a violent shock and a sensation as though a red-hot iron had been drawn across my breech." Yexley instinctly reacted aggressively and was immediately struck harder by a second Ship's Corporal. "This was the practice on all training ships." The Ship's Police, called "Crushers," would run round the decks cutting indiscriminately at the boys. When one boy's eye was put out, the practice temporarily ceased. Yexley, *Inner Life,* pp. 9-10.

  Quite a similar evolution toward elimination of the practice of corporal punishment took place in the American navy. Flogging was abolished in the army in 1812, and after Congressional and public pressure, in the navy in 1850. The heavy hand of the Secretary of the Navy, Gideon Welles, was an influence. Langley, *Social Reform,* pp. 30-31, 138-49, 173; Leo F. S. Horan, "Flogging in the United States Navy: Unfamiliar Facts Regarding Its

Origin and Abolition," *U.S. Naval Institute Proceedings* 76 (September 1950): 972-74.
   49. Yexley, *Inner Life*, p. 9; Noble, *Sam Noble*, p. 43; Claver, *Under the Lash*, p. 267; Charles Christopher Lloyd, "The Mutiny of the *Nereide*," *Mariner's Mirror* 54 (August 1968): 245-52.
   50. Adm 1/5795 of 1862.
   51. The term "marking" more accurately described the practice. The technique was more similar to tattooing than branding. The device consisted of a head with about forty needles about one-half inch long arranged to form a letter, in England either a "D" (deserter) or "BC" (bad character). The device "punched" an outline of the letter, on the right or left breast, which was then treated with some indelible solution so that it could not be obliterated. Claver, *Under the Lash*, pp. 83, 226; *Hansard*, 3rd ser., Vol. 173 (10 March 1864), pp. 1807-13.
   52. Adm 1/5795 of 1862; Adm 1/5913 of 1864; *Admiralty Digest*, IND 12569 of 1865; IND 12582 of 1866; IND 12597 of 1866; IND 18034 of 1868; IND 18036 of 1868; *Hansard*, 3rd ser., Vol. 191 (23 March 1868), pp. 35-37. There was lively debate in the House of Commons over the practice of branding or marking in the army. *Hansard*, 3rd ser., Vol. 173 (10 March 1864), pp. 1807-14. A Royal Commission on Courts-Martial and Military Punishment recommended abolition of the practice. In 1865 the number of men marked "D" was 1615 and "BC," 190. *Sessional Papers*, 12 (1868-69), No. 4114, pp. 147-51, 423; David Tribe, *President Charles Bradlaugh, M.P.* (Hamden, Conn.: Archon, 1971), pp. 201-203.
   53. Burn, *Equipoise*, pp. 181-85. For civilians an interim punishment was used extensively earlier in the nineteenth century, transportation to a penal colony in Australia. The government drastically curtailed its use in the 1840s with abolition occurring in 1857. The navy supervised the actual transfers, paying a bonus (four pounds, ten shillings, six pence) for each convict safely landed. Between 1788 and 1868 over 160,000 persons were transported. See Charles Bateson, *The Convict Ships, 1787-1868* (Glasgow: Brown and Ferguson, 1959); Charles Christopher Lloyd and Jack L. S. Coulter, *Medicine and the Navy, 1200-1900*, 4 vols. (Edinburgh: Livingston, 1957-63), 4: 124-31; Christopher John Bartlett, ed., *Britain Preeminent* (London: Macmillan, 1969), pp. 55-75; Eric Midwinter, *Victorian Social Reform* (New York: Harper and Row, 1971), pp. 42-43.
   54. *Sessional Papers, Report on Crime and Punishment in the Navy*, 1862, p. 7.
   55. Radzinowicz, *Criminal Law*, 1: 313; Burn, *Equipoise*, pp. 188-90; Best, *Mid-Victorian Britain*, p. 286; Richard Standish Hinde, *The British Penal System, 1773-1950* (London: Duckworth, 1951), pp. 81-109; Thomas Archer, *The Pauper, the Thief and the Convict* (London: Groombridge, 1865), pp. 150-208; Claver, *Under the Lash*, p. 32; Derek Lionel Howard, "Transportation and Imprisonment," *Listener* 76, pp. 722-24 and *John Howard: Prison Reformer* (London: Johnson, 1958); Gillespie, "Plymouth Port Orders," p. 56; Ernest Teagarden, "A Victorian Prison Experiment,"

*Journal of Social History* 2 (Summer 1969): 357-66; L. L. Robson, *The Convict Settlers of Australia* (Melbourne: Melbourne University Press, 1965); Marcello Maestro, *Cesare Beccaria and the Origins of Penal Reform* (Philadelphia: Temple University Press, 1973) and *Voltaire and Beccaria as Reformers of Criminal Law* (New York: Columbia University Press, 1942); *Hansard*, 3rd ser., Vol. 160, p. 820; Home Office, *Corporal Punishment Report*, 1961, p. 3; Adm 1/5782 of 1862; Adm 1/5997 of 1866.

One of the responses, that of Captain William Chamberlain, *Royal Oak*, to the Admiralty request for evaluation of reform measures in 1865 applied to the cell aboard his ship. Captain Chamberlain would undoubtedly fit the image of the stereotyped Victorian.

> There should be just enough light for reading. It would afford the prisoner a perfect opportunity of studying his Bible, which should be the only words allowed him. . . . The glass admitting the light could be easily protected and extra punishment and payment for it would stop injury to the Bible.

Adm 1/5997 of 1867, Pro H 568 of 1866, p. 564.

56. For example, men in the first class received meat on Sunday and were required to do less labor. Third class men were required to pick oakum after work. The routine included haircuts every two weeks, linen changes twice a week, and no visitation for the first three months; then one visitor per month in the presence of a warder. Adm 1/5795 of 1862; [William and Robert Chambers], eds., "The Naval Prison at Lewes," *Chamber's Journal* 51 (6 June 1874): 361-63. For a report of a Royal Commission which investigated the disposition of prisoners from the Army see *Sessional Papers*, Vol. 12 (1868-69), No. 4114, pp. 131-51.

57. [Chambers], "Naval Prison," pp. 361-62

58. *Admiralty Digest*, 1850-80, passim.; Claver, *Under the Lash*, pp. 196-97.

59. *Admiralty Digest*, 1850-80, passim.

60. Ibid., 1861-79, passim.

## Notes for Chapter IV

1. Adm 1/6068 of 1868-78.

2. Some examples included immediate execution of any punishment, even capital punishment, without approval from higher authority; any punishment could be executed on Sunday; a punishment could be assigned for mutiny when excluded from all other acts; and a seaman being in the first class for conduct was not exempt from punitive measures.

3. Manwaring, *Floating Republic*, p. vii. The authors are George Ernest Manwaring and Bonamy Dobree.

4. John Greville Bullocke, *Sailors' Rebellion* (London: Eyre and Spottiswoode, 1938), p. 190.

5. There was one violent episode at Spithead aboard H.M.S. *London* when the commanding officer got excited as the Delegates came aboard and a scuffle ensued resulting in three seamen killed and several wounded. Valentine Joyce restored order. Misunderstanding, delay, and lack of communication caused the incident.

6. Claims of from twenty-four to thirty-six can be found. This figure comes from the more reliable studies, Manwaring, *Floating Republic*, p. 242, and Michael Arthur Lewis, *Spithead* (London: Allen and Unwin, 1972), p. 153.

7. J. D. Spinney, "The *Hermione* Mutiny," *Mariner's Mirror* 41 (May 1955): 123-36; Edgar K. Thompson, "Saga of a Mutineer," *Mariner's Mirror* 53 (May 1967): 171-78.

The subsequent capture of one of the *Hermione* mutineers, Jonathan Robbins, in South Carolina apparently contributed to the defeat of President John Adams' bid for re-election.

8. Manwaring, *Floating Republic*, p. 245.

9. Ibid., pp. 59-63, 110-38, 218-45; Lewis, *Spithead*, pp. 118-53; Bullocke, *Sailors' Rebellion*, pp. 189-284; William R. Hunt, "Nautical Autobiography in the Age of Sail," *Mariner's Mirror* 57 (May 1971): 140; James Dugan, *The Great Mutiny* (New York: New American Library, 1967), pp. 78-389; Marcus, *Age of Nelson*, 2: 82-88; D. Bonner-Smith, "The Naval Mutinies of 1797," *Mariner's Mirror* 21 (October 1935): 428-49 and 22 (January 1936): 65-86 and "Some Remarks about the Mutiny of the *Bounty*," *Mariner's Mirror* 22 (April 1936): 200-37; C. Field, "The Marines in the Great Naval Mutinies, 1797-1802," *Journal of the Royal United Service Institution* 62 (1917): 720-46; R. Colvile, "Naval Personnel in the XVIIIth Century," *Journal of the Royal United Service Institution* 87 (1942): 160-76; Charles Christopher Lloyd, "New Light on the Mutiny at the Nore," *Mariner's Mirror* 46 (1960): 286-95 and *St. Vincent and Camperdown* (New York: Macmillan, 1963), pp. 93-116; Kemp, *British Sailor*, pp. 173-77; H. D. Sprule, "James Burney's Opinions on the Naval Mutinies of 1797," *Mariner's Mirror* 46 (February 1960): 61-62; H. W. Wilson, "Discipline in the Old Navy," *Macmillan's Magazine* 78 (1898): 94-96.

The question of the relationship of the mutinies of 1797 to revolution has been much debated. Manwaring's *The Floating Republic*, one of the most solid studies, notwithstanding the title, hardly mentions outside activities and conspiracy, and other accounts such as those of Michael Lewis, Geoffrey Marcus, and Christopher Lloyd discount connections with radicalism. At the opposite extreme is James Dugan's excessively popularized study, *The Great Mutiny*, which attempts to attach the mutiny to every conceivable occurrence. He begins with an account of the storming of the Bastille and ends with a chapter on "1817"! The industrial revolution, trade unionism, moderate reformism, radicalism, Jacobinism, the Irish rebellion, republicanism, and communism, one way or another, are connected to the "Great Mutiny." Appendix I, the "Author's Interjection," sums up:

> In a sense the great mutiny was an isolated major event in industrial history. Considering the Georgian Admiralty, as a major concentrator of wage labor—12,000 men in several 'plants'—the cruising squadrons and fleet anchorages—Valentine Joyce and his confederates at Spithead led the first successful mass sitdown strike in history, and Richard Parker the first defeated one. As a horizontal union, the Spithead strikers forced their will twice upon an employer who had the power of death over every man involved. Belaboring the labor analogy, a comparable event did not happen on such a scale again in Britain until the London dock strikes a hundred years later.
>
> Dugan, Great Mutiny, p. 463.

Two articles in the *Journal of the Royal United Service Institution* make charges without corroboration. Marine Colonel C. Field claimed that the "leaders at Spithead, especially Richard Parker [sic] . . . had imbibed the revolutionary and socialistic doctrines . . . and machinations of the United Irishmen." Navy Lieutenant R. F. Colvile explained that Parker, who in fact led at the Nore, was "probably insane from the peculiar conditions of life at sea," and that some of the Quota-Men had belonged to the Corresponding Societies.

Professor E. P. Thompson in a controversial but brilliant study of radicalism holds a similar view: ". . . there is some evidence of direct Jacobin instigation. . . . " Thompson, *Making of Working Class*, pp. 167-68.

10. Adm 1/5391; Adm 1/5392; Lloyd, *"Nereide,"* pp. 246-51.

11. The American training brig, U.S.S. *Somers*, homeward bound from West Africa, experienced an "incident" resulting in a "drumhead court of inquiry" which decreed the execution of a midshipman son of the Secretary of War and two seamen. This and the subsequent trial of the commanding officer evoked sensational accusations and counter-charges and involved several contemporary writers (Richard Henry Dana, Herman Melville, and James Fenimore Cooper). "Naval and Marine Gazette," *Nautical Magazine* (1843): 207. Harrison Hayford, ed., *The Somers Mutiny Affair* (Englewood Cliffs, N.J.: Prentice-Hall, 1959), pp. 2-5, 22-29; Langley, *Social Reform*, pp. 111-15; Leon David, "An Episode in Naval Justice," *Case and Comment* 62 (July-August 1952): 20-25; Hickman, *Treatise*, pp. 24-40.

Fictionalized accounts have been based on this episode. Herman Melville, *Billy Budd, Sailor* (Chicago: University of Chicago Press, 1962); Howard P. Vincent, *Twentieth Century Interpretations of Billy Budd* (Englewood Cliffs, N.J.: Prentice-Hall, 1971); D. B. Ives, "*Billy Budd* and the Articles of War," *American Literature* 34 (March 1962): 31-39; Henry C. Carlisle, *Voyage to the First of December* (New York: Putnam, 1972).

Evelyn Berckman, in a curious study of persons and things associated with *The Hidden Navy*, claims that "between 1840 and 1850, constant outbreaks of mutiny in the British navy arose from this one cause, efforts of prohibition" of prostitutes aboard ship. After perusal of the sources no evidence to substantiate such "constant outbreaks" can be found. *The Hidden Navy* (London: Hamish Hamilton, 1973).

12. Taylor, "Manning," pp. 215-19.
13. *Admiralty Digest*, IND 12488 of 1860 and IND 12489 of 1860.
14. Ibid.; *Hansard*, 3rd ser., vol. 155 (25 July 1859), pp. 363-65.
15. Adm 1/5753; *Admiralty Digest*, IND 12470 of 1859.
16. *Hansard*, 3rd ser., vol. 155 (11 July 1859), pp. 278-79.
17. The *Times*, 3 December 1860, p. 7e.
18. *Admiralty Digest*, IND 12474 of 1859; IND 12489 of 1860. Admiral Bowles' resignation letter was pubilshed in the *Morning Herald* but he denied responsibility.
19. *Admiralty Digest*, IND 12489 of 1860; IND 12492 of 1860.
20. Adm 1/5997, Pro H568 of 1866, p. 199.
21. Adm 1/5863 of 1863; *Admiralty Digest*, IND 12534 of 1863.
22. *Admiralty Digest*, IND 12537 of 1863.
23. Baynham, "Seaman," p. 349 and *From the Lower Decks*, pp. 123-29; Arthur Durham Divine (pseud. David Divine), *Mutiny at Invergordon* (London: Macdonald, 1970); Dewar, *Navy from Within*, pp. 332-45; Adm 53/8632; *Admiralty Digest*, IND 12566 of 1865; IND 12567 of 1865; IND 12570 of 1865.

A mutiny in some ways comparable to the one at Spithead, where the main concern was pay—this time an announced pay cut—occurred in September 1931 with the Atlantic Fleet at Invergordon. The pay reduction was part of an overall government cutback during an extremely serious financial crisis. The men simply desired to arouse public and Parliamentary sympathy against an Admiralty they believed had abandoned them. As at Spithead the affair was orderly and no violence resulted. About 12,000 men were involved.

24. At this time there were twelve (thirteen after 1865), each with a commander-in-chief; (1) Drill-Home, (2) Home, (3) Cape (of Good Hope), (4) Coast Guard, (5) West African, (6) Pacific, (7) North American and West Indian, (8) East Indian, (9) China, (10) Channel, (11) Mediterranean, (12) Australian, and (13) Southeast American. Adm 1/6011 of 1867.
25. *Admiralty Digest*, IND 12492 of 1860; Bartlett, *Great Britain and Sea Power*, p. 313.
26. The classes were: (1) Special, for men of "good" character to be granted the fullest leave, (2) Privileges, for "less reliable" men to be given leave "when convenient," and (3) Regular, for everyone else, especially all men in the Second Class for Conduct. Adm 1/5999.
27. Baynham, *From the Lower Decks*, pp. 111-17; Kemp, *British Sailor*, pp. 205-10; Taylor, "Manning," pp. 11-12; R. F. Colvile, "The Navy and the Crimean War," *Journal of the Royal United Service Institution* 85 (1940): 73-78.
28. Another source stated ten days. Adm 1/5782 of 1861-65.
29. The commanding officer of H.M.S. *Pioneer*, Commander Reilly, had been questioned about placing "R" beside three men's names "pre-maturely." They had been arrested in disguise aboard an outbound merchant ship. The Law Officer concluded Commander Reilly's action was justified because intent to desert had been demonstrated. Adm 1/5782; *Admiralty*

*Digest,* IND 12519 of 1862; *Hansard,* 3rd ser., vol. 155 (17 August 1860), pp. 1652-64.

30. Adm 1/5974 of 1866; Adm 1/5977 of 1866; Adm 1/6011 of 1867; *Admiralty Digest,* IND 12502 of 1861; IND 12582 of 1866; IND 18034 of 1868; *Sessional Papers* 9 (1857): 619, 633, 642; 15 (1859): 445, 487, 499; 42 (1860): 397;38 (1861): 141; 36 (1863): 1-6; 25, Part II (1865): 141-46; The *Times,* 9 June 1869, p. 9f.

31. In 1859 a total of 2338 men deserted; 86 being apprehended. Seven hundred twelve had received the bounty upon entry which meant £4571 was wasted. In 1862 a total of 1876 men deserted, 774 being apprehended, leaving the loss of 1102 or 2.02 percent of the mean force employed.

The *Times,* 9 June 1860, p. 9f. The losses in 1862 were broken down by squadrons as follows: West African, .69 percent of mean force; Mediterranean, .88 percent; Cape of Good Hope, 2.17 percent; East Indian and China, 2.69 percent; North American and West Indian, 3.022 percent; Home, 3.26 percent; Channel, 4.03 percent; Coast Guard, 4.84 percent; Australian, 8.28 percent; Pacific, 9.69 percent; Southeast American, 13.97 percent. *Sessional Papers,* 25, Part II (1865): 112.

32. The *Times,* 31 December 1860, p. 10b; *Admiralty Digest,* IND 12567 of 1865.

33. Quoted directly from Article XIX of the Naval Discipline Act of 1860. *Sessional Papers,* 42 (1860): 40, 397; Adm 1/5782 of 1861-65.

34. *Admiralty Digest,* IND 12567 of 1865.

35. Ibid.; IND 12587 of 1866; Adm 1/5975 of 1866.

36. *Admiralty Digest,* IND 12503 of 1861; IND 12566 of 1865; IND 12567 of 1865; IND 12570 of 1865; IND 12597 of 1867; Adm 38/7450 of 1863.

In the 1870s leave breakers in foreign ports were hunted by local "vigilantes," who received lucrative rewards for every seaman returned. Riley, *Memories of a Blue-Jacket,* pp. 54-55.

37. The English merchant service was "the worst in the world," the seaman being subjected to gross abuses and flagrant exploitation; e.g., accidents causing a thousand deaths per year. There was no regulatory system. Roberts, *Victorian Origins,* pp. 6-7, 85-89; Roger Warren Prouty, *The Transformation of the Board of Trade, 1830-55* (London: Heinemann, 1957), pp. 30-42; Paul Smith, *Disraelian Conservatism and Socal Reform* (Toronto: University of Toronto Press, 1967), pp. 32-42; Erickson, *Public Career,* pp. 18-25; Lawrence Averell Harper, *The Navigation Laws* (New York: Octagon Books, 1964), pp. 367-68; Bartlett, *Great Britain and Sea Power,* p. 311; Griffiths, *Impressment,* pp. 45-55.

38. Baynham, "Seaman on *Leander,*" p. 349 and *From the Lower Decks,* pp. 116-17; Fenton Aylmer, *A Cruise in the Pacific,* 2 vols. (London: Hurst and Blackett, 1860), 1:25; Leech, *Thirty Years,* p. 40; Alice E. J. Fanshawe, *Admiral Sir Edward Gennys Fanshawe* (London: Spottiswoode, 1904), p. 278; *Admiralty Digest,* IND 12502 of 1861; IND 12503 of 1861; IND 12550 of 1864; *Hansard,* 3rd ser., vol. 111 (23 May 1850), p. 282.

One entry described an instance when a seaman from H.M.S. *Buzzard* was "kidnapped for the United States Army." The officer to whom Admiral Milne referred, Captain Ejerton of H.M.S. *St. George*, received a reprimand. Able Seaman Tilling confessed that several deserters from H.M.S. *Leander* had mistresses ashore who sheltered them.

39. *Admiralty Digest*, IND 12535 of 1863.
40. Ibid.; IND 18116 of 1872.
41. The conclusions of a similar study of the German navy are essentially the same. Holger H. Herwig, *The German Naval Officer Corps* (London: Oxford University Press, 1973); Karsten, *Naval Aristocracy*, pp. 1-37.
42. Baynham, *From the Lower Decks*, p. 120.
43. *Hansard*, 2nd ser., vol 13 (9 June 1825), pp. 1097-1110.
44. Hunt, "Nautical Autobiography," pp. 139-40; Cornelius O'Donoghue, "On Courts-Martial and the Cat-o'-Nine-Tails," *Fraser's Magazine* 13 (May 1836): 543.
45. Clowes, *Royal Navy*, 6:205; Conacher, *Aberdeen Coalition*, p. 255; Lewis, *Navy of Britain*, p. 270 and *Navy in Transition*, pp. 14-15; Lloyd, *Medicine*, 4:12-15; Philip Howard Colomb, *Fifteen Years of Naval Retirement* (Portsmouth: Griffin, 1886), pp. 1-5.
46. One of the officers put ashore at the Nore was the commanding officer of H.M.S. *Director*, Captain William Bligh, his second such experience in eight years. Manwaring, *Floating Republic*, pp. 110-11, 127, 138, 281. Able Seaman Tilling complained about the reprehensible conduct of midshipmen. Baynham, "Seaman on *Leander*," pp. 346-49; Kemp, *British Sailor*, pp. 82-83; Lloyd, *Captain Marryat*, pp. 35-36.
47. A celebrated instance in the 1840s was a case in point. Captain Elliot received a reprimand from a court-martial in Port Royal. Upon returning to his ship he was cheered by his crew, an incident looked upon with disdain. A questioner in Parliament received concurrence from the Admiralty spokesman that it was a "most irregular proceeding, and contrary to all discipline." The Plymouth Port Order made a point of remonstrating: "all such demonstrations of approval or disapproval by Ship's Crews relative to their officers, or to sentences of Courts-Martial, or on other occurrences, are most strictly forbidden." Gillespie, "Plymouth Port Orders," p. 66; *Hansard*, 3rd ser., vol. 68 (31 March 1843), p. 287.

> 48. ". . . laws of subordination rigidly enforced, the forms and ceremonials, a deference to which he is so strictly enjoined, may at first appear of trifling importance, often tedious and superfluous . . . , that without those forms and ceremonials, those nice distinctions, those minute and punctilious observances, subordination would soon be at an end; and without subordination the service must inevitably become a mere negative force, a burthen and an incumbrance, or formidable only to those shores which it was intended to protect."

(London: Ackerman, 1841), pp. 103-104.

49. From minor to serious the punishments were: "Warning to be more careful in the future," censure, reprimand, severe reprimand, "dismiss the ship" (to be transferred), delayed promotion, loss of places—sometimes all the way to the bottom—on the list of officers of equal rank, and in truly

exceptional cases, imprisonment and discharge. *Admiralty Digest,* IND 18071 of 1870.
  50. Wilson, "Discipline in Old Navy," pp. 96-98.
  51. *Admiralty Digest,* IND 18052 of 1869.
  52. Ibid., IND 12518 of 1862; IND 18034 of 1861; IND 18052 of 1869. There were exceptions such as the case of Commander Bulkeley who was threatened with expulsion if he did not pay for a box contracted at the Opera. He promptly paid. *Admiralty Digest,* IND 12550 of 1864.
  53. Ibid., IND 12518 of 1862; IND 12534 of 1863.
  54. Baynham, *From the Lower Decks,* pp. 64-66, 113, 124-29; Busk, *Navies of World,* pp. 198-203; Dewar, *Navy from Within,* pp. 14-17, 22; Leech, *Thirty Years,* p. 37.
  55. Lieutenant Marsden of H.M.S. *Isis* with an army captain in Sierra Leona in 1861. Duelling was quite rare, and illegal. This was the only instance to which official notice was taken between 1850-80. *Admiralty Digest,* IND 12502 of 1861.
  56. Ibid., IND 12566 of 1865.
  57. Ibid., IND 12488 of 1860; IND 12489 of 1860.
  58. Ibid., IND 12534 of 1863.
  59. A. E. Dingle, "Drink and Working-Class Living Standards in Britain, 1870-1914," *Economic History Review* 2nd ser., 25 (November 1972): 608-609.
  60. J. H. Briggs, *Naval Administration,* p. 147.
  61. Agnes Weston, *My Life Among the Blue Jackets* (London: James Nisbet, 1909), p. 2.
  62. Beresford, *Memoirs,* 1: 17-18; Bennett, *Charlie B.,* p. 23.
  63. "Master of a British Merchant Ship," (pseud.), "On the Defective State of Discipline of the Merchant Service: Shewing the Loss Occasioned to the Owners Thereby," *Nautical Magazine* 44 (October 1835): 586-92; Herman Ausubel, *In Hard Times* (New York: Columbia University Press, 1960), pp. 46-47.
  64. Lewis, *Navy of Britain* pp. 295-96.
  65. A. J. Pack, "Note on Alcoholism," *Mariner's Mirror* 58 (May 1972): 193-94.
  66. Admiral Vernon presented the following rationale:

> Whereas it manifestly appears..., to be the unanimous opinion of both Captains and Surgeons, that the pernicious custom of the seamen drinking their allowance of rum in drams, and often at once, is attended with many fatal effects to their morals as well as their health, which are visibly impaired thereby, and many of their lives shortened by it....

Bryan McLean Ranft, ed., *The Vernon Papers* (London: Navy Records Society, 1958), pp. 417-18.
  Leslie Gardiner, *British Admiralty,* pp. 147-48; Kemp, *British Sailor,* p. 79. Commander Kemp claims the grosgrain applied to Admiral Vernon's breeches.
  Royal Navy rum was 95.9 degrees proof: a blend of sixty percent Demerara, 30 percent Trinidad, ten percent Barbados, Australian, and

others. Lawrence Phillips, "The Abolition of the Rum Ration," *U.S. Naval Institute Proceedings* 96 (July 1970): 87.

67. Brian Harrison, "Drink and Sobriety in England, 1815-72: A Critical Bibliography," *International Review of Social History* 12 (1967): 210-22 and "The Power of Drink," *Listener*, 81 (13 February 1969): 204-206; Taylor, "Recruiting System," Part I, pp. 308-309; Baynham, *From the Lower Decks*, p. 40; Leech, *Thirty Years*; Best, *Mid-Victorian Britain*, pp. 218-24; Dingle, "Drink and Living Standards," pp. 608-609; *Admiralty Digest*, IND 18099 of 1871.

68. Great Britain, National Maritime Museum, *Milne Papers*, MLN/P/B/2k, pp. 2-3.

69. *Admiralty Digest*, IND 12518 of 1862; IND 12534 of 1863; IND 12536 of 1863; IND 12550 of 1864; IND 12566 of 1865; IND 18052 of 1869; Adm 1/6112; Montagu, *Middy's Recollections*, p. 16.

70. The variety of temperance movements, in fact, incorporated a wide spectrum of positions from the moderate anti-spirits view to absolute teetotalism. There even developed competition and open conflict among adherents of different movements.

71. Dingle, "Drink and Living Standards," pp. 608-609; Bennett, *Charlie B.*, p. 23; Joseph Montague Kenworthy, *The Real Navy* (London: Hutchinson, 1932), p. 35; Kemp, *British Sailor*, p. 210.

Investigations into the national problem, mostly by select committees, occurred in 1834, 1872, and 1877. See their reports: *Sessional Papers*, 1834; 1872 (242), vol. 11; 1877 (171) (271) (418), vol. 11. Two recent books deal directly with the temperance movements: Brian Harrison, *Drink and the Victorians* (Pittsburgh: University of Pittsburgh Press, 1971) and Norman Longmate, *The Water-Drinkers* (London: Hamilton, 1968). Also see Burn, *Equipoise*, pp. 280-83; Ausubel, *In Hard Times*, pp. 46-47; Elizabeth Isichei, *Victorian Quakers* (New York: Oxford University Press, 1970), pp. 235-43; Harrison, "Drink and Sobriety," pp. 210-22 and "Power of Drink," pp. 205-206; David M. Fahey, "Temperance and the Liberal Party—Lord Peel's Report, 1899," *Journal of British Studies* 10 (May 1971): 132-59; Weston, *My Life*, pp. 85-95, 103-40 and *Temperance Work in the Royal Navy* (London: Hodder & Stoughton, 1879), pp. 2-65, 254-66; Baynham, *From the Lower Decks*, p. 112-19; Beresford, *Memoirs*, 1: 17-18.

72. Bonnett, *Price of Admiralty*, pp. 64-65.
73. Phillips, "Abolition," pp. 87-88.
74. Baynham, *From the Lower Decks*, p. 119.

*Notes for Chapter V*

1. The studies dealing with this aspect of Victorian society include: Steven Marcus, *The Other Victorians* (London: Weidenfeld & Nicolson,

1966); Kellow Chesney, *The Anti-Society* (American title: *The Victorian Underworld)*, (Boston: Gambit, 1970), pp. 354-63; Michael Pearson, *The Age of Consent* (London: David & Charles, 1972); Ronald Pearsall, *The Worm in the Bud* (New York: Macmillan, 1969), pp. 266-78. On various aspects of the double standard see: Keith Thomas, "The Double Standard," *Journal of the History of Ideas* 10 (1959): 195-216; J. A. Banks and Olive Banks, *Feminism and Family Planning in Victorian England* (Liverpool: University of Liverpool Press, 1964) and "The Bradlaugh-Besant Trial and the English Newspapers," *Population Studies* 8 (July 1954): 22-34; Duncan Crow, *The Victorian Woman* (London: Allen and Unwin, 1971); O. R. McGregor, *Divorce in England* (London: Heinemann, 1957); Constance Rover, *Women's Suffrage and Party Politics in Britain* (Toronto: Toronto University Press, 1967); Peter T. Cominos, "Late-Victorian Sexual Respectability and the Social System," *International Review of Social History* 8, Parts I and II (1963): 18-48, 216-50; Brian Harrison, "Underneath the Victorians," *Victorian Studies* 10 (March 1967): 54-55; Margaret Maison, "Insignificant Objects of Desire," *Listener* 86 (July 1971): 105-107; Martha Vicinus, ed., *Suffer and Be Still* (Bloomington: Indiana University Press, 1972), pp. 77-97; Walter E. Houghton, *The Victorian Frame of Mind, 1830-70* (New Haven: Yale University Press, 1964); William Logan, *The Great Social Evil* (London: Hodder & Stoughton, 1871); Theodore K. Rabb and Robert I. Rotberg, eds., *The Family in History* (New York: Harper and Row, 1973); Burn, *Equipoise*, pp. 158-59; *Dictionary of National Biography*, 15: 972-74.

2. *Lancet*, 1840-90, passim.

3. *Admiralty Digest*, IND 12502 of 1861; Adm 1/5974; *Sessional Papers*, 25 (1865), Part II, p. 113; Appleman, *1859*, pp. 202-203; John Lawrence Hammond and Barbara Hammond, *James Stansfeld* (London: Longmans, Green, 1932), pp. 118-19.

4. For example, the Admiralty contributed £400 per year to a lock ward at Shanghai and £800 at Hong Kong. The cost for lock wards in the 1870s was £16,500 a year. *Admiralty Digest*, IND 18207 of 1874; F. B. Smith, "Ethics and Disease in the Later Nineteenth Century: The Contagious Diseases Acts," *Historical Studies* 15 (October 1971): 131.

5. Lloyd, *Medicine*, 4:199. These recommendations were quite perceptive and far-sighted, and all were ultimately instituted.

6. E.g., Mr. Richard Allen of Dublin at the annual meeting of the Social Science Association at Newcastle-upon-Tyne in 1870, *National Association for the Promotion of Social Science, Transactions* (1870): 233.

7. The acts: 27 and 28 Vict c. 85 of 1864; 29 and 30 Vict c. 96 of 1866, and 32 and 33 Vict c. 86 of 1869.

8. In fact the jurisdiction of the special constables extended out to a fifteen mile radius.

9. Portsmouth, Plymouth-Devonport, Woolwich, Chatham, Sheerness, Aldershot, Colchester, Shorncliff, the Curragh, Cork, and Queenstown, all established in the act of 1864.

10. Windsor was added in the act of 1866. Canterbury, Dover, Gravesend, Maidstone, Winchester, and Southampton were all added in the act of 1869. Southampton was not a military or naval facility.
    11. Scott, *Iniquity*, p. 32.
    12. Adm 1/5976 of 1866; Adm 1/6104 of 1869; *Admiralty Digest*, IND 12549 of 1864; IND 18187 of 1875; Amos, *Comparative Survey*, pp. 31-41, 65-137, 344-69, 423-82; *National Association*, 1868, p. 509; Percy Ford and G. Ford, *Select List of British Parliamentary Papers, 1833-99* (Oxford: Blackwell, 1953), p. 34; William Stuart Fowler, *A Study in Radicalism and Dissent* (Westport, Conn.: Greenwood, 1963), p. 28; Scott, *Iniquity*, pp. 12-31; Richard L. Blanco, "The Attempted Control of Venereal Disease in the Army of Mid-Victorian England," *Journal of the Society for Army Historical Research*, 45 (Winter 1967): 234-41; Robert Lawson, "The Operation of the Contagious Diseases Acts Among the Troops in the United Kingdom," *Journal of the Royal Statistical Society*, 54 (1891): 31-69; Smith, "Ethics and Disease," pp. 118-35; Lloyd and Coulter, *Medicine and the Navy*, 4: 197-99; Judith R. Walkowitz, "'We Are Not Beasts of the Field': Prostitution and the Campaign Against the Contagious Diseases Acts, 1869-86," Ph.D. dissertation, University of Rochester, 1974, pp. 110-11, 159-63 and "Notes on the History of Victorian Prostitution," *Feminist Studies* 1 (Summer 1972): 105-14.
    13. *Lancet*, 1823-24, pp. 387-96; *Lancet*, 1867, p. 580; Walkowitz, Ph.D. dissertation, p. 297.
    14. Scott, *Iniquity*, pp. 23-26.
    15. *Dictionary of National Biography*, 15: 972-74.
    16. Adm 7/623, Case 162.
    17. Ibid.; *Dictionary of National Biography*, 15: 972-74.
    18. Lloyd, *Medicine*, 4: 100-101; *Admiralty Digest*, IND 18076 of 1870.
    19. Adm 12/1075 of 1881.
    20. Adm 1/6061 of 1868.
    21. *Hansard*, 3rd ser., vol. 182 (22 March 1866), pp. 814-15.
    22. Josephine Elizabeth Butler, *Social Purity* (London: Morgan & Scott, 1879), pp. 23-31.
    23. Josephine Butler, *Simple Words for Simple Folk, About the Repeal of the Contagious Diseases Act* (Bristol: Arrowsmith, n.d.).
    24. William Robbins, *The Newman Brothers* (Cambridge: Harvard University Press, 1966), p. 150; Cominos, "Late-Victorian Respectability," pp. 45-46; Logan, *Social Evil*, pp. 211-18; Constance Rover, *Love, Morals and the Feminists* (London: Routledge & Paul, 1970), pp. 71-84.
    25. Pearson, *Age of Consent*, p. 73; Glen Petrie, *A Singular Iniquity* (New York: Viking Press, 1971), p. 129.
    26. *Admiralty Digest*, IND 18070 of 1870; IND 18076 of 1870.
    27. *Lancet* (1870): 33; (1871): 46; (1872): 18; (1873): 13; *Saturday Review* 29 (1 January 1870): 11-12; 29 (26 February 1870): 277-78; 29 (28 May 1870): 701-702; Hammond, *Stansfeld*, pp. 132-34; Acton, *Prostitution*, pp. 7-22; Amos, *Comparative Survey*, pp. 11-13.
    28. Lambert, *Sir John Simon*, pp. 405-406.

## REFORM IN THE ROYAL NAVY

29. Adm 12/1075 of 1881; Adm 12/1109 of 1883, Adm 12/1140 of 1885.
30. *Admiralty Digest*, IND 18099 of 1871; IND 18207 of 1874.
31. *Hansard*, 3rd ser., vol. 260, Commons, (5 May 1881), pp. 1815-16; *Admiralty Digest*, IND 18203 of 1876; IND 18204 of 1876; IND 18190 of 1875; Walkowitz, *Feminist Studies*, 1972, pp. 107-11; Walkowitz, Ph.D. dissertation, pp. 189-92, 262-63, 276.
32. *Admiralty Digest*, IND 12502 of 1861; IND 12517 of 1862; IND 12549 of 1864; IND 18070 of 1870; IND 18076 of 1870; Adm 1/5974 of 1866; Adm 1/6061; Adm 1/6113; Adm 12/1106 of 1883. Great Britain, Parliament, *Report of the Royal Commission upon the Administration and Operation of the Contagious Diseases Acts (Not Concerned with Animals)* (London: Her Majesty's Stationery Office, 1871); Petrie, *Singular Iniquity*, pp. 11-35, 119-49, 201-208; Josephine Butler, *Personal Reminiscences of a Great Crusade* (London: Marshall, 1896) and *Simple Words*, pp. 1-4; Hammond, *Stansfeld*, pp. 118-259; Banks, *Feminism and Family Planning*, pp. 94-111; F. B. Smith, "Ethics and Disease," pp. 119-32; Vicinus, *Suffer and Be Still*, pp. 77-97; Brian Harrison, *Drink and the Victorians*, pp. 174-75; Michael St. John Packe, *The Life of John Stuart Mill* (New York: Putnams, 1954), pp. 501-502; Kemp, *British Sailor*, pp. 181-98.
    W. L. Burn used the example of the Contagious Diseases Acts and their repeal as support for his thesis concerning the conflict between regulation and liberty, the pertinent chapter being entitled "The Inverventionism of Panic." He concludes that during the "age of equipoise," which coincides with the period of this study, "England . . . was more notable . . . for discipline than for freedom from discipline." Burn, *Equipoise*, pp. 7-17, 132-36, 154-61.
33. Between 1883 and 1884 there was an increase of 4.79/1000 cases throughout the navy and 11.8/1000 for the Home Fleet, the highest rates since the annual medical statistical report began. Clowes, *Royal Navy*, 7: 67; William H. Lloyd, "Health of the Navy," pp. 451-55.
34. Adm 12/1109 of 1883; 12/1140 of 1885.
35. Kenworthy, *Real Navy*, p. 35.
36. Kemp, *British Sailor*, p. 210; Berckman, *Hidden Navy;* Beresford, *Memoirs*, 1: 3-14; Bennett, *Charlie B.*, p. 23; Scott, *Fifty Years*, pp. v-ix, 1-7.
37. Baynham, *From the Lower Decks*, p. 111.
38. Penrose, *Observations*, pp. 51-65. Elsewhere in the pamphlet Admiral Penrose calls ships of the Royal Navy "ideal schools for youth."
39. Leech, *Thirty Years*, pp. 37-40. Perhaps more perceptively, he calls naval ships "no place for boys."
40. Baynham, *Before the Mast*, p. 39. Also see *From the Lower Decks* and "Seaman from *Leander*."
41. Quoted from Vicinus, *Suffer and Be Still*, p. 86.
42. *Admiralty Digest*, IND 18052 of 1869; IND 18053 of 1869; W. B. Rowbotham, "Soldier's and Seaman's Wives and Children in H.M. Ships," *Mariner's Mirror* 47 (February 1961): 42-48; Kemp, *British Sailor*, pp. 143, 167-73, 195-96; Berckman, *Hidden Navy*, pp. 1-42.

43. Christopher Bartlett incorrectly used the term "dirtiness" when referring to these activities contained in legal charges. The term, in fact, was used to describe neglect to keep clean (i.e., with soap and water), a common problem at the time because of general ignorance and inexperience exemplified by young boys, some barely teenagers, aboard ship. Bartlett, *Great Britain and Sea Power,* p. 312.

44. *Admiralty Digest,* 1850-80, passim.

45. The modern researcher is confronted with dearth, the choices being of highly questionable validity. First, there is *The History of the Rod and Other Corporal Punishments* by Gilbert Oakley, "D. Psy." (There is no explanation of what that signifies). Corporal punishment, the author concludes, is the "fulfillment of the masochistic-sadistic impulse." There is, inevitably, a chapter on "Corporal Punishment in the Navy." The Navy has

> ... always been a breeding ground for homosexual practices because a large number of men are herded together, for long periods, without the natural companionship of females.

In wartime, he continues, "the navy is the most manly service—only in peacetime do seamen "seek other outlets." Flogging began in 1689 [in wartime!]

> At the base of it all was the homosexual urge that existed between officers and men. . . . The victims can become masochists and seek the punishment for sexual pleasure.

Oakley, *History of Rod,* pp. 23, 196-200.

Second, George Ryley Scott emphasizes the title of the revised edition of *The History of Corporal Punishment: Flagellation.* There is, he claims, an "inherent cruelty" in the practice, "an ambivalence of pleasure and pain." Scott, *History,* pp. 17-36.

These presentations fall under what Scott Claver calls "sensationalist . . . pseudo-scientific essays . . . for a basically uncritical market." He laments, correctly, that that is about the extent of the writing in the last century. Claver, *Under the Lash,* p. ix.

46. *Admiralty Digest,* IND 18116 of 1872; IND 18161 of 1874.

47. Robinson, *British Tar,* pp. 90-91.

48. The Articles of War of 1661 called for punishment of death by hanging "without mercy," those of 1749 omitting "without mercy." In the nineteenth century sentences for homosexual acts (something difficult to determine from the records) consisted of death or from seven years to life penal servitude and discharge with disgrace. Some examples included the death penalty for sodomy in 1829, flogging around the fleet, one year imprisonment and discharge with disgrace for two seamen in 1842, and a sentence of capital punishment, commuted to two years' imprisonment and discharge with disgrace for a marine in 1859. Hannay, *Naval Courts-Martial,* pp. xi-xiiii; Kemp, *British Sailor,* p. 87; Hickman, *Treatise,* pp. 233-35;

Langley, *Social Reform*, pp. 172-73; *Admiralty Digest*, IND 12470 of 1859; IND 12518 of 1862; IND 12534 of 1863; IND 12550 of 1864; IND 12597 of 1867; Thring, *Treatise*, 1861 edition, p. 169.

49. Chesney, *Anti-Society*, pp. 327-29.

50. A thorough study of medical and health services throughout the history of the Royal Navy is Christopher Lloyd and Jack Coulter's, *Medicine and the Navy*, 4 vols. See especially vol. 4, *1815-1900*.

51. An inordinate number of naval surgeons came from Scotland where they received excellent medical training but no lucrative job offers. C. Lloyd, *Medicine*, 4: 2-4, 81-82 and "Dr. Baikie," pp. 740-41.

52. Richard Ollard, "Greenwich," *History Today* 5 (November 1955): 777-84; Marcus, *Age of Nelson*, 2: 432-33; letter from Christopher Lloyd, 28 February 1974.

53. The uniform consisted of a blue serge frock with three rows of white tape border on the collar, blue trousers, black silk neckerchief, and straw hat or blue cloth cap. The number of rows of white tape and the color of the neckerchief apparently had no connection with Lord Nelson, although some claimed the number of tapes symbolized his three great victories and the black signified mourning for his death. Sir Gerald Dickens, *The Dress of the British Sailor* (London: Her Majesty's Stationery Office, 1957); Leslie Gardiner, *British Admiralty*, pp. 170-72; Kemp, *British Sailor*, pp. 155-56, 203-204; G. M. Young, *Victorian England*, 2nd ed. (New York: Oxford University Press, 1964), p. 331; Lewis, *Navy in Transition*, p. 15; C. Lloyd, *Medicine*, 4: 281-99; Kenneth Chivers, "Henry Jones versus the Admiralty," *History Today* 10 (April 1960): 247-54; Scott, *Fifty Years*, p. 7; Hans Zinsser, *Rats, Lice and History* (Boston: Little, Brown, 1935), pp. 284-90; *Admiralty Digest*, IND 12501 of 1861.

54. Taylor, "Manning," p. 204; Busk, *Navies of the World*, p. 190; Baynham, *Before the Mast*, p. 134.

55. Reay Tannahill, *Food in History* (New York: Stein & Day, 1973), pp. 226-27; A. G. Bath, "The Victualling of the Navy," *Journal of the Royal United Service Institution* 84 (1939): 744-48, 765.

56. By 1859 the following items or the equivalent in money were issued to incoming men:

| | | | |
|---|---|---|---|
| clothing - | blue jacket | Cost: | 17s 8d |
| | blue trousers | | 11s 7d |
| | serge frock | | 8s 6d |
| | duck frock | | 2s 9d |
| | duck trousers | | 2s 7d |
| | black silk handkerchief | | 2s 10d |
| | shoes | | 6s 7d |
| hammock | | | |
| bedding | | | |
| mess utensils | | | |

Busk, *Navies of the World*, p. 190.

57. Beresford, *Memoirs*, 1:19. Lord Fisher recalled:

> When the first bathroom was introduced . . . , I heard the First Sea Lord (scandalized by the innovation!), "Did you ever wash when you went to sea?" "No!," replied Sidney Dacres, "No more did I," said Sir Alexander Milne . . . , but they were more angry at the water-closet seats being French polished instead of being scrubbed and holystoned, and always damp in consequence!

Marder, *Dread Nought*, 1: 20.

58. Cornewall-Jones, *Merchant Service*, p. 266; Beresford, *Memoirs*, 1: 18; C. Lloyd, *Medicine*, 4: 97; Marder, *Dread Nought*, 1: 20; Busk, *Navies of the World*, pp. 189-90.

59. C. Lloyd, *Medicine*, 4: 2, 97. T. E. Lawrence compared this innovation in the armed services as equivalent to the impact of gunpowder.

60. Bath, "Victualling," pp. 748-49.

61. Baynham, *Before the Mast*, p. 134 from a pamphlet, *The Seamen of the Royal Navy*, 1877.

62. Baynham, *Before the Mast*, pp. 157-60.

63. Sensational and widely publicized scandals occurred in 1850 when 110,000 pounds of meat in large-size cans were condemned and in 1852 when a Hungarian Jew named Goldner was prosecuted for "the stinking meats" episode. Tannahill, *Food*, pp. 353-55; Taylor, "Manning," p. 40.

64. C. Lloyd, *Medicine*, 4: 83-84, 270-71; *Sessional Papers*, vol. 37 (1837-38), No. 371, pp. 253-65.

65. Lewis, *Navy of Britain*, pp. 298-99; Kemp, *British Sailor*, pp. 6, 27, 152.

66. Peter Kemp, *Prize Money* (Aldershot: Gale & Polden, 1946); Lewis, *Navy in Transition*, pp. 231-37.

67. Allotments in force:

| Year | Number of Allotments and Total Force |
|---|---|
| 1796 | 3346 of 106,708 |
| 1812 | 27,019 of 138,204 |
| 1832 | 7600 of 23,484 |
| 1850 | 13,212 of 28,741 |
| 1855 | 23,841 of 49,739 |
| 1858 | 17,308 of 38,704 |

T. Pitcairn, *Report on the Allotment System in the Navy* (1859) in Adm 7/710.

68. Adm 1/5977 of 1866.

69. *Admiralty Digest*, IND 18105 of 1871.

70. Pack, *Britannia*, pp. 24-30; Statham, *Story of the Britannia*, pp. 55-70; Baynham, *Before the Mast*, pp. 19-20; F. Grey, *Organization of the Navy*, pp. 28-29; Charles Christopher Lloyd, "The Royal Naval Colleges at Portsmouth and Greenwich," *Mariner's Mirror* 52 (May 1966): 145-56.

71. Marcus, *Age of Nelson*, 2: 434; Baynham, *Before the Mast*, pp. 117, 125-26, 204-11; Aylmer, *Cruise in the Pacific*, 1:19; *Admiralty Digest*, IND 18210 of 1876.

72. *Admiralty Digest*, IND 12583 of 1866; IND 12597 of 1867; IND 12604 of 1867; Kemp, *British Sailor*, p. 204; Bath, "Victualling," p. 748.

The idea of beer canteens was credited to William Hickman, the Admiralty clerk. The policy precipitated a classic "smart lawyer" success. Three marines on *Revenge* were court-martialed for drunkenness and theft of wine. They pleaded guilty to the former and a lawyer claimed it resulted from the available beer, not any wine that was missing. The marines were acquitted of theft. This may be one of the reasons the Admiralty disliked civilian defense lawyers.

73. Weston, *Temperance Work*, pp. 47-59.

74. Ibid., pp. 59-65; Baynham, *Before the Mast*, pp. 117-19.

75. *Admiralty Memorandum*, BR11, p. 1; Kemp, *British Sailor*, pp. 2-3.

76. *Sessional Papers*, 1 (1960): 320.

77. *Queen's Regulations*, 1862, pp. 103-104; Hannay, *Courts Martial*, p. xl; Adm 1/5782 of 1861-65.

78. *Queen's Regulations*, 1862, p. 104. Earlier in the century a naval chaplain quit because he refused to recognize the close association. Rev. Edward Mangin explained:

> To leave the men unreproved and vicious, was possible; and I dare say it was equally possible to have transformed them all into Methodists, or madmen or hypocrites of some other kind; but to convert a man-of-war's crew into Christians would be a task to which the courage of Loyola, the philanthropy of Howard, and the eloquence of St. Paul united, would prove inadequate.... So I bid adieu to the sameness and (to me) insupportable vexations of a naval life; to the necessity of dwelling in a prison; within whose limits were to be found Constraint, Disease, Ignorance, Insensibility, Tyranny, Sameness, Dirt and Foul Air; and, in addition, the dangers of Ocean, Fire, Mutiny, Pestilence, Battle and Exile.
>
> From C. Lloyd, *British Seaman*, pp. 237-38.

79. Adm 12/1040 of 1879.

80. Clode, *Administration*, p. 36.

81. Vol. 2:465.

82. Lewis, *Navy of Britain*, pp. 190-91.

83. *Queen's Regulations*, 1862, p. 104; Adm 1/6011 of 1867; *Admiralty Digest*, IND 12489 of 1860; IND 12492 of 1860. Roman Catholics were exempted from services and morning prayers.

84. Conrad Dixon, "The Hard Life and Times of Henry Moffat, Seaman," *Mariner's Mirror*, 59 (May 1973):193-203.

85. Adm 116, Case F82 of 1882. This documents the process for acquiring certain administrative recognition for the Wesleyans. All tracts and religious books supplied to ship's libraries were stamped "Presented by the Lords of the Admiralty." Adm 12/1129 of 1884.

86. A typical response was "Their Lordships cannot admit doctrine which would exempt the Chaplain from the authority of the Captain of the Ship." The conduct of a chaplain who refused to report attendance of a recalcitrant midshipman was deemed "unbecoming" by the Admiralty which noted its "grave displeasure." *Admiralty Digest*, IND 12519 of 1862; IND 12554 of 1864; Adm 1/5790 of 1862.

87. *Admiralty Digest* IND 12507 of 1861; IND 12604 of 1867; IND 18034 of 1868; IND 12601 of 1867; IND 18034 of 1868; IND 18056 of 1869.

88. Ibid., IND 18224 of 1877.

89. Langley, *Social Reform*, pp. viii-ix, 45-47; Kemp, *British Sailor*, pp. 109-10; C. Lloyd, *British Seaman*, pp. 220-31; Roberts, *Victorian Origins*, p. 87.

90. Taylor, "Manning," p. 11; C. Lloyd, *British Seaman*, p. 271; Woodward, *Age of Reform*, p. 271.


## Notes for Chapter VI

1. The Milne Papers at the National Maritime Museum, Greenwich, contain a note attached to a copy of this circular indicating that he provided the impetus. He was Junior Lord from 1847-59. *Milne Papers*, MLN/P/B/2k, p. 1; *Dictionary of National Biography*, vol. 22, supplement 3, p. 1048.

2. The following is a sampling:

   1. Drink grog on the Quarterdeck and remain standing there about two hours.
   2. Extra duty, e.g., picking oakum, cleaning the head, pump-well, stoning the galley—never over twenty-one days.
   3. Stop leave for breaking leave. . . .
   4. Stop grog for drunkenness only. . . .
   . . .
   8. Deprive of Good Conduct Badge.
   . . .
   12. Solitary confinement in cell . . . never over ten days.
   13. Imprisonment ashore in jail.
   14. Corporal punishment—rarely expedient for first offense.
   15. Discharge with disgrace. Forfeits all previous service and precludes re-entry into Royal Navy.
   16. [Restricted to boys] Caning Boys on the hand to check inattention and dirty habits—to be resorted to with moderation.

   *Milne Papers*, MLN/P/B/2k, p. 3.

# REFORM IN THE ROYAL NAVY

3. Ibid., pp. 1-7; Kemp, *British Sailor,* p. 186.
4. The *Times,* 14 December 1853, p. 12d.
5. (1) Mutiny, (2) desertion, (3) repeated drunkenness, (4) smuggling liquor, (5) theft, (6) repeated disobedience, (7) desertion of post, and (8) indecent conduct. Adm 1/5718 of 1859.
6. Ibid.; Taylor, "Recruiting System," part II, pp. 52-53.
7. *Admiralty Digest,* IND 12570 of 1865.
8. *Hansard,* 3rd ser., vol. 155 (21 August 1860), pp. 1657-62.
9. Adm 1/5718 of 1859; *Sessional Papers,* vol. 5 (1860), No. 320, p. 1; Laughton, "Preamble," p. 84.
10. *Hansard,* 3rd ser., vol. 159 (29 June 1860), p. 1181; vol. 159 (9 July 1860), pp. 1612-16; vol. 160 (7 August 1860), pp. 819-22; vol. 160 (10 August 1860), p. 1098; vol. 160 (21 August 1860), pp. 1649-66; vol. 160 (23 August 1860), p. 1722; vol. 160 (28 August 1860), p. 1831; the *Times,* 11 October 1860, p. 10c; Adm 1/5782 of 1861; Taylor, "Recruiting System," part II, p. 53; Young, *Victorian England,* p. 322.
11. *Sessional Papers,* vol. 2 (1861), no. 191, pp. 377-400; Adm 1/5782 of 1861; *Admiralty Digest,* IND 12506 of 1861.
12. The dates of the acts: Naval Discipline Act of 1864, 29 July 1864; Naval Discipline Act Amendment Bill of 1865, 5 July 1865; Naval Discipline Act of 1866, 10 August 1866; *Hansard,* 3rd ser., vol. 176, index; 3rd ser., vol. 180, index; 3rd ser., vol. 184, index; *Sessional Papers,* vol. 3 (1864), no. 233, pp. 87-113; vol. 3 (1865), no. 254, p. 119; vol. 3 (1866), no. 231, pp. 557-638; *Admiralty Digest,* IND 12550 of 1864; IND 12551 of 1864; IND 12567 of 1865; IND 12582 of 1866; Burn, *Equipoise,* p. 191. After passage of the act of 1866 the Admiralty printed 1500 copies for distribution.
13. Gordon Rose, *The Struggle for Penal Reform* (London: Stevens, 1961), pp. 1-18.
14. *Admiralty Digest,* IND 12567 of 1865; IND 18033 of 1868; IND 18034 of 1868; IND 18052 of 1869.
15. Ibid., IND 18161 of 1874; IND 18183 of 1875; IND 18184 of 1875; Adm 12/1105 of 1882; Adm 12/1124 of 1884; Thring, *Treatise,* 2nd ed., 1877, pp. iii, 177-79.
16. Adm 1/5997 Pro H 568 of 1866. The responses to Romaine's letter were later edited and published by William Hickman. *Reports and Opinions.*
17. *Committee to Consider the Administration of Justice under the Naval Discipline Act,* 1:8.
18. Quoted from the *Times,* 17 June 1859, and from Sir John Henry Briggs in Colin F. Baxter, "Admiralty Problems," pp. 14-16.
19. William Hurrell Mallock and Lady Guendolen Ramsden, eds., *Letters, Remains, and Memoirs of Edward Adolphus Seymour, Twelfth Duke of Somerset, K.G.* (London: Richard Bentley, 1893), p. 3.
20. Baxter, "Admiralty Problems," p. 185.
21. Quoted from a letter from Colin F. Baxter, 10 July 1972.
22. Moody, "Recruiting for Her Majesty's Service," pp. 587-89, 597-98. "His admirable measures evolved reason out of rowdyism."

23. *Dictionary of National Biography*, vol. 22, supplement 3, p. 1017.
24. L. Gardiner, *British Admiralty*, p. 173; Bridge, *Recollections*, p. 195; Beresford, *Memoirs*, 1: 17; "Naval Officers," *The White Ensign* (London: Roy, 1896), pp. 124-26; Montagu, *Middy's Recollections*, p. 69.
25. [Sir William Fanshawe Martin], "The Admiralty," *Blackwood's Magazine* 107 (June 1870): 763-71 and *Memorandum on Corporal Punishment*; Moody, "Recruiting for Her Majesty's Service," pp. 587-89.
26. Taylor, "Manning," p. 58; Bartlett, *Great Britain and Sea Power*, p. 8.
27. *Admiralty Digest*, IND 18203 of 1876; Bartlett, *Great Britain and Sea Power*, p. 8; Baynham, *Before the Mast*, p. 120.
28. Thring, *Treatise*, 1861 edition.
29. William Schaw Lindsay, *Confirmation of Admiralty Mismanagement* (London: E. Wilson, 1885), pp. 1-35.


## Notes for Appendix

1. Number of Men Borne in the Royal Navy, 1830-75. Clowes, *Royal Navy*, 7: 12-13; Reddie, "On Manning," pp. 355-57.
2. Number of Men Flogged in the Royal Navy, 1830-65. Adm 1/5554 of 1845; Adm 1/5590 of 1848; Adm 1/5974 of 1866; Adm 1/5977 of 1866; Adm 1/6011 of 1867; Adm 1/6158 of 1870; Adm 1/6159 of 1870; Adm 1/6160 of 1870; *Admiralty Digest*, IND 12326 of 1850; IND 12582 of 1866; IND 18071 of 1870; *Hansard*, 3rd ser., vol. 11 (2 April 1832), pp. 1224-31; 3rd ser., vol. 22 (4 March 1834), p. 237; 3rd ser., vol. 20 (15 August 1833), pp. 681-84; 3rd ser., vol. 32 (13 April 1836), p. 974; 3rd ser., vol. 87 (20 July 1846), p. 1343; 3rd ser., vol. 160 (21 August 1860), pp. 1654-56; 3rd ser., vol. 169 (23 February 1863), p. 668; *Sessional Papers*, vol. 42 (1834), no. 393, pp. 371-75; vol. 37 (1837-38), no. 371, pp. 253, 265; vol. 40 (1852-53), p. 395; vol. 34 (1854-55), no. 17, pp. 151-62; vol. 9 (1857), (48 Sess 1), pp. 619, 633, 642; vol. 15 (1859), (Sess 1), pp. 445, 487, 499; vol. 42 (1860), no. 40, p. 397; vol. 38 (1861), no. 82, p. 141; vol. 36 (1863), no. 11, pp. 1-6; vol. 35 (1865), no. 27, Part 2, pp. 141-46. C. Lloyd, *Medicine*, 4: 83-84, 200-201; Bartlett, *Great Britain and Sea Power*, p. 312, n; Langley, *Social Reform*, pp. 172-73; the *Times*, 9 June 1861, p. 9f.
3. Floggings per 1000 Men in the Royal Navy, 1830-65. (Same as number 2.)
4. Average Number of Lashes per Flogging in the Royal Navy, 1830-65. (Same as number 2.)
5. Trend Indicated by the Average Number of Desertions per Month in the Royal Navy, 1800-70. (Same as number 2.)
6. Table of Offenses Not Requiring Courts-Martial in the Royal Navy, 1862-65. (Same as number 2.)

# Selected Bibliography

Acton, William. "Observations on Venereal Diseases in the United Kingdom, from Statistical Reports in the Army, Navy, and Merchant Service." *Lancet* (1846): 703-705.

_____. *Prostitution, Considered in Its Moral, Social and Sanitary Aspects in London and Other Large Cities and Garrison Towns.* 2nd ed. London: J. Churchill, 1870; London: Frank Cass reprint, 1972.

Adams, Henry Brooks. *The Education of Henry Adams.* Cambridge, Ma.: Riverside Press, 1946.

Albion, Robert G. *Forests and Sea Power.* Hamden, Ct.: Archon, 1965.

_____. *Naval and Maritime History.* 4th ed. Mystic, Ct.: Marine Historical Association, 1972.

Allin, Lawrence C. "Abel Parker Upshur and the Dignity of Discipline." *Naval War College Review* (June 1970): 85-91.

Altholz, Josef L. "Victorian England, 1837-1901: Bibliography and Historiography." *Albion* 5 (Winter 1973): 274-78.

_____, ed. *Victorian England, 1837-1901.* New York: Cambridge University Press, 1970.

"American Discipline: From Naval and Marine Gazette." *The Nautical Magazine,* 1843, pp. 207-208.

Amos, Sheldon. *A Comparative Survey of Laws in Force for the Prohibition, Regulation, and Licensing of Vice in England and other Countries.* London: Stevens, 1877.

"Ancora Imparo" (pseud.). "Sir James Graham's Reforms in Administration and Command at the Admiralty." *Fighting Forces* 3 (1927): 404-20.

Anderson, Charles Roberts. *Melville in the South Seas.* New York: Columbia University Press, 1939.

Anderson, Olive. "Early Experiences of Manpower Problems in an Industrial Society at War: Great Britain, 1854-56." *Political Science Quarterly* 82 (December 1967): 526-45.

_____. "The Growth of Christian Militarism in mid-Victorian Britain." *English Historical Review* 86 (January 1971): 46-72.

_____. *A Liberal State at War.* New York: St. Martins Press, 1967.

Anderson, Richard M. "The Navy Ration." *U S. Naval Institute Proceedings* 92 (April 1966): 186-88.
Anderson, Roger Charles. *Naval Wars of the Baltic, 1522-1850.* London: n.p., 1910.
———. *Naval Wars in the Levant, 1559-1853.* Princeton, N.J.: Princeton University Press, 1952; Liverpool: University of Liverpool Press, 1952.
Andrews, William. *Bygone Punishments.* London: Andrews and Co., 1899.
———. *Old-Time Punishments.* London: Andrews and Co., 1890; London: Frederick Muller reprint, 1972.
Appleman, Philip.; Madden, William A.; and Wolff, Michael., eds. *1859: Entering an Age of Crisis.* Bloomington: Indiana University Press, 1959.
Archer, Thomas. *The Pauper, the Thief and the Convict.* London: Groombridge, 1865.
Archibald, Edward H. H. *The Metal Fighting Ship in the Royal Navy, 1860-1970.* Annapolis: U.S. Naval Institute, 1971; London: Blandford, 1971.
———. *The Wooden Fighting Ships in the Royal Navy, A.D. 897-1860.* London: Blandford, 1968; New York: Arco, 1970.
Armstrong, Alexander. *Observations on Naval Hygiene and Scurvy.* London: Churchill, 1858.
Arnstein, Walter L. *The Bradlaugh Case.* London: Oxford University Press, 1965.
———. "The Myth of the Triumphant Victorian Middle Class." *The Historian* 37 (February 1975): 205-21.
———. "Victorian Prejudice Reexamined." *Victorian Studies* 12 (June 1969): 452-57.
Ashworth, William. "Economic Aspects of Late Victorian Naval Administration." *Economic History Review,* 2nd ser. 22 (December 1969): 491-505.
———. *An Economic History of England, 1870-1939.* New York: Barnes and Noble, 1961; London: Methuen, 1961.
Aspinall, Arthur. *Politics and the Press, c. 1750-1850.* London: Home and Van Than, 1949.
Ausubel, Herman. *In Hard Times.* New York: Columbia University Press, 1960.
Aydelotte, William O. "The Conservative and Radical Interpreta-

tions of the Early Victorian Social Legislation." *Victorian Studies* 11 (December 1967): 225-36.
Aylmer, Fenton. *A Cruise in the Pacific.* 2 vols. London: Hurst and Blackett, 1860.
Bach, John. "The Royal Navy in the Pacific Islands." *Journal of Pacific History* 3 (1968): 3-20.
Baker, William T. "Anglo-American Relations in Miniature: The Prince of Wales in Portland, Maine, 1860." *New England Quarterly* 45 (December 1972): 559-68
Banks, J. A. and Banks, Olive. "The Bradlaugh-Besant Trial and the English Newspapers." *Population Studies* 8 (July 1954): 22-34.
―――. *Feminism and Family Planning in Victorian England.* Liverpool: Liverpool University Press, 1964; New York: Schocken, 1972.
Barker-Benfield, Ben. *The Horrors of the Half Known Life.* New York: Harper and Row, 1975.
―――. "The Spermatic Economy: A Nineteenth-Century View of Sexuality." *Feminist Studies* 1 (Summer 1972): 45-72.
Barnaby, Kenneth Cloves. *The Institution of Naval Architects, 1860-1960.* London: Allen and Unwin, 1960.
―――. *Some Ship Disasters and Their Causes.* South Brunswick: Barnes, 1970.
Barnaby, Sir Nathaniel. *Naval Development in the (Nineteenth) Century.* London: Linscott, 1902.
Barnett, Correlli. *Britain and Her Army, 1509-1970.* New York: Morrow, 1970.
Bartlett, Christopher John, ed. *Britain Pre-eminent.* London: Macmillan, 1969.
―――. *Great Britain and Sea Power, 1815-1853.* New York: Oxford University Press, 1963.
Barzun, Jacques. *Darwin, Marx, Wagner: Critique of a Heritage.* 2nd ed. Garden City, N.Y.: Doubleday Anchor, 1958.
Bateson, Charles. *The Convict Ships, 1787-1868.* Glasgow: Brown and Ferguson, 1959.
Bath, A. G. "The Victualling of the Navy." *Journal of the Royal United Service Institution* 84 (1939): 744-68.
Baxter, Colin F. "Admiralty Problems during the Second Palmerston Administration, 1859-65." Ph.D. dissertation, University of Georgia, 1965.

Baxter, James Phinney III. *The Introduction of the Ironclad Warship.* Cambridge: Harvard University Press, 1933.

Baylen, Joseph O. "W. T. Stead and the 'New Journalism.' " *Emory University Quarterly* 21 (Fall 1965): 196-206.

Baynham, Henry W. F. "A Seaman in H.M.S. *Leander,* 1863-66." *Mariner's Mirror* 51 (1965): 343-52.

―――― *Before the Mast.* London: Hutchinson, 1971.

―――― *From the Lower Decks.* London: Hutchinson, 1969.

Beales, Derek. *From Castlereagh to Gladstone, 1815-1885.* New York: Norton, 1969.

[Bechervaise, John]. "By the Old Quarter Master." *A Farewell to My Old Shipmates and Messmates.* Portsea: Woodward, 1847.

―――― *Thirty-Six Years of a Seafaring Life, By an Old Quartermaster.* Portsea: Woodward, 1839.

Bell, Enid Moberly. *Josephine Butler.* London: Constable, 1962.

Bell, Frederick Jackson. *Room to Swing a Cat.* New York: Longmans, Green, 1938.

Bell, Herbert Clifford Francis. *Lord Palmerston.* 2 vols. London: 1936; Hamden, Ct.: Archon, 1966.

Bell, R. C. *Diaries from the Days of Sail.* London: Barrie and Jenkins, 1974.

Bennett, Geoffrey. *Charlie B.* London: Dawnay, 1968.

Berckman, Evelyn. *The Hidden Navy.* London: Hamish Hamilton, 1973.

Beresford, Lord Charles. *The Memoirs of Admiral Lord Charles Beresford.* 2 vols. Boston: Little, Brown, 1914; London: Methuen, 1914.

Besant, Annie. *A Selection of the Social and Political Pamphlets of Annie Besant.* John Saville, ed. New York: Kelley reprint, 1970.

Best, Geoffrey. *Mid-Victorian Britain, 1851-75.* London: Weidenfeld and Nicolson, 1971; New York: Schocken, 1972.

[Blackwood, William], ed. "The Impressment of Seamen, A Review." *Blackwood's Magazine* 20 (November 1826): 745-54.

―――― , ed. "Sir James Graham." *Blackwood's Magazine* 93 (April 1863): 436-57.

Blake, Robert. *The Conservative Party from Peel to Churchill.* London: Eyre and Spottiswoode, 1970.

―――― *Disraeli.* New York: St. Martins, 1966; New York: Doubleday Anchor, 1967.

Blanc, Louis. *Letters on England.* 2 vols. London: 1866-67.
Blanco, Richard L. "Army Recruiting Reforms, 1861-67." *Journal of the Society for Army Historical Research* 46 (Winter 1968): 37-46.
_____ "The Attempted Control of Venereal Disease in the Army of Mid-Victorian England." *Journal of the Society for Army Historical Research* 45 (Winter 1967): 234-41.
_____ "Attempts to Abolish Branding and Flogging in the Army of Victorian England Before 1881." *Journal of the Society for Army Historical Research* 47 (Autumn 1968): 137-45.
Boase, Frederic. *Modern English Biography.* 6 volumes. London: Cass, 1965.
Bodelsen, Carl A. G. *Studies in Mid-Victorian Imperialism.* London: Heinemann reprint, 1960; New York: Fertig reprint, 1968; orig. 1924.
Bolt, Christine. *Victorian Attitudes to Race.* Toronto: University of Toronto Press, 1971; London: Routledge and Paul, 1971.
Bond, Brian James. "The Introduction and Operation of Short Service and Localisation in the British Army, 1868-92." M.A. thesis, King's College, London, 1962.
_____ "The Late-Victorian Army." *History Today* 11 (September 1961): 616-24.
_____ "Recruiting in the Victorian Army, 1870-92." *Victorian Studies* 5 (June 1962): 331-38.
_____ *The Victorian Army and the Staff College, 1854-1914.* New York: Barnes and Noble, 1972; London: Eyre Methuen, 1972.
_____ *Victorian Military Campaigns.* New York: Praeger, 1967.
Bond, Maurice F. *Guide to the Records of Parliament.* London: Her Majesty's Stationery Office, 1971.
Bonner-Smith, D. and Lumby, E. W. R., eds. *The Second China War, 1856-60.* Greenwich: Navy Records Society, 1954.
_____ and Dewar, A. C., eds. *Russian War.* 3 vols. London: Navy Records Society, 1943.
Bonnett, Stanley. *The Price of Admiralty.* London: Robert Hale, 1968.
Bourne, Kenneth. "British Preparations for War with the North." *English Historical Review* 76 (October 1961): 600-32.
_____ *The Foreign Policy of Victorian England, 1830-1902.* New York: Oxford University Press, 1970.
_____ and Watt, D. C., eds. *Studies in International History.* Hamden, Ct.: Archon, 1967; London: Longmans, 1967.

Bowen, Frank Charles. *His Majesty's Coastguard.* London: Hutchinson, 1928.
───── *History of the Royal Naval Reserve.* London: Lloyds, 1926.
Brassey, Lord Thomas. *The British Navy.* 5 vols. London: Longmans, 1882-83.
───── "Manning the Navy." *Brassey's Naval Annual* (1886): 104-106.
───── "Our Reserves of Seamen." London: Longmans, Green, 1872.
───── *Papers and Addresses.* 5 vols. London: Longmans, Green, 1894-95.
Brebner, J. B. "Laissez-Faire and State Intervention in 19th Century Britain." *Journal of Economic History,* supplement 3 (1948): 59-73.
Brent, Harry W. "Three Years in the Royal Naval Reserve." *Journal of the Royal United Service Institution* 18 (1874): 358-82.
Bridge, Sir Cyprian. *Some Recollections.* London: Murray, 1919.
Briggs, Asa. *The Age of Improvement.* New York: Longmans, Green, 1959; New York: McKay, 1962.
───── "Crimean Centenary." *Virginia Quarterly Review* 30 (1954): 542-55.
───── *Victorian People.* New York: Harper and Row, 1963.
───── *William Cobbett.* New York: Oxford University Press, 1967.
Briggs, Sir John Henry. *Naval Administrations, 1827-92.* London: S. Low, 1897.
Brighton, John George. *Admiral of the Fleet Sir Provo Wallis.* London: Hutchinson, 1892.
Brine, Lindesay. "The Best Method of Providing an Efficient Force of Officers and Men for the Navy, Including the Reserves." *Journal of the Royal United Service Institution* 26 (1882): 183-338.
*The British Public Record Office.* Richmond: Virginia State Library, 1960.
Brown, Lucy. *The Board of Trade and the Free Trade Movement, 1830-42.* Oxford: Clarendon Press, 1958.
Bullocke, John Greville. *Sailors' Rebellion.* London: Eyre and Spottiswoode, 1938.
Burn, W. L. *The Age of Equipoise.* New York: Norton, 1964.
Busk, Hans. *The Navies of the World.* New York: Routledge, Warnes, 1859; London: Richmond reprint, 1972.

Butler, Charles. "On the Legality of Impressing Seamen." 3rd ed. *The Pamphleteer* 23 (1824): 225-87.
Butler, Josephine Elizabeth. *Address Delivered at Croydon, July 3, 1871.* London: National Association, 1871.
_____ *Government by Police.* London: Dyer, 1879.
_____ *A Grave Question (the System of Officially Organized Prostitution) that Needs Answering by the Churches of Great Britain.* London: Dyer, 1886.
_____ *Josephine E. Butler.* George W. Johnson and Lucy A. Johnson, eds. Bristol: Arrowsmith, 1909.
_____ *Legislative Restrictions on the Industry of Women, Considered from The Women's Point of View.* London: Matthews, 1874.
_____ *Personal Reminiscences of a Great Crusade.* London: Marshall, 1896.
_____ *Simple Words for Simple Folk, about the Repeal of the Contagious Diseases Acts.* Bristol: Arrowsmith, n.d.
_____ *Social Purity.* London: Morgan and Scott, 1879.
_____ *Some Thought on the Present Aspect of the Crusade against the State Regulation of Vice.* Liverpool: Brakell, 1874.
"By a Captain, R.N." (pseud). "Hints on Education and Manning the Navy." Bath: Hayward and Payne, 1855.
Caborne, W. F. "The Royal Naval Reserve." *Journal of the Royal United Service Institution* 33 (January 1889): 41-67.
Callender, Sir Geoffrey Arthur R. *Bibliography of Naval History.* 2 parts. London: Historical Association, 1924-25.
_____ "An Educational Centenary: December 1838-December 1938." *Mariner's Mirror* 25 (January 1939): 11-23.
_____ and Hinsley, F. H. *The Naval Side of British History.* Boston: Little, Brown, 1924; London: Chatto and Windus, 1960.
Carlisle, Henry C. *Voyage to the First of December.* New York: Putnam, 1972.
"A Cautious (and therefore a true) Friend to the Sea-Service," (pseud.). "Corporal Punishment in the Mercantile Marine." *Nautical Magazine* (1843): 367-68.
[Chambers, William and Chambers, Robert], eds. "The Naval Prison at Lewes." *Chambers Journal* 51 (6 June 1874): 361-63.
[Chapman, John]. "Our Seamen." *Westminster Review* n.s. 43 (April 1873): 504-28.
_____ "Prostitution: Governmental Experiments in Controlling It." *Westminster Review* n.s. 37 (January 1870): 119-79.

———. "Prostitution: How to Deal with It." *Westminster Review* n.s. 37 (April 1870): 477-535.
Checkland, S. G. *The Rise of Industrial Society in England, 1815-85.* London: Longmans, 1964.
Chesney, Kellow. *The Victorian Underworld,* (English title: *The Anti-Society.*) Boston: Gambit, 1970; New York: Schocken, 1972.
Childers, Edmund Spencer Eardley. *The Life and Correspondence of the Right Honorable Hugh C. E. Childers, 1827-96.* 2 vols. London: John Murray, 1901.
Chivers, Kenneth. "Henry Jones versus the Admiralty." *History Today* 10 (April 1960): 247-54.
Claver, Scott. *Under the Lash.* London: Torchstream, 1954.
Clode, Charles M. *The Administration of Justice under Military and Martial Law.* 2nd ed. London: John Murray, 1874.
Clokie, Hugh McDowall and Robinson, J. William. *Royal Commissions of Inquiry.* Stanford: Stanford University Press, 1937.
Clowes, Sir William Laird. *The Royal Navy, A History.* 7 vols. London: S. Low and Marston, 1897-1903.
Cohen, Emmeline Waley. *Growth of the British Civil Service.* New York: Norton, 1940; London: Allen and Unwin, 1941.
Cole, Arthur Harrison, ed. *A Finding-List of British Royal Commission Reports, 1860-1935.* Cambridge: Harvard University Press, 1935.
Cole, G. D. H. and Postgate, Raymond. *The British People, 1746-1938.* New York: Barnes and Noble, 1961.
Colgate, Hugh Arthur. "Trincomalee and the East Indies Squadron, 1746-1844." M.A. thesis, University of London, 1959.
Colledge, James Joseph. *Ships of the Royal Navy.* 2 vols. New York: Kelley, 1969; London: Newton Abbot, 1969.
Collingridge, J. H., et al. *Catalogue of an Exhibition of Naval Records at the Public Record Office.* London: His Majesty's Stationery Office, 1950.
Collinson, Joseph. *Facts about Flogging.* Revised ed. London: Fifield, 1905.
Colomb, Philip Howard. *Fifteen Years of Naval Retirement.* Portsmouth: Griffin, 1886.
———. *The Memoirs of Admiral Sir Astley Cooper Key.* London: Methuen, 1898.

———. *Slave-Catching in the Indian Ocean.* New York: Longmans, Green 1873; New York: Negro University Press reprint, 1969.

Colson, Percy, ed. *Lord Goschen and His Friends.* London: Hutchinson, n.d.

Colvile, R. F. "The Baltic as a Theatre of War: the Campaign of 1854." *Journal of the Royal United Service Institution* 86 (February 1941): 72-80.

———. "Naval Personnel in the XVIIIth Century." *Journal of the Royal United Service Institution* 87 (1942): 160-76.

———. "The Navy and the Crimean War." *Journal of the Royal United Service Institution* 85 (1940): 73-78.

Cominos, Peter T. "Late-Victorian Sexual Respectability and the Social System." *International Review of Social History* 8, Parts I and II, (1963): 18-48, 216-50.

"Commander, R.N.," (pseud), ed. *Crime and Punishment in the Navy, A.D. 1862-63.* Portsea: Griffin, 1866.

Compton, Piers. *Cardigan of Balaclava.* London: Hale, 1972.

Conacher, James B. *The Aberdeen Coalition, 1852-55.* New York: Cambridge University Press, 1968.

———. *The Peelites and the Party System, 1846-52.* Hamden, Ct.: Archon, 1972; London: David and Charles, 1972.

"The Contagious Diseases Act." *The Saturday Review* 29 (1 January 1870): 11-12.

Corbett, Julian S. "Education in the Navy." *Monthly Review* 6 (March 1902): 34-49.

Cornewall-Jones, R. J. *The British Merchant Service.* London: Low, Marston, 1898; London: Cornmarket Press reprint, 1969.

———. *Ships, Sailors, and the Sea.* London: Cassell, 1887.

"Corporal Punishments, and Penal Reformation." *Frasers Magazine* 71 (February 1865): 154-66.

Costigan, Giovanni. *A History of Modern Ireland.* New York: Pegasus, 1969.

Cotton, Sir Harry Evan Auguste. *East Indiamen.* London: Batchworth, 1949.

Course, A. *The Merchant Navy.* London: Muller, 1963.

Cox, John George, ed. *Cox and the Ju Ju Coast.* Jersey: Ellison, 1968.

Creswell, William Rooke. *Close to the Wind.* London: Heinemann, 1965.

Cromwell, Valerie. "Interpretations of Nineteenth Century Administration: An Analysis." *Victorian Studies* 9 (March 1966): 245-55.

Crow, Duncan. *The Victorian Woman*. London: Allen and Unwin, 1971.

Cunningham, Hugh. *The Volunteer Force*. Hamden, Ct.: Shoe String Press, 1976; London: Croom-Helm, 1976.

"D." (pseud). *A Clean Anchor: The Board of Admiralty*. 2nd ed. London: n.p., 1871.

Daniell, J. F. "Discipline: Its Importance to an Armed Force and the Best Means of Promoting and Maintaining It." *Journal of the Royal United Service Institution* 33 (1889): 287-470.

David, Leon. "An Episode in Naval Justice." *Case and Comment* 62 (July 1952): 20-25.

Day, Sir Archibald. *The Admiralty Hydrographic Service, 1795-1919*. London: Her Majesty's Stationery Office, 1967.

"Death of Joseph Hume, Esq., M.P." *Littell's Living Age* 2nd ser., 9 (14 April 1855): 83-85.

"The Debate on the Contagious Diseases Acts." *The Saturday Review* 29 (28 May 1870): 701-702.

DeVico, Anthony J. "Evolution of Military Law." *The J.A.G. Journal* 21 (December 1966): 63-68.

Dewar, Kenneth Gilbert Balmain. *The Navy from Within*. London: Gollancz, 1939.

DeWatteville, H. *The British Soldier*. New York: Putnams, 1955.

Dickens, Sir Gerald. *The Dress of the British Sailor*. London: Her Majesty's Stationery Office, 1957.

Dingle, A. E. "Drink and Working-Class Living Standards in Britain, 1870-1914." *Economic History Review* 2nd ser., 25 (November 1972): 608-22.

DiRoma, Edward and Rosenthal, Joseph A., compilers. *A Numerical Finding List of British Command Papers Published, 1833-1961/62*. New York: New York Public Library, 1967.

"Dirt-Pies." *Saturday Review* 29 (26 February 1870): 277-78.

Divine, Arthur Durham (pseud., Divine, David). *Mutiny at Invergordon*. London: Macdonald, 1970.

Dixon, Conrad. "Hard Life and Times of Henry Moffat, Seaman." *Mariner's Mirror* 59 (May 1973): 193-203.

Don, W. G. "Recruits and Recruiting." *Journal of the Royal United Service Institution* 33 (1889): 827-53.

Douglas-Home, Charles. *Britain's Reserve Forces*. London: Royal United Service Institution, n.d. (1970?).
DuBois, W. E. B. *The Suppression of the African Slave-Trade to the U. S. of A., 1638-1870*. Harvard Historical Series, 1896. New York: Schocken, 1969.
Dugan, James. *The Great Mutiny*. New York: Putnams, 1965; New York: New American Library, 1967.
Dutcher, George Matthew, et al. *Guide to Historical Literature*. New York: Macmillan, 1931; reprint, 1949.
Dyos, Harold J. and Wolff, Michael, eds. *The Victorian City: Images and Realities*. 2 vols. Boston: Routledge and Paul, 1973.
Earle, Edward Mead, ed. *Makers of Modern Strategy*. Princeton: Princeton University Press, 1941; New York: Atheneum, 1966.
Eder, Richard. "Caning in British Schools." *New York Times*, 15 October 1972, p. A-3.
Edgell, Sir John. *Sea Surveys*. London: Her Majesty's Stationery Office, 1965.
Egerton, Mrs. Fred. *Admiral of the Fleet Sir Geoffrey Phipps Hornby*. Edinburgh: Blackwood, 1896.
Elliot, Arthur Ralph Douglas. *The Life of Lord Goschen, First Viscount Goschen, 1831-1907*. 2 vols. London: Longmans, Green, 1911.
[Elliot, G. A.] "Reform in the Navy." *Cornhill Magazine* (January 1861): 90-94.
Elton, Geoffrey R. *Modern Historians on British History, 1485-1945*. Ithaca, N.Y.: Cornell University Press, 1970.
*Encyclopaedia Britannica*. 9th ed. New York: Allen, 1890.
Ensor, Robert Charles Kirkwood. *England, 1870-1914*. London: Oxford University Press, 1949.
Erickson, Arvel B. "Abolition of Purchase in the British Army." *Military Affairs* 23 (Summer 1959): 65-76.
――― *Edward T. Cardwell: Peelite*. Philadelphia: American Philosophical Society, 1959.
――― *The Public Career of Sir James Graham*. Cleveland: Western Reserve University Press, 1952.
Fahey, David M. "Temperance and the Liberal Party—Lord Peel's Report, 1899." *Journal of British Studies* 10 (May 1971): 132-59.
Fanshawe, Alice E. J. *Admiral Sir Edward Gennys Fanshawe*. London: Spottiswoode, 1904.

Field, C. "The Marines in the Great Naval Mutinies, 1797-1802." *Journal of the Royal United Service Institution* 62 (1917): 720-46.

Fielden, Kenneth. "Samuel Smiles and Self-Help." *Victorian Studies* 12 (December 1968): 155-76.

Finer, Samuel Edward. *The Life and Times of Sir Edwin Chadwick.* London: Methuen, 1952.

Finlason, William Francis. *Commentaries upon Martial Law.* London: Stevens, 1867.

Fisher, Sir Frederic William. *Naval Reminiscences.* London: Muller, 1938.

Fisher, Lord John. *Memories and Records.* 2 vols. New York: George Dorna, 1920.

"Flogging Soldiers." *Tait's Edinburgh Magazine* old ser., (August 1832): 635-36.

Forbes, Archibald. "Flogging in the Army." *The Nineteenth Century* 6 (October 1879): 604-14.

Ford, Percy and Ford, G. *A Guide to Parliamentary Papers.* 2nd ed. Oxford: Blackwell, 1955; 3rd ed., 1972.

———. *Hansard's Catalogue and Breviate of Parliamentary Papers, 1696-1834.* Reprint. Oxford: Blackwell, 1953.

Forester, Cecil Scott, ed. *The Adventures of John Wetherall.* New York: Doubleday, 1954.

Fortescue, John W. *History of the British Army.* 13 vols. London: 1889-1930.

Foulke, Robert D. "Life in the Dying World of Sail, 1870-1910." *Journal of British Studies* 3 (November 1963): 105-36.

Fraser, Sir Thomas. "A Century of Empire." *Fortnightly Review* 77 (1905): 1112-25.

Fremantle, Sir Edmund Robert. *The Navy as I Have Known It, 1849-99.* London: Cassell, 1904.

Furber, Elizabeth Chapin, ed. *Changing Views on British History.* Cambridge: Harvard University Press, 1966.

Gardiner, A. G. *Life of Sir William Harcourt.* 2 vols. London: Constable, 1923.

Gardiner, Leslie. *The British Admiralty.* London: Blackwood, 1968.

Gardner, G. H. "On the Formation of Reserves of Officers and Seamen for the Royal Navy, and the Evils and Inadequacy of Impressment to Provide the Same." *Journal of the Royal United Service Institution* 15 (1871): 601-42.

Gardner, James Anthony. *Above and Under Hatches.* London: Batchworth Press, 1955.
Gaynor, James K. "The French Code of Military Justice: A Comparison with the Uniform Code of Military Justice." *George Washington Law Review* 22 (1954): 318-36.
Gerry, Elbridge T. "Must We Have the Cat-o'-Nine Tails?" *The North American Review* 160 (1895): 318-24.
Gillespie, T. P. "The Plymouth Port Orders of 1858." *Mariner's Mirror* 46 (February 1960): 54-60.
Giuseppi, M. S. *Guide to the Contents of the Public Record Office.* 2 vols. London: His Majesty's Stationery Office, 1923-24.
[Glascock, William Nugent]. *Naval Sketch-book.* 2 vols. London: Colburn, 1826; Philadelphia: n.p., 1835.
Gosnell, Harold F. "British Royal Commissions of Inquiry." *Political Science Quarterly* 49 (1934): 84-118.
Graham, Gerald S. "By Steam to India." *History Today* 14 (May 1964): 301-12.
_____ *Great Britain in the Indian Ocean.* London: Oxford University Press, 1967; New York: Oxford University Press, 1968.
_____ and Humphreys, R. A., eds. *The Navy and South America, 1807-23.* London: Navy Records Society, 1962.
_____ *The Politics of Naval Supremacy.* New York: Cambridge University Press, 1965.
_____. *Sea Power and British North America, 1783-1820.* Cambridge: Harvard University Press, 1941; New York: Greenwood reprint, 1969.
Gray, Ernest A. "The Stone Frigates of Sebastopol: The Navy's Role on Land and Sea in the Crimean Campaign." *History Today* 19 (June 1969): 388-96.
Gray, Thomas. *Under the Red Ensign.* London: Simpkin, Marshall, 1878.
Great Britain, Admiralty. *Admiralty Memorandum on Naval Court-Martial Procedure.* BR 11/1958. 2nd ed. London: Her Majesty's Stationery Office, 1958.
_____, Admiralty. *Black Book of the Admiralty.* 4 vols. London: Longmans, 1871-76.
_____, Admiralty. *Committee to Consider the Administration of Justice under the Naval Discipline Act.* 2 vols. London: Her Majesty's Stationery Office, 1950-51.

_____, Admiralty. *Committee on Venereal Diseases in the Army and Navy*. London: Her Majesty's Stationery Office, 1867.

_____, Admiralty. *Naval Courts-Martial Returns*. (various).

_____, Admiralty. *The Queen's Regulations for the Government of H.M. Naval Service*. London: Her Majesty's Stationery Office, 1844.

_____, Admiralty. *The Queen's Regulations and the Admiralty Instructions*. London: Her Majesty's Stationery Office, 1862.

_____, Admiralty. *The Queen's Regulations for the Royal Navy*. London: Her Majesty's Stationery Office, 1967.

_____, Central Office of Information. *The Treatment of Offenders in Britain*. London: Her Majesty's Stationery Office, 1960.

_____, Her Majesty's Stationery Office. *British National Archives*. London: Her Majesty's Stationery Office, n.d.

_____, Home Department. *Report of the Departmental Committee on Corporal Punishment*. London: His Majesty's Stationery Office, 1938.

_____, Home Office. *Corporal Punishment Report*. London: Her Majesty's Stationery Office, n.d.

_____, National Maritime Museum. *Journals and Diaries, Logs*.

_____, National Maritime Museum. *Personal Papers*. Admirals Sir Henry Codrington, Sir Alexander Milne, and Sir Geoffrey Phipps Hornby.

_____, Orders-in-Council. *The Orders in Council and Some of the Acts of Parliament for the Regulation of the Naval Service*. 5 vols. London: Her Majesty's Stationery Office, 1856-88.

_____, Parliament. *A Bibliography of Parliamentary Debates of Great Britain*. London: Her Majesty's Stationery Office, 1956.

_____, Parliament. *British Sessional Papers*. New York: Readex Microprint, 1966.

_____, Parliament. *Hansard's Parliamentary Debates*. New York: Readex Microprint, 1962-63.

_____, Parliament, House of Commons. *Catalogue of Parliamentary Papers, 1801-1900*. London: King, n.d.

_____, Parliament, House of Commons. *General Index to the Accounts and Papers*. London: His Majesty's Stationery Office, 1938.

_____, Parliament. *Report of the Royal Commission upon the Administration and Operation of the Contagious Diseases Acts (Not Con-*

cerned with Animals). London: Her Majesty's Stationery Office, 1871.

―――, Parliament. *Report on the Discipline and Management of the Military Prisons, 1857.* London: Her Majesty's Stationery Office, 1858.

―――, Parliament. *Report of the Commissioners: Manning the Navy.* London: Her Majesty's Stationery Office, 1871.

―――, Public Record Office. *Admiralty Courts-Martial Records.* (Adm 1).

―――, Public Record Office. *Admiralty Digests: Heads and Sections.* London: Public Record Office, 1935.

―――, Public Record Office. *Admiralty Digests: IND Numbers.*

―――, Public Record Office. *Admiralty In-Letters* (Adm 1).

―――, Public Record Office. *Summary of Records.* 2 vols. London: Her Majesty's Stationery Office, 1962-69.

Grey, Sir Frederick William. *On the Organization of the Navy.* London: n.p., 1860.

―――. *Suggestions for Improving the Character of Our Merchant Seamen and for Providing an Efficient Naval Reserve.* London: n.p., 1873.

Griffiths, Anselm John. *Impressment Fully Considered.* London: Norie, 1826.

Grisewood, Harman, ed. *Ideas and Beliefs of the Victorians.* New York: Dutton, 1949.

Guy, William Augustus. "On the Sanitary Condition of the British Army; and Especially on the Want of Space in Barracks." *Journal of the Royal United Service Institution* 2 (1858): 1-34.

Haight, Gordon S. "Male Chastity in the Nineteenth Century." *Contemporary Review* 219 (November 1971): 252-62.

Halevy, Elie. *A History of the English People in the Nineteenth Century.* 6 vols. Trans.: E. I. Watkin and D. A. Barker. New York: Barnes and Noble, 1924-47.

Hammond, John Lawrence and Hammond, Barbara. *James Stansfeld.* London: Longmans, Green, 1932.

Hannay, David. *Naval Courts-Martial.* London: Cambridge University Press, 1914.

Harper, Lawrence Averell. *The Navigation Laws.* New York: Octagon, 1964.

Harrison, Brian. "Drink and Sobriety in England, 1815-72: A

Critical Bibliography." *International Review of Social History* 12 (1967): 204-76.
―――― *Drink and the Victorians.* Pittsburgh: University of Pittsburgh Press, 1971; London: Faber and Faber, 1971.
―――― "Drunkards and Reformers: Early Victorian Temperance Tracts." *History Today* 13 (March, 1963): 178-85.
―――― "The Power of Drink." *Listener* 81 (13 February 1969): 204-206.
―――― "Underneath the Victorians." *Victorian Studies* 10 (March 1967): 239-62.
―――― "A World of Which We Had No Conception: Liberalism and the English Temperance Press, 1830-72." *Victorian Studies* 13 (December 1969): 125-58.
Harrison, John Fletcher Clews. *The Early Victorians, 1832-51.* New York: Praeger, 1971; London: Weidenfeld and Nicolson, 1971.
―――― *Learning and Living, 1790-1960.* Toronto: University of Toronto Press, 1961.
―――― "Recent Writing on the History of Victorian England." *Victorian Studies* 8 (March 1965): 263-70.
―――― "The Victorian Gospel of Success." *Victorian Studies* 1 (December 1957): 155-64.
Hart, Jenifer. "Nineteenth-Century Social Reform: A Tory Interpretation of History." *Past and Present* 31 (July 1965): 39-61.
Hartman, Mary and Banner, Lois W. *Clio's Consciousness Raised.* New York: Harper and Row, 1974.
Hayford, Harrison, ed. *The Somers Mutiny Affair.* Englewood Cliffs, N.J.: Prentice-Hall, 1959.
Herwig, Holger H. *The German Naval Officer Corps.* London: Oxford University Press, 1973.
Heasman, Kathleen Joan. *Evangelicals in Action.* London: Bles, 1962.
Hickman, William, ed. *Reports and Opinions of Officers on the Acts of Parliament and Admiralty Regulations for Maintaining Discipline and Good Order in the Fleet, Passed and Issued since the Year 1860.* London: Harrison, 1867.
―――― *A Treatise on the Law and Practice of Naval Courts-Martial.* London: Murray, 1851.
Higham, Robin and Wing, Karen Cox, eds. *The Consolidated Author and Subject Index to the Journal of the Royal United Service Institution, 1857-1963.* Ann Arbor, Mi.: University Microfilms, 1964.

Higham, Robin, ed. *A Guide to the Sources of British Military History.* Berkeley: University of California Press, 1971; London: Routledge and Paul, 1971.

Hill, Berkeley. "Statistical Results of the Contagious Diseases Acts." *Journal of the Royal Statistical Society* 33 (1870): 463-85.

Hill, L. M. "The Admiralty Circuit of 1591: Some Comments on the Relations between Central Government and Local Interests." *Historical Journal* 14 (1971): 148-70.

Himmelfarb, Gertrude. "The Writing of Social History: Recent Studies of Nineteenth-Century England." *Journal of British Studies* 11 (November 1971): 148-70.

Hinde, Richard Standish. *The British Penal System, 1773-1950.* London: Duckworth, 1951.

Hirst, Francis Wrigley. *The Six Panics and Other Essays.* London: Methuen, 1913.

[Hodgskin, Thomas]. "The Abolition of Impressment: Review Article." *Edinburgh Review* 41 (1824): 154-81.

Hogg, Peter C. *The African Slave Trade and Its Suppression.* London: Cass, 1974.

Hollis, Patricia, ed. *Pressure from Without in Early Victorian England.* New York: St. Martins, 1974.

[Holman, Tom]. *Life in the Royal Navy.* 3rd ed. London: Sampson Low, 1892.

Horan, Leo F. S. "Flogging in the United States Navy: Unfamiliar Facts Regarding Its Origin and Abolition." *U.S. Naval Institute Proceedings* 76 (September 1950): 969-75.

Houghton, Walter E. *The Victorian Frame of Mind, 1830-70.* New Haven: Yale University Press, 1964.

―――, Altholz, Josef L., et al. *The Wellesley Index to Victorian Periodicals, 1824-1900.* 2 vols. Toronto: University of Toronto Press, 1966-73.

Hovgaard, William. *Modern History of Warships.* London: Spon, 1920.

Howard, Derek Lionel. *John Howard: Prison Reformer.* New York: Archer House, 1958; London: Johnson, 1958.

―――. "Transportation and Imprisonment." *Listener* 76: 722-74.

Howe, George Frederick, et al. *Guide to Historical Literature.* New York: Macmillan, 1961.

Howitt, William. "Military Flogging." *The People's Journal* 2 (1847): 78-79.

Hugill, Stan. *Sailortown*. London: Routledge and Paul, 1967.
Hunt, William R. "Nautical Autobiography in the Age of Sail." *Mariner's Mirror* 57 (May 1971): 135-42.
Hutchinson, J. R. *The Press-Gang Afloat and Ashore*. London: Nash, 1913.
Hyde, H. M. *The Love That Dared Not Speak Its Name*. Boston: Little, Brown, 1970.
Iliasu, A. A. "The Cobden-Chevalier Commercial Treaty of 1860." *Historical Journal* 14 (March 1970): 67-98.
Imlah, Albert Henry. *The Economic Elements in the Pax Britannica*. Cambridge: Harvard University Press, 1958; New York: Russell and Russell reprint, 1969.
"The Inner Life of a Man-of-War." *The Cornhill Magazine* 7 (1863): 172-88.
Isichei, Elizabeth. *Victorian Quakers*. New York: Oxford University Press, 1970.
Ives, D. B. "Billy Budd and the Articles of War." *American Literature* 34 (March 1962): 31-39.
Jameson, Sir William Scarlett. *The Fleet That Jack Built*. New York: Harcourt, Brace, 1962; London: Hart-Davis, 1962.
Johnson, Roy Frank. *The Royal George*. London: Charles Knight, 1971.
Johnson, William Branch. *The English Prison Hulks*. London: Phillimore, 1970.
Jones, Philip D. "The British Army in the Age of Reform, 1830-54." Ph.D. dissertation, Duke University, 1968.
Jones, Stephen. "Blood Red Roses: The Supply of Merchant Seamen in the Nineteenth Century." *Mariner's Mirror* 58 (November 1972): 429-44.
Jones, Wilbur Devereux. *Lord Derby and Victorian Conservatism*. Athens, Ga.: University of Georgia Press, 1956; London: Basil Blackwell, 1956.
Karsten, Peter Daggett. *The Naval Aristocracy*. Riverside, N.J.: Free Press, 1971.
Keating, P. J. *The Working Classes in Victorian Fiction*. New York: Barnes and Noble, 1971; London: Routledge and Paul, 1971.
Kelly, Mrs. Tom. *From the Fleet in the Fifties*. London: Hurst and Blackett, 1902.
Kemp, Peter Kemp. *The British Sailor*. London: Dent, 1970.

_____. *Prize Money.* Aldershot: Gale and Polden, 1946.
Kenworthy, Joseph Montague. *The Real Navy.* London: Hutchinson, 1932.
Keppel, Henry. *A Sailor's Life under Four Sovereigns.* 3 vols. London: Macmillan, 1899.
Kerr, James Lennox and Granville, Wilfred. *The R.N.V.R.* London: Harrap, 1957.
Kinglake, Arthur William. *The Invasion of the Crimea.* 6 vols. London: 1863-80.
Kitson Clark, George S. R. *The Making of Victorian England.* Cambridge: Harvard University Press, 1962; New York: Atheneum, 1967.
_____. "Statesmen in Disguise: Reflections on the History of the Neutrality of the Civil Service." *Historical Journal* 2 (1959): 19-39.
Kuehl, Warren F. *Dissertations in History.* Lexington: University of Kentucky Press, 1965.
Laffin, John. *Jack Tar.* London: Cassell, 1969.
_____. *Tommy Atkins.* London: Cassell, 1966.
Lambert, Royston J. *Sir John Simon, 1816-1904.* London: MacGibbon, 1963.
Langley, Harold D. *Social Reform in the United States Navy.* Chicago: University of Illinois Press, 1967.
Lathrop, Constance. "Grog: Its Origin and Use in the United States Navy." *U.S. Naval Institute Proceedings* 61 (March 1935): 377-80.
Laughton, Sir John Knox. "The National Study of Naval History." *Transactions of the Royal Historical Society* n.s., 12 (1898): 81-94.
_____. *Studies in Naval History—Biographies.* London: Longmans, 1887.
Laughton, L. G. Carr. "The Preamble to the Articles of War." *Mariner's Mirror* 7 (March 1921): 82-86.
Lawson, Robert. "The Operation of the Contagious Diseases Acts among the Troops in the United Kingdom." *Journal of the Royal Statistical Society* 54 (1891): 31-69.
Leech, Samuel. *Thirty Years from Home.* London: H. Collins, 1851; Boston: Tappan, 1843; New York: Abbatt reprint, 1909.
Lewis, Michael Arthur. *England's Sea Officers.* London: Allen and Unwin, 1939.

———. "An Eye-Witness at Petropaulovski, 1854." *Mariner's Mirror* 44 (November 1963): 265-72.
———. *The Navy in Transition, 1814-64.* Mystic, Ct.: Lawrence Verry, 1965; London: Hodder and Stoughton, 1965.
———. *The Navy of Britain.* London: Allen and Unwin, 1948.
———. *A Social History of the Navy, 1793-1815.* London: Allen and Unwin, 1960.
———. *Spithead.* London: Allen and Unwin, 1972.
Lindsay, William Schaw. *Confirmation of Admiralty Mismanagement.* London: E. Wilson, 1855.
———. *History of Merchant Shipping and Ancient Commerce.* 4 vols. London: Sampson Low, 1874-76.
———. *Manning the Royal Navy and the Mercantile Marine.* London: Pewtress, 1877.
Lindsay-MacDougall, K. F. *A Guide to the Manuscripts at the National Maritime Museum.* Greenwich: National Maritime Museum, 1960.
"Lines on the Lash: To the Queen." *Punch* 11 (1846): 71.
*List of Admiralty Records Preserved in the Public Record Office.* New York: Kraus, 1963.
Lloyd, Charles Christopher. *The British Seaman, 1200-1860.* London: Collins, 1968; Cranbury, N.J.: Fairleigh Dickinson University Press, 1970.
———. *Captain Marryat and the Old Navy.* London: Longmans, 1939.
———. "Dr. Baikie and the Niger." *History Today* 21 (October 1971): 740-46.
———. *The Health of Seamen.* London: Navy Records Society, 1965.
———. *Lord Cochrane.* London: Longmans, 1947.
——— and Coulter, Jack L. S. *Medicine and the Navy, 1200-1900.* 4 vols. Edinburgh: Livingston, 1957-63.
———. *Mr. Barrow of the Admiralty.* London: Collins, 1970.
———. "The Mutiny of the *Nereide*." *Mariner's Mirror* 54 (August 1968): 245-52.
———. *The Nation and the Navy.* New York: Macmillan, 1954; London: Cresset reprint, 1961; reissue, 1965.
———. *The Navy and the Slave Trade.* New York: Longmans, Green, 1949; London: Cass, 1968.

———. "New Light on the Mutiny at the Nore." *Mariner's Mirror* 46 (1960): 286-95.

———. "The Press Gang and the Law." *History Today* 17 (October 1967): 683-90.

———. "The Royal Naval Colleges at Portsmouth and Greenwich." *Mariner's Mirror* 52 (May 1966): 145-56.

———. *St. Vincent and Camperdown*. New York: Macmillan, 1963.

———. *Search for the Niger*. London: Collins, 1973.

———. "The Torpedo." *History Today* 1 (August 1956): 552-55.

Lloyd, William H. "Health of the Navy: Report for 1884—presented to Parliament." *Brassey's Naval Annual* (1886): 451-58.

[Lockwood, John A.] "Flogging in the Navy." *United States Magazine and Democratic Review* 25 (1849): 97-115, 225-42, 318-37, 417-32.

Logan, William. *The Great Social Evil*. London: Hodder and Stoughton, 1871.

Longmate, Norman. *The Water-Drinkers*. London: Hamilton, 1968.

Luvaas, Jay. *The Education of an Army*. Chicago: University of Chicago Press, 1964.

Lyne, Sir Thomas J. Spence. *Something About a Sailor*. London: Jarrolds, 1940.

MacCoby, Simon. *English Radicalism*. 6 vols. London: Allen and Unwin, 1935-61.

Mccord, Norman. "The Impress Service in Northeast England during the Napoleonic War." *Mariner's Mirror* 54 (May 1968): 163-80.

———. "A Naval Scandal of 1871: The Loss of H.M.S. *Megaera*." *Mariner's Mirror* 57 (May 1971): 115-34.

MacDonagh, Oliver. "The Nineteenth-Century Revolution in Government: A Reappraisal." *Historical Journal* 1 (1958): 52-67.

———. *A Pattern of Government Growth, 1800-60*. London; MacGibbon, 1961.

MacDonald, D. F. *The Age of Transition*. New York: St. Martins, 1967.

MacDonald, John Denis. *Outlines of Naval Hygiene*. London: Smith, Elder, 1881.

MacDonald, Robert H. "The Frightful Consequences of Onanism: Notes on the History of Delusion." *Journal of the History of Ideas* 28 (1967): 423-31.

McGregor, O. R. *Divorce in England*. London: Heinemann, 1957.
———. "The Social Position of Women in England, 1850-1914: A Bibliography." *British Journal of Sociology* 6 (March 1955): 48-60.
———. "Social Research and Social Policy in the Nineteenth Century." *British Journal of Sociology* 8 (1957): 146-57.
MacIntyre, Donald and Bathe, Basil W. *The Man-of-War*. London: Methuen, 1969.
MacKay, Ruddock. *Fisher of Kilverstone*. New York: Oxford University Press, 1973.
MacLeod, R. M. "The Edge of Hope: Social Policy and Chronic Alcoholism, 1870-1900." *Journal of the History of Medicine* (July, 1967).
Madden, Lionel. *How to Find Out About the Victorian Period*. Oxford: Pergamon, 1970.
Maestro, Marcello T. *Cesare Beccaria and the Origins of Penal Reform*. Philadelphia: Temple University Press, 1973.
———. *Voltaire and Beccaria as Reformers of Criminal Law*. New York: Columbia University Press, 1942; New York: Octagon reprint, 1972.
Maison, Margaret. "Insignificant Objects of Desire." *Listener* 86 (22 July 1971): 105-107.
Mallock, William Hurrell and Ramsden, Lady Guendolen, eds. *Letters, Remains, and Memoirs of Edward Adolphus Seymour, Twelfth Duke of Somerset, K.G.* London: Richard Bentley, 1893.
Mannix, Daniel Pratt and Cowley, Malcolm. *Black Cargoes*. New York: Viking, 1965.
Mansergh, Nicholas. *Ireland in the Age of Reform and Revolution*. Toronto: University of Toronto Press, 1965.
Manwaring, George Ernest. *A Bibliography of British Naval History*. London: Routledge, 1930; London: Conway Maritime, 1970.
——— and Dobree, Bonamy. *The Floating Republic*. New York: Harcourt, Brace, 1935; London: Geoffrey Bles, 1935.
Marcus, Geoffrey Jules. *The Age of Nelson*, Vol. II of *A Naval History of England*. London: Allen and Unwin, 1971; New York: Viking, 1971.
Marcus, Steven. *The Other Victorians*. New York: Bantam, 1966; London: Weidenfeld and Nicolson, 1966.
Marder, Arthur J. *The Anatomy of British Sea Power*. New York: Knopf, 1940; New York: Octagon reprint, 1972.

———. *Fear God and Dread Nought*. 3 vols. London: Cape, 1952-59.
———. *From the Dreadnought to Scapa Flow*. 5 vols. London: Oxford University Press, 1961-70.
Markham, Sir Albert H. *The Life of Sir Clements R. Markham*. London: John Murray, 1917.
Marryat, Frederick. *Suggestions for the Abolition of the Present State of Impressment in the Naval Service*. London: Richardson, 1822.
———. *Works*. 5 vols. Hartford: Andrus, 1849.
Martin, B. Kingsley. *The Triumph of Lord Palmerston*. London: Allen and Unwin, 1924.
[Martin, Sir William Fanshawe]. "The Admiralty." *Blackwood's Magazine* 107 (June 1870): 763-71; 2nd ed., Portsmouth: Griffin, 1870.
———. *Memorandum on Corporal Punishment*. Portsmouth: Griffin, 1881.
"Master of a British Merchant Ship," (pseud.). "On the Defective State of Discipline of the Merchant Service: Shewing the Loss Occasioned to the Owners Thereby." *Nautical Magazine* 44 (October 1835): 586-96.
Melada, Ivan. *The Captain of Industry in English Fiction, 1821-71*. Albuquerque: University of New Mexico Press, 1970.
Melville, Herman. *Billy Budd, Sailor*. Chicago: University of Chicago Press, 1962.
———. *White-Jacket*. Boston: Page, 1892.
Mends, Bowne Stilon. *Life of Admiral Sir W. R. Mends, 1812-97*. London: Murray, 1899.
Midwinter, Eric. *Nineteenth-Century Education*. New York: Harper and Row, 1971.
———. *Victorian Social Reform*. New York: Harper and Row, 1971.
Miles, E. and Miles, Lawford. *An Epitome, Historical and Statistical, Descriptive of the Royal Naval Service of England*. London: Ackermann, 1841.
Milne, A. T., comp. *Writings on British History, 1901-33*. 12 vols. London: Jonathen Cape, 1968-70.
Milroy, G. *The Health of the Navy Considered*. London: Hardwicke, 1862.
Minchinton, W. E. "Michael Oppenheim, 1853-1927." *Mariner's Mirror* 54 (February 1968): 85-93.
*Minute by the First Lord of the Admiralty (H. C. E. Childers), with*

Reference to H.M.S. Captain, with the Minutes of the Proceedings of the Court Martial, and the Board Minute Thereon. London: Eyre and Spottiswoode, 1870.

Montagu, Victor A. *A Middy's Recollections, 1853-60.* London: Black, 1898.

Moody, J. M. "Recruiting for Her Majesty's Service." *Journal of the Royal United Service Institution* 29 (1885): 565-629.

Moore, E. Majorie. *Adventure in the Royal Navy.* Liverpool: (private publication), 1964.

Moore, W. Harrison. "Executive Commissions of Inquiry." *Columbia Law Review* 13 (1913): 500-23.

Moorehead, Alan. *Darwin and the Beagle.* New York: Harper and Row, 1969; London: Hamilton, 1969.

Morris, James. "The Royal Navy." *U.S. Naval Institute Proceedings* 98 (March 1972): 63-73.

———. "A View of the Royal Navy." *Encounter* 40 (March 1973): 15-37.

Murray, Oswyn. "The Admiralty." *Mariner's Mirror* 23, 24, and 25 (series in 9 installments: January 1937 - July 1939).

Napier, E. Elers. *Life and Correspondence of Admiral Sir Charles Napier.* 2 vols. London: Hurst and Blackett, 1862.

"Naval and Marine Gazette." *Nautical Magazine* (1843): 207.

"Naval Officer." (pseud). "The Feeding of Seamen and Marines on Board H.M. Ships and Those in the Navy of the U.S." *Journal of the Royal United Service Institution* 35 (November 1891): 1149-51.

"Naval Officers." (pseud). *The White Ensign.* London: Roy, 1896.

Neale, H. I. Vansittart. "Manning the Navy—Seamen." *Naval Library Pamphlets* 3 (February 1883): 253-56.

"A Necessarian." (pseud). "The Contagious Diseases Acts and the Royal Commission." Manchester: Ireland, 1871.

Nicol, John. *The Life and Adventures of John Nicol, Mariner.* New York: Farrar and Rinehart, 1936.

Nield, Keith, ed. *Prostitution in the Victorian Age.* Westmead: Gregg, 1973.

Noble, Samuel. *Sam Noble, Able Seaman: 'Tween Decks in the Seventies.* New York: Stokes, 1925.

Norman, Edward R. *Anti-Catholicism in Victorian Britain.* New York: Barnes and Noble, 1968.

Oakley, Gilbert. *The History of the Rod and other Corporal Punishments.* London: Walton Press, 1964.
"Obituary of Admiral Sir George Cockburn, Bart." *Gentleman's Quarterly* new ser., 40 (1853): 406-10.
"Obituary of Vice-Admiral Sir Charles Napier, K.C.B." *Gentleman's Magazine* 10 (1861): 209-16.
O'Broin, Leon. *Fenian Fever.* New York: New York University Press, 1971.
"Observations on the Preparation and Discipline of the British Navy with Suggestions for a Better System." London: Dalton, 1837.
O'Donoghue, Cornelius. "Corporal-Punishment Commission, Defects in Military Education, and Promotion from the Ranks." *Fraser's Magazine* 13 (June 1836): 645-56.
———. "On Courts-Martial and the Cat-o'-Nine Tails." *Fraser's Magazine* 13 (May 1836): 539-52.
"Old Officer," (pseud). "A Chapter on Flogging." *Tait's Edinburgh Magazine* n.s., 1: 316-22.
Ollard, Richard. "Greenwich." *History Today* 5 (November 1955): 777-84.
Orpen, H. "The Origin, Evolution, and Future of the Personnel of the British Royal Navy." *Journal of the Royal United Service Institution* 47 (15 January 1903): 18-38.
Pack, A. J. "Note on Alcoholism." *Mariner's Mirror* 58 (May 1972): 193-94.
Pack, S. W. C. *Admiral Lord Anson.* London: Cassell, 1960.
———. *Britannia at Dartmouth.* London: Redman, 1966.
Packe, Michael St. John. *The Life of John Stuart Mill.* New York: Putnams, 1954; London: Secker and Warburg, 1954.
Padfield, Peter. *Aim Straight.* London: Hodder and Stoughton, 1966.
Palmer, Roy, ed. *The Valiant Sailor.* London: Cambridge University Press, 1973.
Parker, Charles Stuart. *Life and Letters of Sir James Graham.* 2 vols. London: Murray, 1907.
Parkes, Oscar. *British Battleships;* London: Seeley, 1957. Hamden, Ct.: Shoe String Press reprint, 1972.
Parkinson, Cyril Northcote. *Britain in the Far East.* Singapore: D. Moore, 1955.

———— *Edward Pellew, Viscount Exmouth.* London: Methuen, 1934.
———— *The Life and Times of Horatio Hornblower.* Boston: Little, Brown, 1970; London: Michael Joseph, 1970.
———— *Portsmouth Point.* Liverpool: Hodder and Stoughton, 1948.
Parris, Henry. *Constitutional Bureaucracy.* New York: Kelley, 1969; London: Allen and Unwin, 1969.
———— "The Nineteenth-Century Revolution in Government: A Reappraisal Reappraised." *Historical Journal* 3 (1960): 17-37.
Parry, Ann. *The Admirals Fremantle.* London: Chatto and Windus, 1971.
Pasley, Robert S. "A Comparative Study of Military Justice Reforms in Britain and America." *Vanderbilt Law Review* 6 (1953): 305-32.
———— and Larkin, Felix E. "The Navy Court Martial: Proposals for its Reform." *Cornell Law Quarterly* 33 (1947): 195-234.
Patterson, M. W. *Sir Francis Burdett and His Times, 1770-1844.* 2 vols. London: Macmillan, 1931.
Pearsall, Ronald. *The Worm in the Bud.* New York: Macmillan, 1968; London: Weidenfeld and Nicolson, 1968.
Pearson, Michael. *The Age of Consent.* London: David and Charles, 1972.
Peckham, Morse. *Victorian Revolutionaries.* New York: Braziller, 1970.
Penn, Geoffrey. *"Up Funnel, Down Screw."* London: Hollis and Carter, 1955.
Penrose, Sir Charles Vinicombe. *A Friendly Address to the Seamen of the British Navy.* London: Liddell, 1820.
———— *Observations on Corporal Punishment.* London: Bodmin, 1824.
Perkin, Harold James. *The Origins of Modern English Society, 1780-1880.* Toronto: University of Toronto Press, 1969; London: Routledge and Paul, 1969.
Perry, George and Mason, Nicholas, eds. *The Victorians.* New York, 1974.
Petrie, Glen. *A Singular Iniquity.* New York: Viking Press, 1971; London: Macmillan, 1971.
Phillips, J. Roland. "The Punishment of Flogging." *Gentleman's Magazine* n.s., 14 (March 1875): 355-64.
Phillips, Lawrence. "The Abolition of the Rum Ration." *U.S. Naval Institute Proceedings* 96 (July 1970): 86-88.

"Philo-Palinurus." (pseud). *No Impressment or Flogging.* London: Thomas, 1839.
Pike, G. Holden. *Among the Sailors.* London: Hodder and Stoughton, 1897.
Pool, Bernard. "Navy Contracts after 1832." *Mariner's Mirror* 54 (August 1968): 209-26.
Pope, Dudley. *At Twelve Mr. Byng Was Shot.* Philadelphia: Lippincott, 1962.
―――― *The Black Ship.* Philadelphia: Lippincott, 1964.
Poynter, F. N. *Medicine and Science in the 1860's.* London: Wellcome, 1968.
Preston, Anthony. "The End of the Victorian Navy," *Mariner's Mirror* 60 (November 1974): 363-81.
―――― and Major, John. *Send a Gunboat!* London: Longmans, Green, 1967.
Prouty, Roger Warren. *The Transformation of the Board of Trade, 1830-55.* London: Heinemann, 1957.
Rabb, Theodore K. and Rotberg, Robert I., eds. *The Family in History.* New York: Harper and Row, 1973.
Radzinowicz, Sir Leon. *A History of English Criminal Law and Administration from 1750.* 4 vols. New York: Macmillan, 1948-68.
[Ragan, William H.] *Admiralty Administration.* 2nd ed. London: Longmans, Green, 1861.
Ranft, Bryan McLean, ed. *The Vernon Papers.* London: Navy Records Society, 1958.
Ransford, Oliver. *The Slave Trade.* London: Murray, 1971.
Rasor, Eugene L. "The Problem of Discipline in the Mid-Nineteenth Century Royal Navy." Ph.D. dissertation, University of Virginia, 1972.
Reddie, James. "On Manning the Navy." *Journal of the Royal United Service Institution* 11 (1867): 279-362.
Reed, E. J. "The Great Naval Revolution." *Cornhill Magazine* 5 (May 1862): 550-59.
"Review of Major General Charles J. Napier, Remarks on Military Law and the Punishment of Flogging, 1837." *The Monthly Review* 143 (July 1837): 380-92.
Richardson, Joanna. "The Most English of Englishmen: an Impression of Tennyson." *History Today* 23 (November 1973): 776-84.

Richardson, Patrick. *Empire and Slavery*. New York: Harper and Row, 1968.
Richmond, Sir Herbert William. *Invasion of Britain*. London: Methuen, 1941.
―――. "Sir James Graham's Reforms in Administration and Command at the Admiralty." *Naval Policy and National Strength*. London: Longmans, Green, 1928, pp. 231-54.
Ridley, Jasper. *Lord Palmerston*. New York: Dutton, 1970; London: Constable, 1970.
"The Right and Practice of Impressment as Concerning Great Britain and America, Considered." *The Pamphleteer* 14 (1819): 381-416.
Riley, Patrick. *Memoirs of a Bluejacket*. London: Sampson Low, n.p., 1931.
Ritcheson, Charles R. and Hargrave, O. T. *Current Research in British Studies by American and Canadian Scholars*. 6th ed. Dallas: Southern Methodist University Press, 1969.
Ritchie, George Stephen. *The Admiralty Chart*. New York: American Elsevier, 1967; London: Hollis and Carter, 1967.
Robbins, William. *The Newman Brothers*. Cambridge, Harvard University Press, 1966; London: Heineman, 1966.
Roberts, David. "Jeremy Bentham and the Victorian Administrative State." *Victorian Studies* 2 (March 1959): 193-210.
―――. *Victorian Origins of the British Welfare State*. New Haven: Yale University Press, 1960; Hamden, Ct.: Shoe String Press reprint, 1969.
Robinson, Arthur Howard W. *Marine Cartography in Britain*. Leicester: Leicester University Press, 1961.
Robinson, Charles Napier. *The British Fleet*. London: G. Bell, 1894.
―――and Leyland, John. *The British Tar in Fact and Fiction*. New York: Harper, 1909.
Robson, L. L. *The Convict Settlers of Australia*. London: Cambridge University Press, 1965; Melbourne: Melbourne University Press, 1965.
Robson, Robert, ed. *Ideas and Institutions of Victorian Britain*. New York: Barnes and Noble, 1967; London: Bell, 1967.
Ropp, Theodore. *War in the Modern World*. Durham, N.C.: Duke University Press, 1959; New York: Collier, 1962.

Rose, Gordon. *The Struggle for Penal Reform.* London: Stevens, 1961.
Rose, John Holland. "The Royal Navy and the Suppression of the West African Slave Trade, 1815-65." *Mariner's Mirror* 22 (1936): 54-64, 162-71.
Rosebury, Theodore. *Microbes and Morals.* New York: Viking, 1971.
Ross, Joseph E. "The Military Justice Act of 1968: Historical Background." *The J.A.G. Journal* 23 (May-June 1969): 125-30.
Rover, Constance. *Love, Morals and the Feminists.* London: Routledge and Paul, 1970.
―――― *Women's Suffrage and Party Politics in Britain, 1866-1914.* Toronto: University of Toronto Press, 1967.
Rowbotham, W. B. "The Burning of H.M.S. Bombay." *Journal of the Royal United Service Institution* 106 (1961): 264-69.
―――― "The Loss of H.M.S. Bulldog, 1865." *Journal of the Royal United Service Institution* 103 (1958): 549-58.
―――― "Nile Gunboats, 1884-85." *Journal of the Royal United Service Institution* 101 (1956): 80-91.
―――― "Soldier's and Seaman's Wives and Children in H.M. Ships." *Mariner's Mirror* 47 (February 1961): 42-48.
Royal United Service Institution. *Catalogue of the Library.* London: Royal United Service Institution, 1908.
Runciman, Sir Walter. *Before the Mast and After.* London: Unwin, 1924.
―――― *The Shellback's Progress in the Nineteenth Century.* London: Walter Scott, 1904
Rutter, Owen, ed. *The Court Martial of the Bounty Mutineers.* London: Hodge, 1931.
Ryker, George C. "The New French Code of Military Justice." *Military Law Review* 44 (April 1969): 71-96.
Sala, George Augustus, ed. "Tried by Court-Martial." *Temple Bar* 5 (July 1862): 280-86.
Salt, Henry Stephens. *The Ethics of Corporal Punishment.* London: Humanitarian League, 1906.
―――― *The Flogging Craze.* London: Allen and Unwin, 1916.
Sanderson, Michael, ed. *National Maritime Museum Catalogue of the Library.* 2 vols. London: Her Majesty's Stationery Office, 1968-70.

Sandler, Stanley. "'In Deference to Public Opinion': The Loss of H.M.S. *Captain*." *Mariner's Mirror* 59 (February 1973): 57-68.
Scheuerle, William H. "Henry Kingsley and the Governor Eyre Controversy." *Victorian Newsletter* 37 (Spring 1970): 24-27.
Schurman, D. M. *The Education of a Navy*. Chicago: University of Chicago Press, 1965.
Scott, George Ryley. *The History of Corporal Punishment*. London: Torchstream, 1948; London: Tallis reprint, 1968.
Scott, Sir Percy. *Fifty Years in the Royal Navy*. London: Murray, 1919.
Semmel, Bernard. *Democracy vs. Empire*. Garden City, N.Y.: Doubleday, 1962; New York: Anchor, 1969.
Senior, William. "The Navy as Pententiary." *Mariner's Mirror* 16 (October 1930): 313-18.
"Sidney Herbert, First Baron Herbert of Lea." *Fraser's Magazine* 65 (February 1862): 313-18.
Skallerup, Harry R. *Books Afloat and Ashore*. Hamden, Ct.: Archon, 1974.
[Sloane-Stanley, Cecil George]. *Reminiscences of a Midshipman's Life from 1850-56*. 2 vols. London: Eden, Remington, 1893.
Smiles, Samuel. *Self Help*. New York: Sphere, 1968.
_____ *Lives of the Engineers*. 3 vols. London: David and Charles, 1861-62.
Smith, D. Bonner. "The Naval Mutinies of 1797." *Mariner's Mirror* 21 and 22 (October 1935 and January 1936): 428-49 and 65-86.
_____ "Some Remarks about the Mutiny of the *Bounty*." *Mariner's Mirror* 22 (April 1936) 200-37.
_____ and Dewar, A. C. eds. *Russan War*. 3 vols. London: Navy Records Society, 1943-45.
Smith, F. B. "Ethics and Disease in the Later 19th Century: the Contagious Diseases Acts." *Historical Studies* 15 (October 1971): 118-35.
Smith, Paul. *Disraelian Conservatism and Social Reform*. Toronto: University of Toronto Press, 1967.
Snedeker, James. *A Brief History of Courts-Martial*. Annapolis: U.S. Naval Institute, 1954.
Somerville, J. F. "The Lower Deck, Past and Present." *Journal of the Royal United Service Institution* 81 (February and May 1936): 109-25, 303-14.

Southgate, Donald. *"The Most English Minister."* New York: St. Martins, 1966.
Spinner, Thomas J., Jr. *George Joachim Goschen.* New York: Cambridge University Press, 1973.
──────. "George Joachim Goschen: The Man Randolph Churchill 'Forgot'." *Journal of Modern History* 39 (December 1967): 405-24.
Spinney, J. D. "The *Hermione* Mutiny." *Mariner's Mirror* 41 (May 1955): 123-36.
Sproule, H. D. "James Burney's Opinions on the Naval Mutinies of 1797." *Mariner's Mirror* 46 (February 1960): 61-62.
Stansfeld, James. "On the Validity of the Annual Government Statistics on the Operation of the Contagious Diseases Acts." *Journal of the Royal Statistical Society* 39 (1876): 540-72.
Statham, Edward Phillips. *The Story of the Britannia.* London: n.p., 1904.
[Stephen, Fitzjames]. "Courts-Martial." *Cornhill Magazine* 5 (June 1862): 682-94.
Stephen, Sir Leslie and Lee, Sir Sidney, eds. *The Dictionary of National Biography.* 21 vols. London: Oxford University Press, 1937-38.
Stewart, James. "The Press-Gangs of the Royal Navy." *U.S. Naval Institute Proceedings* 86 (October 1960): 81-87.
Stuart, Vivian. *The Beloved Little Admiral.* London: Hale, 1967.
Sulivan, George Lydiard. *Dhow Chasing in Zanzibar Waters.* London: Dawson, 1967.
Sulivan, Henry Norton. *The Life and Letters of Admiral Sir Bartholomew James Sulivan, 1810-90.* London: Murray, 1896.
Sutherland, Gillian, ed. *Studies in the Growth of Nineteenth-Century Government.* Boston: Routledge and Paul, 1972.
Sweetman, John. "Military Transport in the Crimean War, 1854-56." *English Historical Review* 88 (January 1973): 81-91.
Tannahill, Reay. *Food in History.* New York: Stein and Day, 1973.
Tappe, E. D. "Meat Canning in Rumania for the British Navy: An Appendix." *Slavonic and East European Review* 39 (December 1960): 214-15.
Taylor, Roy. "Manning the Royal Navy: The Reform of the Recruiting System, 1852-62." *Mariner's Mirror* 44 and 45 (November 1958 and February 1959): 302-13 and 46-58.

———. "Manning the Royal Navy: The Reform of the Recruiting System, 1847-61." M.A. thesis, Birkbeck College, University of London, 1954.
Teagarden, Ernest. "A Victorian Prison Experiment." *Journal of Social History* 2 (Summer 1969): 357-66.
Temperley, Howard. *British Antislavery, 1833-70*. Columbia: University of South Carolina Press, 1972; London: Longmans, 1972.
Thomas, Keith. "The Double Standard." *Journal of the History of Ideas* 20 (1959): 195-216.
Thompson, Edgar K. "Note on Keelhauling." *Mariner's Mirror* 58 (May 1972): 171-72.
———. "Saga of a Mutineer." *Mariner's Mirror* 53 (May 1967): 171-78.
Thompson, Edward Palmer. *The Making of the English Working Class*. New York: Random House, 1963; New York: Vintage, 1966.
Thompson, Paul, ed. *Close to the Wind*. London: Heinemann, 1965.
[Thomson, Henry]. "Punishments in the Army." *Blackwood's Magazine* 15 (April 1824): 399-406.
Thornton, John N. *Warships, 1860-1970*. New York: Arco, 1973; Newton Abbot: David and Charles, 1973.
Thring, Theodore, *A Treatise on the Criminal Law of the Navy*. London: Stevens, 1861.
——— and Gifford, E. C. *Thring's Criminal Law of the Navy*. 2nd ed. London: Stevens, 1877.
Traill, Henry Duff and Mann, James Saumarez, eds. *Social England*. 6 vols. London: Cassell, 1897.
Tribe, David. *President Charles Bradlaugh, M.P.* Hamden, Ct.: Archon, 1971; London: Elek, 1971.
Tunstall, William C. Brian. *Realities of Naval History*. London: Allen and Unwin, 1936.
Tuttle, Elizabeth Orman. *The Crusade against Capital Punishment in Great Britain*. London: Stevens, 1966.
Uden, Grant. *British Ships and Seamen*. 2 vols. London: Macmillan, 1969.
Van Der Voort, P. J. *The Pen and the Quarter Deck*. London: Leiden University Press, 1972.
Van de Water, Frederic F. *The Captain Called It Mutiny*. New York: Ives Washburn, 1954.

Vicinus, Martha, ed. *Suffer and Be Still.* Bloomington: Indiana University Press, 1972.
Vincent, Howard P. *Twentieth Century Interpretations of Billy Budd.* Englewood Cliffs, N.J.: Prentice-Hall, 1970.
Walker, Charles Frederick. *Young Gentlemen.* London: Longmans, Green, 1938.
Walkowitz, Judith R. "Notes on the History of Victorian Prostitution." *Feminist Studies* 1 (Summer 1972): 105-14.
──────. "'We Are Not Beasts of the Field': Prostitution and the Campaign Against the Contagious Diseases Acts, 1869-86." Ph.D. dissertation, University of Rochester, 1974.
Wallace, Elisabeth. *Goldwin Smith.* Toronto: University of Toronto Press, 1957.
Walpole, Frederick. *Four Years in the Pacific in Her Majesty's Ship Collingwood from 1844 to 1848.* 2 vols. London: R. Bentley, 1849.
Walrond, Mary L. *Launching Out into the Deep.* London: Society for Promoting Christian Knowledge, 1904.
Walton, Clifford Elliott. *History of the British Standing Army.* 3 vols. London: Harrison, 1894.
Ward, J. T. *Sir James Graham.* New York: St. Martins, 1967.
Ward, William Ernest Frank. *The Royal Navy and the Slavers.* London: Allen and Unwin, 1969; New York: Schocken, 1970.
Warner, Oliver. *Captain Marryat.* London: Constable, 1953.
Warner, Philip. *The Crimean War.* London: Weidenfeld and Nicolson, 1972.
Waters, C. D. "Recruiting to the Regular Forces." *Journal of the Royal United Service Institution* 102 (1957): 55-60.
Weston, Agnes. *My Life Among the Blue Jackets.* London: James Nisbet, 1909.
──────. *Temperance Work in the Royal Navy.* London: Hodder and Stoughton, 1879.
White, A. S. "Flogging in the Army." *Journal of the Society for Army Historical Research* 20 (Summer 1941): 114-15.
Wiley, Byron A. "Non-judicial Punishment in the Royal Navy." *U.S. Naval Institute Proceedings* 93 (July 1967): 139-41.
Williamson, James A. *The Ocean in English History.* New York: Oxford University Press, 1941.
Wilson, H. W. "Discipline in the Old Navy." *Macmillan's Magazine* 78 (1898): 94-101.

Wilson, J. C. "Is Our Merchant Service Any Longer a Feeder to the Royal Navy?" *Journal of the Royal United Service Institution* 20 (1876): 61-84.

───── "Seamen of the Fleet; their Training and How Employment of Marines Afloat in Peace-time Affects Them." *Journal of the Royal United Service Institution* 19 (1875): 604-30.

Wilson, Leonard G. "The Clinical Definition of Scurvy and the Discovery of Vitamin C." *Journal of the History of Medicine and Applied Science* 30 (January 1975): 40-60.

Woodham-Smith, Cecil. *The Reason Why*. New York: Dutton, 1960.

Woodward, Ernest L. *The Age of Reform, 1815-70*. New York: Oxford University Press, 1938.

Wright, Maurice. *Treasury Control of the Civil Service, 1854-74*. Oxford: Clarendon Press, 1969.

Yates, R. W., ed. "From Wooden Walls to Dreadnoughts in a Lifetime." *Mariner's Mirror* 48 (November 1962): 291-303.

Yexley, Lionel, (pseud), [Wood, James]. *The Inner Life of the Navy*. London: Pitman, 1908.

───── *Our Fighting Sea Men*. London: S. Paul, 1911.

Yonge, Charles Duke. *The History of the British Navy*. 3 vols. London: R. Bentley, 1863-66.

Young, G. M. *Early Victorian England*. 2 vols. New York: Oxford University Press, 1934; 2nd ed., 1951.

───── *Victorian England*. 2nd ed. New York: Oxford University Press, 1964.

Young, Robert T. *The House that Jack Built*. Aldershot: Gale and Polden, 1955.

Zegger, Robert E. "Victorians in Arms: The French Invasion Scare of 1859-60." *History Today* 23 (October 1973): 705-14.

Zinsser, Hans. *Rats, Lice and History*. Boston: Little, Brown, 1935.


Newspapers, Journals, and Periodicals

*Annual Register*
*Army and Navy Gazette*
*Blackwood's Magazine*

*Brassey's Naval Annual*
*Chamber's Journal*
*Contemporary Review*
*Edinburgh Review*
*Fortnightly Review*
*Fraser's Magazine*
*Gentleman's Magazine*
*Illustrated London News*
*Journal of the Royal United Service Institution*
*Lancet*
*Macmillan's Magazine*
*Meliora*
*National Reformer*
*Nautical Magazine*
*Nineteenth Century*
*Quarterly Review*
*Saturday Review*
*The Shield*
*Temple Bar*
*The Times* (London)
*Westminster Review*

# Index

Acton, Dr. William (1814-75), 87, 95
Adams, Henry Brooks (1838-1918), 13
Admiralty, definition of, 9; policies of, 16, 19, 34-35, 70, 115, 122. *See also* Royal Navy.
*Admiralty Digests,* 20, 41, 43-44, 59-60, 65, 68, 69, 98-99, 115, 117
Alcoholism, 10, 79, 80-86, 96, 113, 120, 159, 167
Anson, Admiral Lord George (1697-1762), 39, 50
*Army and Navy Gazette,* 18, 52, 137
Army, relations with Royal Navy, 15, 21, 22, 38, 50, 51, 87, 88, 92, 104, 141, 146, 148-50
Articles of War. *See* Naval Discipline Acts
Barracks ashore, 88, 100, 107, 121
Baxter, Colin, naval historian, 14
Baynham, Henry W. F., naval historian, 97-98, 132
Bechervaise, John, naval gunner, 7
Beresford, Admiral Lord Charles William de la Poer (1846-1919), 80, 81, 95, 101
Berkeley, Admiral Sir Maurice Fredcrick Fitzhardinge (1788-1867), 28, 121
Birching, method of punishment, 49, 55-56, 168
Bluejacket, enlisted man of the Royal Navy, 7, 14, 20, 34, 47, 56, 70, 73, 74, 75, 98, 110, 111, 112, 119, 122, 123
Bounty, method of recruiting, 22, 29-30, 65, 74, 120, 141, 157
Bowles, Admiral William, 66-67
Boys, category of shipboard intraining status, 28, 34, 55-56, 99, 121, 168

Brassey, Lord Thomas (1836-1918), 33
Briggs, Sir John Henry, chief clerk, Admiralty (1808-97), 81
British Empire, development in the nineteenth century, 10, 12
Burdett, Sir Francis (1770-1844), 51, 77
Burnett, Sir William, physician-general of the Royal Navy (1779-1861), 100
Butler, Josephine Grey (1828-1906), 93-95
Cat-of-nine tails, 49, 53, 56
Chamier, Captain Frederick (1796-1870), 53, 150
Childers, Hugh Culling Eardley (1827-96), 121
Classifications of conduct (e.g., first class, third class), 14-15, 32, 54, 113, 114-15
Clowes, Sir William Laird, naval historian, 77, 131, 137
Coast Guard, 31, 41
Cobbett, William (1762-1835), 51
Cobden-Chevalier Treaty of 1860, 13
Conditions on the lower deck, 14, 15-16, 131
Confinement. *See* Imprisonment
Contagious Diseases Acts, 18, 88-97, 131, 161-63. *See also* Venereal Disease
Continuous Service, method of recruiting, 23, 27-32, 35, 36, 48, 101, 106, 111
Corporal punishment, in American navy, 18, 51, 116, 151-52; in other foreign countries, 51, 53, 116; method of punishment, 10, 14, 35, 38, 41, 43, 44-58, 59, 61, 66, 67, 80, 83, 96, 114-15, 116, 128, 129, 138, 144, 146-53, 168

207

Corry, Henry Thomas Lowry (1803-73), 56, 117
Court-martial, 39-42, 46, 47, 55, 66, 84, 99, 114, 115, 116, 118, 121, 130, 143
Crimean War. *See* Russian War
Derby, Lord (fourteenth Earl, 1799-1869), 14, 27
Desertion, 27, 65, 70-75, 96, 115, 116, 129, 156-57, 158
Discharge as Objectionable alternative to punishment, 48, 118
Discharge with Disgrace, method of punishment, 45, 48, 118, 168
Discipline in the Royal Navy, 16, 37, 38-48, 62-63, 71, 104, 107-10, 113-14, 115, 119, 121
Drunkenness. *See* Alcoholism
Eighteen fifth-nine, significance of, 12, 20, 30, 62, 67, 110, 115, 135
Enlisted men of the Royal Navy. *See* Bluejacket
Fenianism, 109-10
Financial matters of the Royal Navy, 14, 36, 79, 88, 91, 107, 159
Fisher, Admiral Lord John (1841-1920), 85, 97
Flogging. *See* Corporal punishment
France, relations with Great Britain, 12, 13, 22-23, 29, 31, 115, 141
Gladstone, William Ewart (1809-98), 13, 120
Good Conduct Badge and Pay, 67, 104, 121, 168
Goschen, George Joachim (1831-1907), 54-55, 75
Graham, Sir James Robert George (1792-1861), 24, 30, 31, 36, 122
Grey, Admiral Sir Frederick William (1805-78), 122
Griffiths, Captain A. J., 25
Grog. *See* Rum Ration
Habitability, 100-107

Harris, Captain Robert (1809-65), 36, 122
Health of seamen, 82, 83, 85, 87-88, 100-107, 131, 165-66
Herbert, Sir Sidney (Baron Herbert of Lea, 1810-61), 31
Hickman, William, Admiralty clerk, 42, 46, 47, 117, 121, 167
Hire-and-Discharge, method of recruiting, 23, 26-27, 111
Homosexuality, 98-100, 164
Hornby, Admiral Sir Geoffrey T. Phipps (1825-95), 65
Hume, Joseph (1777-1855), 14, 25, 43, 51, 148-49
Hutchinson, J. R., naval historian, 25
Impressment, method of recruiting, 10, 23-26, 35, 38, 61, 64, 139
Impress Service, 23, 24
Imprisonment, method of punishment, 48, 57-59, 116, 117, 153
Judicial review by the Admiralty, 40-41
Karsten, Peter, naval historian, 27, 76
Key, Admiral Sir Astley Cooper (1821-88), 52
Leave and liberty, 10, 23, 35, 65, 67, 70-75, 97, 99, 107, 118-19, 168
Leech, Seaman Samuel, 97
Lewes, naval prison in Sussex, 59, 73, 153
Lewis, Michael, naval historian, 36, 82
Lindsay, William Schaw (1816-77), 32, 108, 122
Lloyd, Charles Christopher, naval historian, 7, 8, 27, 102, 132
Manning the Royal Navy, 12, 21, 26-27, 65, 70, 115, 121, 127, 140. *See also* Recruiting
Marder, Arthur J., naval historian, 20
Marryat, Captain Frederick (1792-1848), 18, 25, 53, 138

Martin, Admiral Sir William Fanshawe (1801-95), 52, 56, 88, 104, 117, 120-21
Melville, Herman (1819-91), 18, 53, 150
Merchant marine, relations with Royal Navy, 19, 30-32, 74, 122, 151, 157-58
Midshipmen or officer cadets, 56, 80, 84
Mill, John Stuart (1806-73), 12, 93
Milne, Admiral Sir Alexander (1806-96), 56, 75, 76, 100, 104, 113, 121, 166, 168
Mortality, 103
Mutiny, definition of, 9, 62-63, 116; disturbances of 1859-60, 62-67, 71, 79, 101, 155; instances of, Spithead (1797), 22, 61, 63-64, 78, 154-55; the Nore (1797), 22, 61, 63-64, 78, 154-55; Sepoy or Indian of 1857, 11, 13, 63; other instances of, 55, 63, 64, 67-69, 155-56
Napier, Admiral Sir Charles (1786-1860), 13, 26, 29, 116, 121
Naval Discipline Acts (formerly Articles of War), 8, 10, 14, 38-41, 67, 72, 107, 112-19, 132-33, 142, 169
Officers of the Royal Navy, 15, 16-17, 44-48, 64, 65, 70, 75-80, 84, 100, 106, 110, 158-59
Paget, Admiral Lord Clarence Edward (1811-95), 30, 115, 116
Pakington, Sir John Somerset (1799-1880), 18, 32, 46, 122
Palmerston, Lord (third Viscount, 1784-1865), 13, 14, 120, 136
Parker, Admiral Sir William (1781-1866), 28
Pay and allowances, 32, 64, 67, 73, 92, 100, 101, 103-105, 107, 117, 121, 166
Pennell, Sir Charles Henry, Admiralty clerk (1805-98), 28

Pension, naval retirement, 27, 28, 32, 70, 111
Press gang, 23, 64
Prostitution, 88-98, 155. *See also* Contagious Diseases Acts
Public opinion, pressure of, 10, 17-19, 24, 48, 51, 52, 53-54, 56, 58, 65, 69-70, 92-96, 112, 116, 122, 137
Punishment practices, 37, 38-61, 73-74, 77, 79, 83, 92, 99, 113-15, 116, 118-19, 121, 144, 152, 158-59, 164, 168-69; keelhauling, 49; marking or branding, 49, 57; starting, 56-57. *See also* Corporal Punishment, Imprisonment, Discharge with Disgrace, Birching
Quarterly Punishment Returns, 42, 43, 46, 55-56, 113
*Queen's* or *King's Regulations and Admiralty Instructions*, 39, 50, 54, 107-108, 115
Quota-men, 22, 64, 71
Quota system, method of recruiting, 22
Ranft, Bryan, naval historian, 8
Recreation, 83, 88, 97, 100, 106, 111
Recruiting, 19, 21-23, 26-37, 70, 76, 121. *See also* Manning
Reform in the Royal Navy, 7, 9, 10, 17, 20, 43-48, 54-61, 67-68, 71, 79, 85, 87, 100-107, 118-19, 120-21, 122-23, 132-33
Religion, 107-10, 167-68
Remission of punishment, 45-46, 60, 79
Repeal of the Contagious Diseases Acts, 92-97
"Revolution in government," nineteenth century administrative, 13, 135-36
Romaine, William Govett, Admiralty secretary (1815-93), 46, 118, 121

Royal Commission on Manning the Navy of 1858-59, 26, 27-28, 30, 32
Royal Marines, 15, 33, 41, 49, 65, 67
Royal Navl Coastal Volunteers, 31-32, 33
Royal Naval Reserve, 23, 32-37
Royal Navy, history of, 7, 11, 38-39, 76-77, 107, 119-20; organization and operations of, 10-11, 14-16, 70, 156. *See also* Admiralty
*Royal United Service Institution, Journal of,* 18, 27, 52, 137, 155
Rum ration, 82-83, 85-86, 159-60
Russell, Lord John (1792-1878), 13, 14, 136
Russian War of 1854-56, 11, 26, 28-29, 122, 134
Scott, Admiral Sir Percy Moreton (1853-1924), 11
Sexuality, 87-100
*The Shield,* journal, 93
Simon, Sir John (1816-1904), 95
Somerset, twelfth Duke of (Edward Adolphus Seymour, prior to 1855 Lord St. Maur, 1804-85), 10, 116, 118, 119-20, 122
Stansfeld, Sir James (1820-98), 93-96
Storks, General Sir Henry Knight (1811-74), 88, 94

Sulivan, Admiral Sir Bartholomew James (1810-90), 17, 32
Summary punishment, 39-40, 42, 50, 99, 113-14, 118-19
Taylor, Roy, naval historian, 47-48
Temperance campaign, 80, 84-85, 106, 110, 111, 160
Tennyson, Alfred Lord (1809-92), 13
Thring, Theodore (1816-91), 39, 51-52, 99, 132
Tilling, Abe Seaman, diarist, 68-69, 79-80, 158
the *Times* (London), coverage of naval matters, 13, 18, 52, 65, 73, 114
Training and education within the Royal Navy, 36, 55, 83, 97, 100, 105-106, 110, 121
Uniform, naval, 101, 165
Venereal disease, 10, 87-88, 90-98, 117, 120, 122, 163. *See also* Contagious Diseases Acts
Victualing, 101-102, 166
Volunteer, method of recruiting, 21-22, 71
Volunteer Rifle Corps of 1859, 13
Warrant, document required prior to punishment, 40-41, 50
Weston, Dame Agnes, 81, 84-85, 107
Williams, William (1789-1865), 66, 116
Wood, Sir Charles (1800-85), 32

## LIBRARY OF DAVIDSON COLLEGE

**Books** on regular loan may be checked out for **two weeks**. Books must be presented at the Circulation Desk in order to be renewed.

A fine is charged after date due.

Special books are subject to special regulations at the discretion of library staff.

| | | | |
|---|---|---|---|
| 11-22-86 ILL- | | | |
| MAY 23 1990 | | | |